ww news

Waterford Whispers News
2022

COLM WILLIAMSON

Gill Books

Gill Books
Hume Avenue
Park West
Dublin 12
www.gillbooks.ie

Gill Books is an imprint of M.H. Gill & Co.

9780717192588

Designed by seagulls.net
Copy-edited by Neil Burkey
Printed and bound by GraphyCems, Spain

Waterford Whispers News is a satirical newspaper and comedy website published by Waterford Whispers News. Waterford Whispers News uses invented names in all the stories in this book, except in cases when public figures are being satirised. Any other use of real names is accidental and coincidental.

For permission to reproduce photographs, the author and publisher gratefully acknowledge the following: © Adobe: 2, 6C, 12BR, 15B, 17B, 20BL, 21C, 26T, 27, 28T, 28B 29T, 30C, 32B, 32T, 33B, 34T, 35B, 36T, 36B, 37T, 38T, 39C, 41T, 42TR, 44T, 45B, 46B, 48T, 48B, 49T, 50C, 51B, 51T, 51B, 56B, 58B, 59T, 61T, 62T, 64B, 66T, 66B, 67T, 71, 73T, 75B, 79B, 81B, 82B, 85T, 86B, 88T, 90T, 93T, 93B, 94B, 95T, 95B, 96T, 96B, 97T, 99T, 100T, 100B, 101T, 101B, 102C, 103B, 103T, 105B, 106T, 107T, 108T, 109C, 111T, 111B, 112T, 112B, 113T, 114T, 114B, 116T, 117T, 117B, 118T, 118B, 119T, 119B, 120T, 120B, 122B, 123C, 126T, 129T, 133B, 135B, 138T, 139C, 140T, 141T, 142B, 143T, 144B, 145C, 146C, 148T, 148B, 150B, 151B, 152B, 153T, 154T, 155, 156C, 157T, 159B, 160B,161T, 162T, 163B, 163T, 165C, 167T, 168B, 169T, 170B, 172T; © Alamy: 6C, 11T, 14B, 20B, 21T, 22T,24T, 31B, 54T, 57T, 60T, 61B, 64B, 65T, 68C, 72BL, 72BR, 75T, 77T, 81T, 82T, 84T, 87T, 88B, 89T, 90B, 131T, 136T, 139C, 166C, 167T; © Alexey Nikolsky/Getty Images: 135T; © Andrew Steinmetz/Wikimedia Commons: 83T; © Duncan Hull/Wikimedia Commons: 52TR; © Eamon Farrell/RollingNews.ie: 147B; © Fars Media Corporation/Wikimedia Commons: 132T; © Gage Skidmore/Wikimedia Commons: 52TL; © INPHO: 126B, 128T, 130C; © iStock: 5C, 6C, 7B, 9C, 13C, 16T, 17T, 18B, 25C, 27, 31T, 34B, 42T, 44B, 47T, 55C, 57B, 58T, 60C, 61B, 63C, 65B, 69B, 71, 78C, 83C, 94T, 98T, 103T 106B, 107T, 114B, 121, 123C, 128B, 131B, 133B, 137, 140B, 167B; © Maurizio Pesce/Wikimedia Commons: 73B; © Courtesy of the National Library of Ireland: 85B; © Northern Ireland Office/Wikimedia Commons: 40T; © Palm Beach County Sheriff's Department/Wikimedia Commons: 86C; © Redadeg/Wikimedia Commons: 52C; © Shutterstock: 4T, 4B, 7T, 8T, 8B, 10B, 11B, 12T, 12B, 14T, 19C, 22B, 23C, 24B, 31T, 37T, 43T, 47B, 49T, 53, 56T, 62B, 68T, 70T, 70B, 72C, 74T, 76T, 76B, 78T, 79T, 80T, 87T, 89B, 91, 92T, 98B, 104T, 110T, 115B, 122T, 124T, 125T, 125B, 127B, 132B, 134B, 135B, 136B, 137, 138B, 149B, 151T, 164B, 171T; © Sinn Féin Ireland/Wikimedia Commons: 18T; © U.S Government/Wikimedia Commons: 22T, 69T; © Wikimedia Commons: 86L, 86R, 108B, 131T, 158T.

The author and publisher have made every effort to trace all copyright holders, but if any have been inadvertently overlooked we would be pleased to make the necessary arrangement at the first opportunity.

The paper used in this book comes from the wood pulp of sustainably managed forests. For every tree felled, at least one tree is planted, thereby renewing natural resources.

A CIP catalogue record for this book is available from the British Library.

5 4 3 2 1

CONTENTS

ABOUT THE AUTHOR

Colm Williamson created *Waterford Whispers News* in 2009 when he was unemployed. Though it began as a hobby, with Colm sharing stories with family and friends, his unique brand of topical, distinctly Irish satire quickly attracted thousands of fans. Now *Waterford Whispers News* has over 666,000 Facebook, 240,000 Twitter and 173,000 Instagram followers, and an average of 4 million page views on the website every month. Colm runs *Waterford Whispers News* from his home town of Tramore in Co. Waterford.

LETTER FROM THE EDITOR

Dear readers,

First off, I would like to thank you, dear reader, for ignoring the mass climate change delusion people are spouting on about and purchasing this former tree. I also thank you a second time for reading the groundbreaking journalism contained within these pages – some of you even made it through an entire article without trying to scroll it like it was an Instagram feed, I'm proud of you!

Without our loyal readers, this publication would suffer the same fate as the RTÉ Player – sure it's there, but if no one uses it does it even make a sound?

Some time ago *Waterford Whispers News* reached 250 million 'internet newspaper readers' 250,000,000! Nearly as many convictions as Conor McGregor. And like Mr Notorious, we're equally as proud and arrogant about the whole thing. Truly, I can't thank you enough for reading.

However, what the internet is exactly is anyone's guess. The IT guys try to explain it to me but, much like Sinn Féin, it remains a mysterious beast that is probably secretly plotting to take over the world and kill us all.

Speaking of the world and killing, this year saw a number of unique issues and conflicts arise, with much of the pain, injury and anguish undoubtedly the fault of one evil figure unable to control his ego and anger … but that's the last time I'll mention Will Smith.

As various crises and catastrophes reared their heads, *Waterford Whispers News* didn't shirk its responsibilities, instead, under my guidance, it embraced its journalistic duties.

I'm proud of our series of articles on the cost of living crisis, which included saving tips for the poorest in society, available behind our paywall for just €16.99 a day.

Housing once again hit the headlines, and this publication wasn't afraid to give column inches and opinion pieces to the marginalised voices of the developer and landlord communities.

We took on a number of Ukrainian refugees as staff at Whispers HQ, not because it was an easy thing to do but because they were so desperate that they worked for peanuts, and we didn't need to inform the taxman.

Women's rights finally entered its 'common sense' era with the nuns getting to run the National Maternity Hospital, no one believing Amber Heard and all that *Roe v Wade* business.

Waterford Whispers News embraced the 21st-century modern newsroom by making its debut on TickleTok – getting our news out to the youth of today and doing our part to help the Chinese government collect a disturbing amount of data on them all. We're sure that'll work out fine.

Who knows where the world is headed next, but let's hope it will mean increased revenues for media companies like this one, which is more than happy to print whatever those in charge tell us to.

Yours factually,

Bill Badbody
Deputy Stand-In Temporary Editor of *WWN*, Landlord, Philanthropist and Man of the People.

PRINTED USING THE €1.6MN LEINSTER HOUSE PRINTER   JUNE 2022

NATIONAL CATASTROPHIC

Is this the most structurally unsound building in Ireland?

Airport queues: What your dumb ass can do to avoid fucking things up for everyone

Homelessness to be rebranded 'Fresh Air Time'

FREE PROMISES INSIDE

National Children's Hospital: Do we really need one?

DRINK! SPORTS! REALITY TV! DISTRACT YOURSELF WITH THESE THINGS WHILE WE RUN DOWN THE CLOCK TO PENSION TIME

25002 74135

POLITICS

BREXIT

'WE'RE TELLING THE US ON YOU' IRELAND WARNS UK OVER PROTOCOL

RUNNING IN THE DIRECTION of Joe Biden as fast as its little legs could carry it, Ireland, speaking a million miles an hour, snot bulging from its nose and short of breath, is trying to tell the US what the UK is always saying the second everyone's backs are turned.

'And then they're all like "Article 16 is coming out", but then they're all "we never said", then the media is saying "the UK privately says it's an all-out trade and culture war", and then the UK is like "as if",' said Ireland, tugging on the suit jacket of the US in a bid to get its attention.

'Seriously, look, look, look, do you hear that? They just said "who has two thumbs and doesn't give a fuck about the Good Friday Agreement",' an exasperated Ireland said.

Rowing back on threats to trigger Article 16 of the Northern Ireland Protocol, Lord David Frost informed the US that he never said such things, while also pulling on his ears and sticking his tongue out at Ireland.

'Shut up, the adults are talking. What have I told you about speaking out of turn?' Frost said, covering the mouth of Northern Irish businesses touting the many positives to come from the implementation of the Protocol.

Elsewhere, in a bid to distract the public from just about everything, Boris Johnson, now sporting a full face tattoo of a poppy, has announced his intention to legalise magic mushrooms, thus making hallucinating Brexit success a possibility.

DIRECT PROVISION RESIDENTS REMINDED 'SPECIAL REFUGEE STATUS' ONLY FOR UKRAINIANS

THE IRISH GOVERNMENT, praised for waiving visa requirements for terrified Ukrainians fleeing aerial bombardments and potential death as Vladimir Putin's invasion rages on, has been quick to ask Direct Provision residents not to get their hopes up.

'We appreciate that such welcome acknowledgement of the innate humanity of all individuals fleeing war and persecution might give you false hope that this might be extended to yourselves, but c'mon now, this is strictly a Ukraine thing,' confirmed the coalition government.

Ireland is expected to take in as many as 20,000 refugees from

Ukraine, who will be granted identical rights to EU citizens, something the government has pointed out is a reasonable exception to make for a European neighbour.

'Yeah, but in fairness, geographically speaking, they are European,' the government explained

to a variety of DP residents from as far away as Russian-invaded Georgia.

'And don't forget, we've pledged to end DP by the end of 2024, and it's not like we have a history of failing to meet deadlines, so just hang on in there until then, time will fly,' said the government that has presided over the Children's Hospital, National Broadband and Metrolink projects.

Meanwhile, the Department of You're Only Making It Worse defended the distinction by stating, 'But Ukrainians are just like us, they have jobs and are normal people with … no hang on, we didn't mean it like that, ah shite.'

CLIMATE CRISIS

ONE-THIRD OF IRISH FARMERS TO BE HUMANELY CULLED UNDER NEW CLIMATE PLEDGE

'We promise to focus only on ageing farmers who don't have much time left anyway'

FOLLOWING A PLEDGE by the government to reduce carbon emissions across the island of Ireland, nearly one-third of Irish farmers will be humanely culled by the army by 2030, *WWN* has learned.

'We promise to focus only on ageing farmers who don't have much time left anyway,' Taoiseach Micheál Martin said, in an attempt to ease tensions while defending the future deaths of some 41,000 farmers over the next eight years. 'I'm sure many of them will probably die off before then anyway, either naturally or by becoming so distraught and depressed with Dublin rules that they take their own lives, but look, at least we won't have to worry about cow farts ruining our EU targets anymore and costing the more wealthy of us an arm and a leg.'

With an estimated 35 per cent of national greenhouse gases coming from the agriculture sector, the highest level in Europe, which has an 11 per cent average, some farmers accepted the problem and even offered themselves up to be culled for the sake of the nation.

'Cull away, lads. I'm ready to take one for team Ireland,' Waterford farmer Davey Price urged, pointing to an area between his eyes to shoot. 'Bolt gun job ... bam, over in seconds. And about time, too. I can't even sleep thinking that Ireland is producing three times the emissions of countries on the mainland. Sure, it's because we're an island, and importing beef doesn't make any fucking sense whatsoever, as we've the best land for raising and feeding cattle, but if the EU or the UN says we have to sacrifice our agricultural sovereignty, then pull the trigger and dump me in a slurry tank right now.

'Besides, what country wants to be self-sufficient these days anyway? It's not like there's ever going to be things like trade or supply issues – best leave countries that won't adhere to greenhouse gas emissions to supply all our meat and veg via diesel-chugging container ships – it all makes perfect sense.'

Classifieds

Christmas Shopping Done

Not looking to buy anything but I just want as many people to know that I've already done my Christmas shopping and it's only November. I'm so organised. I mean I have absolutely everything – kids, husband, nieces, nephews, brothers, sisters, Mam and Dad, the cleaner, the guys in work, the woman I say hello to every day on the way to the bus, I've got them all. I'm fucking brilliant, I am.

Call Rachel to congratulate her on 087-895-6478

EXCLUSIVE

50FT-TALL EAMON RYAN LAYS WASTE TO RURAL IRELAND

A DEMONIC BICYCLE-wielding Eamon Ryan with data centres for eyes is on a rural ransacking rampage in Ireland, if reports from the vivid nightmares of some rural TDs are to be believed.

'He's shooting quinoa lasers from his eyes – watch yourself. Oh Christ, he has yoga mats for fingers, aaaah!' screamed those fleeing Ryan, whose monstrous growth spurt was down to him eating the Miracle-Gro he usually gives to the lettuce in his window box.

'It's the turf ban, it's making him stronger,' alerted some TDs, among them one who owned a commercial turf-cutting business, happy to misrepresent the bill if it wins them some gullible votes.

Eating village supplies of cars like they were delicious salads, Ryan, now more like 100 feet tall, has left rural dwellers with no choice but to share the one tricycle between them for transport.

'Is that jumped-up fucker flying?' shocked onlookers said as they observed Ryan attaching wind turbines to his back like he was some sort of energy-efficient helicopter of doom.

Despite the best efforts of a small band of farmers aiming a hose of tainted river water at Ryan, the Minister for Rural End Times remained standing.

'The IPCC says there's three years to save the planet!' madman Ryan's booming disembodied voice said, echoing across the valleys as he forced a family at gunpoint to accept a grant for improved insulation in their Celtic Tiger-era home, which has a building energy rating of 'medieval mud hut'.

Just as it appeared all was lost, Sinn Féin disabled the solar panel on Ryan's head from which he drew power, and in the process saved the small minority of people who want to buy inefficient and expensive commercial turf instead of cheaper alternatives.

> **'He's shooting quinoa lasers from his eyes – watch yourself. Oh Christ, he has yoga mats for fingers, aaaah!'**

Predictions for 2023

Large businesses will continue to fail to make the connection between increasing resignations and anger among employees and not increasing wages but paying out record dividends to shareholders.

'THIS FEELS WRONG, TAKE IT BACK' DONOHOE TELLS MULTINATIONALS AFTER RECORD TAX TAKE

A RECORD TAX TAKE just shy of €69 billion has plunged the Department of Finance into a worrying apology whirlpool as it searches for ways to send any portion of the proceeds back to large companies.

Despite the bulk of the tax take being derived from income tax, Minister for Finance Paschal Donohoe, acting out of pure muscle memory, has been lost in second-hand guilt and grief, tortured by the thought that such levels of revenue have come at the ultimate cost – the welfare of multinationals.

'Rebates, incentives, special designations, can we turn Achill Island into the Caymans of Connacht? I need solutions, people – €69 billion! Who let this happen?' a panicked Donohoe

said, rushing around the Department of Finance offices.

'Large companies invented jobs. Before multinationals, Irish people had never heard of an office or things like money. We owe them everything,' confirmed a frazzled-looking department official as they staged a whip-round for large companies.

Pleas to spend the record tax take on some of the programmes and services that were promised last year but failed to materialise, such as addiction and mental health services, were met with an outbreak of uncontrollable laughter.

Multinationals have thus far politely declined the Department of Finance's offers, leading officials to confirm it'll just leave the money

there on the table and if it's magically gone in the morning sure these things happen.

MAN WHO VOTED ALLIANCE PARTY GLAD REPUBLICAN GRANDFATHER NOT AROUND TO KNEECAP HIM

NOT YET FULLY COMFORTABLE in declaring himself out of the woods, local Down man Sean O'Gorman remains thankful his Republican grandfather wasn't around to quiz him over the assembly elections, because he'd collapse like a soggy biscuit in hot tea.

'Alliance, aye,' whispered O'Gorman, one of many across

the sectarian divide to vote for the party this time around, representing a historic shift in the politics of Northern Ireland.

'I could tell Granda all about how it's a tactical vote against the DUP in a Unionist stronghold but he'd be having none of it,' said O'Gorman, nervously looking over his shoulder despite the fact that his grandfather, Eamon O'Gorman, died in 2006.

Reflexively feeling his knees just to confirm their presence, O'Gorman shifted nervously as he talked about voting for who he thought was the best candidate in his area.

'So why do I feel dirty?' O'Gorman said, interrogating himself like he had been caught looking up Unionist-themed pornography.

O'Gorman, out of an abundance of caution, had visited his grandad's graveside in the days leading up to the election, just to be sure there would be no risk of ramifications for voting with the future and not the past in mind.

'I suppose one bit of comfort in supposedly betraying my family and my community is that none of this MLA shower will ever actually get to do a day's work in Stormont after the DUP threw a Brit-fit,' concluded O'Gorman.

On This Day

In 323 BC, Alexander the Great takes time out of conquering to have a little 'Alex time'.

7 May

CLIMATE CRISIS

SEEKING TO REASSURE the public after a damning UN-backed IPCC report on climate change suggested drastic measures and decisive interventions must be made to avert decades of weather-based catastrophes, the Irish government has said 'hey, we got this', despite the fact that they're rolling out the red carpet for resource-sapping and emission-generating data centres.

'Yes, it's true we've agreed to let Amazon level Leitrim and convert it into a giant data centre, but don't forget our pledge to plant one tree by the end of the decade,' confirmed the government, who all took separate cars to a press conference that was walking distance from Leinster House.

'And yes, just one single data centre will use more electricity than … ~~when really? That much? I've never~~ more than Kilkenny? Wow … but as we said, climatey changey stuff is our top priority,' added one government TD, fresh from lodging 57 separate objections to cycling infrastructure.

Responding to suggestions that perhaps begging big tech companies to build data centres, which create next to no long-term employment, cause a huge demand on local water supply and will soon account for

'WE TAKE CLIMATE CHANGE SERIOUSLY' SAYS GOVERNMENT OF NATION COVERED IN DATA CENTRES

30 per cent of the national electrical grid, is proof that this government is as capable of tackling the greatest threat to humanity as a fish is of playing for the LA Lakers, the government remained bullish.

'Now that's not fair, we have all these carbon taxes in the pipeline that will really cripple the bank account of those truly responsible for climate change: the average person,' explained Minister for Leaving the Multinationals the Fuck Alone, Paschal Donohoe.

Asked if now might be the time to engage with the farming sector on how to phase out the most inefficient and damaging forms of farming, the government leapt for cover under the nearest bush and cowered in fear.

WHAT WOULD IT TAKE FOR IRISH PEOPLE TO PROTEST?

WWN PARTNERED WITH all of Ireland's major survey companies for the most extensive poll conducted on the Irish public's attitude to social issues, scandal and matters of international importance.

After hearing from 4.5 million people on these many issues, we can produce the definitive list of outrages, atrocities and inequalities that would result in a mass protest movement:

- If RTÉ threatened to bring back *Fade Street*.
- If Carling launched a drink called English Guinness.
- If radical housing policies aimed at ensuring first-time buyers could access truly affordable housing resulted in house prices dropping for those already on the 'property ladder'.
- If anyone tried to introduce accountability in public office.
- If multinationals profits took a hit of anything greater than one cent.

TECHNOLOGY

PROS AND CONS OF DATA CENTRES IN IRELAND

IRELAND HAS BECOME the premier location for the world's leading tech companies to plonk a data centre, but is this a good thing for the country? *WWN* weighs up the pros and cons:

- **Pro:** There will be work for builders, who would otherwise face unemployment in Ireland, as there is no other demand for buildings of any other types currently.
- **Con:** Ireland won't meet any of its climate targets.
- **Pro:** It provides a small amount of employment in the short-term.

- **Con:** It provides a large amount of environmental damage in the short, medium and long-term.
- **Pro:** Data centres are vitally important in this era of online business and data storage.
- **Con:** We're only one click of an intern's mouse away from deleting the whole thing.
- **Pro:** Ireland is one of just two countries with a climate uniquely suited to housing data centres, meaning politicians have big multinationals wishing to build them here by the balls and can secure all manner of commitments to help offset the emissions and demand that the centres are put on the electricity grid.
- **Con:** These are Irish politicians we're talking about.
- **Pro:** Data centres can be used

to cover otherwise useless land, such as Longford.
- **Pro:** Becoming home to the storage of the world's data makes Ireland a country of huge importance and influence.
- **Con:** The Irish security forces tasked with securing such facilities are no match for Russian spies.
- **Pro:** The excessive heat generated by the centres can be re-routed and used to heat residential homes.
- **Con:** This is being sold as some sort of amazing innovation we should be grateful for, whereas, in reality, such things have been possible for 40-plus years.
- **Pro:** If one is located near the airport there is the possibility of tricking the government into building a Metrolink to it.

HERE ARE THE ONLY WAYS SINN FÉIN COULD LOSE THE NEXT ELECTION

WITH A COMMANDING LEAD in successive polls, Sinn Féin remains the party with the largest support and look on course to become the leading governing party after the next election.

However, could they let their lead slip? *WWN* examines how it could all go wrong for the Mary Lou McDonald-led party.

Game-changing events that could undo the party's progress in the polls include:

- The *Irish Independent* gains editorial control of all media outlets.
- In a masterstroke of Machiavellian political plotting, Leo Varadkar declares his support for Sinn Féin and tanks the party's poll numbers overnight as a result.
- Pearse Doherty finally reveals he is actually Danny Dyer and devotes himself to becoming a cockney geezer full-time.
- Sinn Féin accidentally hires whoever is in charge of Fianna Fáil's social media accounts.
- They interrupt any government minister who is in the middle of digging a massive hole for themselves during Dáil speeches.
- They produce a policy document stating that Nordie Tayto is the superior Tayto.
- Any of Gerry Adams's connections to the IRA are discovered by the public.

- The party loosens their vetting process for party candidates to include people with anti-vax beliefs, a history of xenophobic and sexist comments, senators who pocketed Covid grants, MLAs who don't bother turning up to Stormont and other assorted eejits.
- They extend their strong pronouncements in the Dáil for supporting women and the need to believe and support victims of all kinds to former members of the party who left amid accusations of being driven out and bullied.
- Voters discover a party in Northern Ireland called Sinn Féin that moved to make sure hunting with dogs was not banned, reversed its calls to reduce the tax rate to 12.5 per cent after discovering it would result in a cut to public spending and gutted sections of a new defamation law aimed at making it harder to cynically silence journalists by threatening them with legal action.
- They produce a housing report that suggests the crisis would take more than just Sinn Féin winning an election to solve.
- Mary Lou McDonald's middle-class background is revealed.
- We're all wiped out by a meteor before the next election takes place.

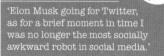

NORTHERN IRELAND

A STRESSED-OUT DUP leader, Jeffrey Donaldson, and his party of fossils are said to be longing for the simpler times before the introduction of the immovable presence of the Northern Ireland Protocol when the hardest problem to solve was eradicating gay cakes.

'It's much easier pretending gay cakes are the biggest threat to humanity than it is to sell the Protocol as a bad thing for the citizens of Northern Ireland when a lot of them realise it's the one thing keeping the DUP from obliterating the Good Friday Agreement and all economic green shoots available to them,' confirmed a DUP spokesperson after the drafting of a cross-party declaration opposing the protocol alongside other Unionist parties.

The declaration, which was signed by the DUP, UUP, TUV, PUP and the two remaining members of TLC, is set to have absolutely no impact on how Northern Ireland is viewed/ignored by the rest of the UK.

DUP LONG FOR SIMPLER TIMES OF FIGHTING HOMOSEXUAL CAKES

'Those were the days, huh? The Gay Cakes Wars, we call 'em. I have my medal at home. Jeffrey actually met with an LGBT group the other day, but

that was just to make sure they weren't putting in any orders with bakeries,' a misty-eyed Unionist remarked.

'It's hell on earth, frankly. We're here in pure misery with food on shelves in supermarkets and an ample supply of petrol at the forecourts – why can't we be like the rest of the UK? We should be tearing each other limb from limb in petrol station queues. It's our right as loyal subjects of the Crown,' cried one DUP member.

The DUP's mood was temporarily lifted by a visit from Prince William and Kate Middleton, who remarked that the Queen was being kind when she said of Northern Ireland, 'Don't visit that godforsaken place, it's the toilet where all other toilets go to take a shit.'

GOVERNMENT WAS HOPING YOU WOULDN'T FIND OUT ABOUT €36BN WORTH OF RUSSIAN ASSETS IN IRELAND

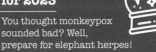
'AH, RIGHT, well, it's just, you see, em … shite,' confirmed the coalition government after it came under sustained questioning in the Dáil over

the presence of €36 billion in Russian assets sloshing around the IFSC in special purpose vehicles.

While several prominent government ministers have taken a tough line on Russia's invasion of Ukraine, it is believed the government was really hoping no one would be bringing up the sort of Russian assets, many of them linked to oligarchs, that would be ripe for being frozen.

'New email, who dis?' responded Minister for Finance Paschal Donohoe, some 24 months after Sinn Féin TD Mairéad Farrell first began asking what the government was going to do about the problem of Russia moving assets to Ireland to avoid sanctions.

'Actually, technically, it's not "dirty money" – what a ridiculous claim.

You think financial institutions charged with funnelling Russian money through Ireland would drop it on the floor or spill coffee on it? Cop on,' offered the Taoiseach in response to questions from the Social Democrats' Catherine Murphy.

Officials from the Department of Finance confirmed that they would be unable to act on these claims because if they looked into them they would be proven true and therefore they would have to act on them and face up to the fact that Ireland is a tax haven for criminals and war-crime-loving regimes.

Meanwhile, the MEPs who voted against measures to prevent refugees from drowning at sea have criticised other MEPs for not voting to fast-track Ukraine's membership to the EU.

JUDGE LEO VARADKAR CLEARS LEO VARADKAR OF ANY WRONGDOING AT LEO VARADKAR COURTS

IN A LEGAL JUDGMENT believed to be the first of its kind in Ireland, Tánaiste Leo Varadkar cleared himself of any wrongdoing at a special sitting of the Leo Varadkar Courts, presided over by Judge Leo Varadkar in front of a jury of himself.

'I guess it's pointless for the Director of Public Prosecutions to deliver its final decision on the matter in December,' confirmed Varadkar during the in camera proceedings, at which the Fine Gael leader and now full-time judge and jury tasked himself with finding himself not culpable for the leaking of documents he himself admitted to leaking.

Witnesses called to the stand included Leo Varadkar, who became quite emotional when cross-examined by himself. Somewhat out of breath due to his scurrying from the witness stand to the floor of the court, Varadkar threw a series of softball questions to himself before commending the witness for his courage and fortitude.

Innovative self-administered one-person courts with responsibility for settling accusations of alleged law breaking may not be confined to Varadkar, with the legal profession admitting that there is scope to extend this to anyone.

'Just think of the money saved on solicitor and barrister fees, and

with building, maintaining and staffing courts and police resources no longer needed. I've a few clients who would happily inform everyone that they've done nothing wrong and therefore that's the end of that,' confirmed one solicitor.

However, not everyone is happy. 'I would have liked a little more warning about the complete and unceremonious overhaul of the Irish legal system. What am I going to teach students now?' harped one disgruntled lecturer in criminal law.

Elsewhere, Mountjoy Prison lies empty today after inmates confirmed they'd all learned their lesson and deserved to go home.

HSE CEO PAUL REID CRUSHED TO DEATH BY PAY PACKET

CONDOLENCES HAVE FLOODED in from around the country after the untimely death of HSE CEO Paul Reid, who was crushed in a workplace accident earlier today, *WWN* has learned.

It is understood that Mr Reid was collecting his annual pay packet today but underestimated exactly how much money was in it before struggling to take his salary home.

'Unfortunately, Paul must have forgotten the extra pension allowance of €48,977 for 2020 in his pay packet today, and it was all too much for him to carry,' a HSE source confirmed today. 'The little legs on him gave way and that was it – splat!'

Despite making €238k more than the HSE's second-best-paid non-medical staff member, and €197k more than the Taoiseach, Reid was unaware of the sheer weight of his

€411,777 take-home pay packet and buckled under the pressure.

'It's mad that he didn't buckle under the pressure of all the scandals of the last few years,' another source stated. 'We really thought the Kerry CAMHS

thing would have been the final nail in his coffin, but it was the massive pay cheque that got him in the end. May he rest in peace.'

Reid leaves behind a whole catalogue of scandals, mismanagement and a not-fit-for-purpose national health system that continually fails its staff and citizens, who continue to pay €21 billion per year for it.

LOCAL MAN OKAY WITH BEING NUKED BY RUSSIA IF IT TAKES OUT BRITAIN TOO

A DISTURBING NEWS REPORT carried by Russian state TV depicting Ireland being obliterated by a giant wave caused by a nuclear strike has been labelled as 'regretful sure, but did you see what happens to Britain? Yeoow!' by local man Ciarán Earley.

'Will I miss being alive? Of course. Will I be sad that the entirety of the country will be gone too? Yes, obviously, but you've got to weigh up the pros and cons of these things, and the fact that Buckingham Palace will be sitting at the bottom of a nuclear underwater aquarium gets my vote,' Earley explained.

> **'Can you film the part where Big Ben goes Big Boom from a helicopter or something?'**

Earley is far from being an outlier in terms of his reaction, as vast swathes of Irish people have asked for further detail from Russian state broadcasters.

'Can you give us a rough date? "At a speed of 200kph"? Can it not go faster? Can you film the part where Big Ben goes Big Boom from a helicopter or something? A zoom-in on Nigel Farage's face even, that'd be class,' urged a growing number of Irish people, who are finally coming around to this whole World War III business.

Elsewhere, local woman Fidelma Gough has urged Russian military drones carrying underwater nuclear missiles to hold off visiting until she has had a chance to give the sitting room the once over, as it's a right mess currently.

Meanwhile, in retaliation to the provocative and worrying broadcast by the Russian station, RTÉ will tonight run a report that details the devastating damage to the Kremlin if a herd of drunken Healy-Raes were unleashed in the Russian capital.

My Highlight of 2022: Will Smith

'Probably getting the windshield wipers on my car to stop squeaking. Quiet enough year otherwise.'

COVENEY TO WITNESS FIRST-HAND THE HORRORS OF DUBLIN AIRPORT

MINISTER FOR FOREIGN AFFAIRS Simon Coveney has described his visit today to Dublin Airport as 'harrowing' and 'a testament to the strength and resilience of the human spirit', while on his way to meet Ukrainian government representatives in Kyiv today.

The flight from Dublin marks the first time Coveney had visited the war-torn airport since the start of the weeks of chaos that have followed the DAA's lay-off of huge numbers of staff. The Cork TD had extra army security assigned to him to ensure he made it to Kyiv safely.

'You don't know how lucky you have it until you've witnessed first-hand the horrors of Dublin Airport,' said a visibly moved Coveney as he met with a very sympathetic Volodymyr Zelenskyy.

'Men, women, children, families – all in upheaval, all trying their best to get out of the country. Some of them were there for hours at a time. Atrocious scenes, just ghastly. I had heard how bad it was and I thought I understood, but it's only when you see it with your own eyes that you really appreciate the humanitarian cost of it all. God help them, the poor divils. Anyways, how's yourself? Up to much these days?'

Coveney concluded his trip to Kyiv by pleading with Zelenskyy to donate

provisions to Dublin Airport to help with the crisis – personnel, equipment, weapons, anything.

IRISH TRUCK REAR-ENDED BY RUSSIAN EMBASSY GATES

IRISH STATE-CONTROLLED MEDIA – An innocent truck carrying valuable religious items was completely destroyed by a reckless set of stationary gates operated by the Russian Embassy.

The truck, which has already had a statue built to it and a special commemorative stamp issued bearing its likeness, is sadly not expected to make a full recovery despite mechanics arriving on the scene quickly, so grave were the injuries suffered during the shocking unprovoked attack by the gates.

'We have no knowledge of a truck, this is a clear act of aggression on the part of Russia,' said Supreme Leader Micheál Martin as he continued his exceptionally heroic leadership today, stating that the de-gate-ification of the Russian Embassy is proceeding as planned.

An Irish Defence Forces intelligence report proves beyond doubt that this was a pre-planned barbaric attack by the embassy, which installed the gates years ago in clear preparation for springing this surprise cowardly attack.

Legal professionals suggest the innocent driver is in line for significant damages after sustaining whiplash.

'This was a special reversing operation, there are no reversing truck crashes, Ireland does not participate in such things, stop swallowing Russian propaganda,' confirmed the Minister for the Removal of Gates, Simon Coveney.

Despite the vile subterfuge used by enemies of innocent trucks, Ireland has offered to open up a humanitarian corridor allowing safe passage for the gates to a safer area, such as the M50.

HEALTH

ON A HSE WAITING LIST FOR SURGERY? HERE ARE SOME HOME SURGERY HACKS

WAITING LISTS REMAIN a huge issue in the health service, and those awaiting surgery of the minor/major variety face serious delays amid a critical lack of access to healthcare.

Marketing and PR companies hired by the government with funds that probably could have been better spent going towards reducing waiting lists have been given the hard task of imploring people to think once more about their surgery and to consider having a go themselves.

Having talked with PR specialists who are pioneering new 'Waiting lists: a state of mind' and 'Trust your gut when performing gut surgery on yourself' campaigns, *WWN* can provide some essential tips on performing your own essential operation:

Glue
Stitches seem hard, right?

The sharpest knife in your house that has jagged edges
Oh, and something to bite down on.

Netflix
With a large library of TV shows, movies and documentaries, there's probably a lot of medical jargon to pick up on the fly while also being entertained.

YouTube
YouTube was great when you wanted to take up the guitar again, right? They've got to have lessons for non-invasive keyhole surgeries too?

More glue, some Pritt Stick? Blu-Tack? Duct tape?
As the saying probably goes – more adhesive, less chance this will go horribly wrong.

Don't panic when you're told this
It's really important you don't pass out after seeing all that blood.

What not to do
Do not make any public appeals, go on radio phone-ins, pressure local TDs or mobilise your family, friends and community to apply pressure on the faceless bureaucracy. They don't like that at all.

Sign this form
This just absolves the HSE of any responsibility. Yeah, sign right there, thanks.

MONOPOLY MAN EMERGES AS LAST-MINUTE FRONT-RUNNER FOR TORY LEADERSHIP

JUST AS Rishi Sunak was plotting a hometown celebration in New York to ring in his crowning as Tory leader and next British PM, a last-minute front-runner has emerged in the shape of board game baron and Monopoly man, Rich Uncle Pennybags.

'Comparing Rishi and Pennybags, it's clear that Pennybags edges it in the common touch stakes,' said one Conservative MP who has recently switched allegiance to the top hat-wielding mogul.

Tories who are now stating their new preference for Pennybags have denied that the man's access to Get Out of Jail Free cards had anything to do with their decision.

'With a fortune of just £500mn, he's much less wealthy than Sunak,

'Rishi thinks slumming it is taking the smaller yacht to Monaco'

so when he says "one doth hath knowledge of a plethora of kinfolk from the Sodom and Gomorrah council estates" you know he's being truthful, whereas Rishi thinks slumming it is taking the smaller yacht to Monaco,' confirmed one political insider.

'You have to factor in too that Pennybags was born with a monocle on his eye AND a spoon in his mouth, and us Tories can relate to that better than Rishi's humble beginnings,' confirmed one MP, who felt Sunak's impoverished family background of a GP and a successful pharmacist made some Tories feel dirty.

In the latest polling among Britons, 87 per cent of respondents said they would vote for the Monopoly man as they would prefer that their amoral vacuum of a leader who takes a flamethrower to the most vulnerable in society wear a funny hat.

No.1

On This Day

1987: The Wall Street crash brings an end to humanity's pursuit of wealth accumulation and greed.

19 October

HEALTH

REVEALED: OUR HOSPITAL WAITING LIST BLACKSPOTS

A NEW REPORT on hospital waiting times has revealed that where you live in Ireland can determine how soon you are treated, kind of, *WWN* finds.

The report, which pinpoints blackspot areas across the 26 counties, has left very few areas untouched, forcing the HSE to subsequently release areas where hospital waiting lists are not an issue.

'If you're on a waiting list and you live in the waters of the Atlantic Ocean or the Celtic or Irish Sea, then you've a good chance of being seen to in the next five years,' a HSE spokesperson confirmed, squinting at the black-dot-riddled map of Ireland in a bid to find anywhere else not in a black spot area. 'Nope, that's about it, everywhere else is screwed, basically.'

The waiting lists, which were a long-standing issue before the pandemic, have now evolved into third-world levels of health care, with some patients travelling to Africa in a bid to be seen by a specialist.

'I said we'd be faster cycling to Ethiopia for my nine-year-old son's scoliosis surgery,' explained one desperate father, now on his way back with his teenage son on the crossbar after a successful operation. 'We set off in June 2019 and were seen just last week, incredible level of care here. Really impressed. We should be home in time to cancel his place on the HSE waiting list later this year.'

Despite its ever-increasing budget year-on-year, a legacy of underfunding, poor management and governance, alongside a lack of beds and specialist healthcare workers and

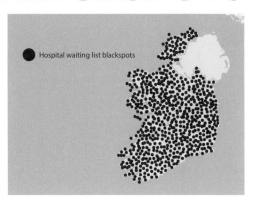

Hospital waiting list blackspots

staff redeployment to pandemic care, has taken its toll on the Irish health care system, leaving it almost obsolete, except for one thing.

'But look at all the lives we saved from Covid by parking all the other healthcare for two years,' a spokesperson concluded, before being consumed by an angry mob.

'ARE YOU SURE? Double-check,' Department of Housing officials stated when a secretary confirmed that, despite the recent news from DRHE that 115 homeless people died in Dublin last year, there was no angry mob outside on the street demanding inquiries, accountability and a basic level of humanity.

'So do we even bother with a serious-wordy-very-sad-must-do-better-policies-are-working-type statement?'

'Well, if a statement is issued about 115 people dying and no one is bothered to fucking read it, does the statement even exist?'

Shaking with relief that such a seismic and hard-to-comprehend story hadn't caused a single ripple, officials themselves struggled to comprehend the apathy and malignant disinterest.

'Not even the usual crowd taking the news as an opportunity to explain it all away with "some choose to

RELIEF IN GOVERNMENT AS 115 HOMELESS DEATHS IN DUBLIN NOT REALLY BOTHERING PUBLIC

sleep in tents", "they're all addicts" or "define homeless", no?' a bewildered official said, quadruple-checking outside the window for even one single person incensed enough to show up.

'Jesus, these heartless motherfuckers are almost as cold, distant and unfeeling as our housing policies,' remarked one full-time landlord, part-time TD.

Another official considered for a moment contemplating the eventual public outrage when nationwide homeless deaths were collated before realising how stupid and naïve he sounded.

'Whoa, wait a second, there are a few articles here about homeless figures being down by 27 per cent from last year … not a single person making the connection. Christ on a bike, we're getting good PR out of this!' said one distraught, guilt-ridden official before it all became too much and they left the building to start a lone protest against themselves.

BREAKING

SINN FÉIN REPULSED BY FACT THEY'RE NOW THE PARTY OF BOURGEOIS MIDDLE CLASS VOTERS TOO

REACTING to an *Irish Times* poll that places them as the top-performing party across a significant number of demographics, Sinn Féin have confirmed 'ew' when it dawned on them that this meant traditionally non-RAing middle-class voters too.

'Like, 4x4 mother at school gates in D4land middle-class? Shops in M&S and doesn't even moan about how expensive it is middle class? Belts out "Ireland's Call" at the Aviva middle class? I think I'm going to be sick,' said a Sinn Féin spokesperson, while also giving it the 'yeah, yeah, sure we're a party for everyone' line.

'I can just hear them now, confidently enunciating foreign words even though they're not remotely fluent in Italian or French,' continued the SF man, who confirmed that leader Mary Lou McDonald's middle-class credentials don't count, as she has reached the necessary 'shouting *tiocfaidh ár lá'* quota for 100 people.

Despite the dawning realisation of their new status, Sinn Féin largely welcomed the poll, while ignoring the fact that it also found Leo Varadkar to be more popular than McDonald.

'Look it, we'll take these voters I suppose, as long as they don't start moaning when our "solving housing and health solutions" turns out to be just us shouting "everyone voted for us to force a border poll immediately" 24/7,' added the spokesperson.

'We're not "eat the rich" communists, but we're also not willing to listen to someone say that a rioja has notes of fermented nutty pineapple or whatever. Wine is just tipsy Ribena, and that's the party's official stance,' concluded the spokesperson, beginning to wonder if winning an election would even be worth it if it involves representing people who willingly watch those Michael Portillo train programmes.

Elsewhere, in an attempt to win over working-class voters, Fine Gael have unveiled an advertising campaign called 'Sure didn't we give you no-good moochers the PUP'.

POLITICIANS' BRAINS TO BE HIT HARD BY VACANT PROPERTY TAX

A LOOPHOLE in a government-proposed vacant property tax could see a significant levy applied to Irish politicians' brains, *WWN* can reveal.

'Sadly there is no more dilapidated a structure, none more cavernous and neglected, than that of a politician's brain,' explained one housing expert. 'The echo within the structure can be heard for miles around.

'Leaving any brain vacant is a moral failing, and with the definition of what a vacant property is left suitably vague, politicians have left themselves open to being taxed for never using them,' added the expert, describing a loophole that is sure to prove lucrative for the exchequer.

Meant to form part of the government's Housing For All plan, the overabundance of derelict brains belonging to politicians could create a new tax revenue stream in the millions that is sure to bankrupt the worst-offending politicians.

'Just imagine the taxes levied on some independent TDs, never mind government ministers, who try to cover their arses with excuse after excuse,' chimed in one member of the public, delighted to see a new tax that doesn't gouge him for once.

However, the scenes of jubilation have been tempered somewhat by the realisation that civil servants will be the ones responsible for collecting the tax and ensuring compliance.

'Another loophole has civil servants identified as untouchable protected structures too,' sighed one housing expert.

HEALTH

STAFF SHORTAGES in the nation's ICU units may have been solved by an innovative contraption currently under trial in St Vincent's University Hospital in Dublin, where a tethered farm animal following a carrot on a stick is 'pretty much running the show'.

Conditions at St Vincent's have reached such a critical stage that staff were reported to be keeping an eye on patients using baby monitors earlier this week, prompting the need to find a solution to the staffing crisis but without having to go to the government looking for more money.

As such, the donkey-wheel device that operates a pulley that distributes medicines, changes pillows and presses the button that won't stop beeping has been implemented, with HSE bosses confident that they can have one operating in every ICU in the country by the end of the month.

Cost of Living Tips

Begin charging friends and family a small fee for replies to their WhatsApp messages.

HOSPITAL ICU CURRENTLY BEING RUN BY DONKEY WALKING AROUND CIRCLE CHASING CARROT

'There was one nurse complaining about receiving €126 for a 13-hour shift the other day. Ha! Do you know how much carrots and baling twine that would buy?'

'You hear a lot of ICU nurses complain about the 18-hour shifts, the lack of time off due to shortages and the supposedly "laughable" wages, but ol' Donk over there hasn't given out once,' beamed a HSE spokesperson.

'There was one nurse complaining about receiving €126 for a 13-hour

My highlight of 2022: Mary Lou McDonald

'Living rent-free in Leo Varadkar's head, 24/7, 365.'

shift the other day. Ha! Do you know how much carrots and baling twine that would buy? Honestly, we were worried that we'd have a major staffing crisis on our hands with the number of nurses quitting under the strain or leaving our shores to find decent work, but it looks like Eeyore and the gang might save the day.'

The HSE went on to say that they now had dozens of 'donkey consultant' roles that needed to be filled by civil servants, with a starting salary of €250k a year, no questions asked.

RURAL TRANSPORT SOLUTIONS

- Build one particularly long bus that stretches from Malin to Mizen Head.
- Move isolated rural villages closer to each other, inch by inch, every year. By the time locals realise it will be too late and they'll be living in a city.
- Eamon Ryan announces a grant for people to buy saddles that they can attach to wolves once they're reintroduced into the wild in Ireland.
- Solve the school bus shortage by painting the words 'school bus' on a horse and cart.
- Force-feed rural couples oysters; the aphrodisiac will help boost town populations over 10,000 so they will qualify for a town bus service from the NTA.
- Alter and repair potholes to make them more ramp-like in structure so that they help to propel vehicles to their destination more efficiently.
- Establish clear 'drink driving only' times on roads, giving those who wish to refrain from such activity advanced notice.
- Finally, give up the pretence of speed limits and replace all signs with 'fucking floor it, sure'.

Waterford Whispers News

VOL 1, 6136   WATERFORD, TUESDAY, 6 DECEMBER, 1921   2p

American Politician Joe Biden Oversees Anglo-Irish Treaty

VETERAN US politician Joseph Biden congratulated the British and Irish delegations on signing the Anglo-Irish Treaty today, hailing it as the first step towards peace between the warring nations after decades of unrest, WWN reports.

The ageing Mr Biden stated that the agreement will likely avoid further bloodshed and that Northern Ireland, which had been created earlier by the Government of Ireland Act, could serve as a 'bacon of cross-community hope'. Asked to clarify if he meant to say 'beacon' Mr Biden instead hugged the Treaty in an overly familiar manner.

'There will be some wrinkles to iron out, but I'm sure this is the last time we'll hear of any more fisticuffs between these two fine nations,' a tired and wrinkled Mr Biden said, nodding off slightly from what he claimed was 'boat-lag' before continuing, 'with Michael [Collins] and Arthur [Griffith] representing the new republic for years to come, I can't see how this Treaty, despite its imperfections, will lead to anything but political, religious and social harmony for centuries to come.'

Vowing to see the Treaty through, the 54-year-old Delaware man said he would continue to nurture the agreement to its end, no matter how long it takes.

'I will do everything in my power to see Ireland gets its entire island back and will remain on this earth until my mission is complete,' Biden concluded, before putting on a pair of unusual blackened-out spectacles.

FINANCE

PENSION SCHEME LAUNCHED SO YOU POOR FUCKS CAN PAY €2,000 RENT WHEN YOU RETIRE

Project Ireland 2040
Building Ireland's Future

WHAT FIRST APPEARED to be a sensible way to help lower- and middle-income individuals to enrol in a pension scheme has been confirmed by the government as yet another way for them to not bother addressing the housing crisis.

'See, a lot of you paupers will never own a home, and once you're 67 you won't be able to pay your €2,000 rent with the measly state pension alone. We needed to act to

make sure landlords can keep raking it in,' confirmed Minister for Social Protection Heather Humphreys.

The atmosphere at the official launch of the new pension scheme had a celebratory air as the horror movie nightmare scenario of actually building large-scale social housing was once again avoided.

'If we hadn't acted we would have been looking at an awful scenario where build-to-rent properties owned by foreign pension funds might have been adversely affected in years to come. Thankfully, you get to work hard and put away a few euros each month for 40 years so that you can grow old in an extortionate place not of your own, using your pension to

fund someone else's fatter pension,' continued the minister.

Questions about how the pension pot money will be invested by the state remain unanswered, but it is believed that this will all become clear whenever the government raids the pension scheme in the future to pay for the next bank and developer bailout.

'It's hardly our concern anyway. We've more pensions than you've had hot dinners,' concluded the cabinet.

Your Census Time Capsules

'Time to come clean, I kept Shergar in my back garden.' - Gerry (74), Louth

NUNS PROMISE THEY WON'T HAVE ANYTHING TO DO WITH MATERNITY HOSPITAL OR YOUR STUPID WHORE VAGINA

MINISTER FOR HEALTH Stephen Donnelly has expressed exasperation at the public's continued questions about the Church's involvement with the new maternity hospital, and insists that he has assurances from high-ranking nuns that the hospital will offer a full range of services to 'even the dirtiest of trollops'.

'Okay, we'll admit that wasn't his best interview on the subject,' said one of Donnelly's PR team, after the minister became aggravated and expressed a desire for everyone to 'get over it, for the love of God' during an appearance on RTÉ radio this morning.

'But what more can he say on the subject? Everyone from the Taoiseach to the Tánaiste to that old nun over there with the gnarled hands and the worn-to-nothing rosary beads have stated that there will be no Catholic ethos at play in the new maternity hospital. What, are you telling me that

people don't trust the leaders of this country teaming up with a big load of nuns? I can see why Stephen went full trampoline out there.'

While the debate on the dealings behind the NMH continues, legal experts have concurred that although

the services that will be provided for pregnant women at the site will be in keeping with current laws surrounding abortion, there was a lot of quite old-fashioned language used that was cause for concern.

'This framework document does indeed tally with what we would expect from a completely secular institution, but did they really need to say that terminations would be available for "anyone who couldn't keep their legs closed"?' said one legal advisor.

'And the mention of a "silly girl" ward, that seems unnecessary. Sometimes you can see where they should have written "woman" but instead they've written "hussy". Things like that. But other than that, no concerns.'

If you would like to congratulate the government on a deal well done, go to the 'Contact us' page at www.oireachtas.ie.

21

COVID

VARADKAR LAST SEEN SWIMMING TO WASHINGTON AS TAOISEACH TESTS POSITIVE FOR COVID

JUST MOMENTS AFTER Taoiseach Micheál Martin was diagnosed with Covid-19 while in Washington for St Patrick's Day events, Tánaiste Leo Varadkar was spotted frantically swimming for the American capital, *WWN* can confirm.

Mr Martin was due to meet with US President Joe Biden in the White House later today, but this has since been cancelled. However, a spokesperson for Varadkar has stated that he is already halfway there, and is expected to deliver a bowl of shamrock to the US President, no matter what.

'Literally seconds after hearing it, Leo was gone,' a source said, recalling

the moment. 'Leo was in Chile doing the Saint Patrick's Day rounds, but has now cancelled all official events here and took off like a torpedo in his Speedos.'

Varadkar was spotted overtaking cargo ships in the Panama Canal with a large bowl of shamrock in tow and is expected to reach Washington around lunchtime.

'If he treated the urgency of the housing crisis in Ireland with such haste we'd all be settled into a gaff by Monday,' our source added. 'Micheál rang him to tell him he was sick and he just dropped the phone, whipped off his clothes and was already wearing swimming gear like he was prepared – he didn't even say get well soon to the Taoiseach or ask how he was, he just dived in and tore off like a rocket-powered Fungie.'

THE NEWLY INSTALLED LEADER of fanatical pro-austerity political outfit the Labour Party, Ivana Bacik, has confirmed that her party are very much forgotten but not gone, as she targets reclaiming lost support.

'We're relying heavily on the public developing mass amnesia and young people not being smart enough to Google "Labour Party in government". I hope my becoming leader gives people pause to realise "wait, are Labour still a thing?" and we can build from there,' confirmed Bacik, who replaces Alan 'The Power' Kelly as the party's leader.

Plans are already in place to inform the public that, while everyone presumed that Labour

BACIK REMINDS PUBLIC THAT LABOUR PARTY ARE FORGOTTEN BUT NOT GONE

were a figment of their imagination, they actually remain a fully malfunctioning political entity.

'Voters have said we should apologise for our time in government, and we've heard that feedback, which is why we've said "Ah that was ages ago, anyway follow us on TikTok",' confirmed Labour's head of brand rehabilitation.

Large posters and leaflets are to be distributed around the country bearing the party's new slogan, 'Vote for Labour if you can't bear voting for Fine Gael but don't mind us being in government to help deliver their policies'.

Labour's new campaign seems to be working, as members of the public *WWN* spoke with certainly remember Ireland's former premier left-wing party.

'Is that the lot that cut the dole for the under-25s during a recession? Think I recall them,' offered one man, defecating on a Labour Party leaflet.

IN-DEPTH REPORT

UNLIMITED SNACK BOXES, ALL-IRELAND FINAL TICKETS, COPPERS GOLD CARDS: INSIDE GARDAÍ ON THE TAKE

WITH THE NATIONAL BUREAU OF CRIMINAL INVESTIGATION (NBCI) raiding the homes of three serving members of the Gardaí over connections to criminal gangs, *WWN* goes deep undercover and chats with several members of the force who are 'on the take'.

'People might think an unlimited supply of snack boxes might be a strange request, but I'm saving myself around €50 a day on lunch and dinners,' one Garda explains, admitting to receiving free food from a local fast-food business known for laundering money for gangs. 'It's harder to trace freebies, especially ones you can eat and shit back down the jacks.'

According to a Tipperary Garda working in Dublin, Coppers Gold Cards have become more expensive than gold thanks to nightclub restrictions and a now undermanned, underfunded force.

'Can you distort my voice?' the guard asked

WWN, before being told his voice cannot be heard in printed form. 'Ah grand, mad what ye can do these days with technology, isn't it?'

'Yeah, Coppers cards, that's the new currency, lad. I could get three to five of them babies a month for tipping off local pushers.

Frontliners are screaming out for them at the mo ahead of the big reopening, with one card going for €1,100 – twice my average weekly wage. I usually charge nurses less, though, if they agree to give me a snaky shift.'

In some instances, ham sandwiches wrapped in tinfoil were offered as bribes, along with half-price All-Ireland tickets or, in more extreme cases, new Garda uniforms.

'Things are tight at HQ, so I had to barter for a new pair of shoes and stab vest in exchange for tipping off a grow house,' another cash-strapped Garda said. 'I'm not proud of it, but we're all

at it – I know an ambulance paramedic who swapped morphine for a working defibrillator one time so he could save a man's life.'

With bribery seemingly rife in the force, many Gardaí we spoke to pointed to not earning enough money, long hours and not being treated with respect by senior Gardaí as viable excuses for breaking their code of honour.

'I don't think there's a guard out there who would turn down Croke Park box tickets in exchange for the whereabouts of a known informant,' concluded one guard. 'At the end of the day, both sides absolutely hate rats.'

BREAKING NEWS

YURI FILATOV OVERWHELMED BY OFFERS OF FREE LIFTS TO DUBLIN AIRPORT

AFTER HIS STAR TURN in an interview with RTÉ's David McCullagh, Yuri Filatov has been on the receiving end of Ireland's notorious friendliness, hospitality and generosity.

'I'm heading out that way meself anyway, so I'll drive you. No, I insist, you monumental prick,' one person outside the Russian Embassy offered, bringing a tear to the eye, such was the selflessness on display.

'Fuck the Port Tunnel fee, Yuri, I'll pay it for you. Speeding fines mean nothing to me either, if I can say I got you to the airport quickly,' added a learner driver whose 1.1-litre engine was going to be tested to its limits.

Regardless of current work commitments, school drops or social occasions, Irish people have said they'd be willing to cancel all that at the drop of a hat just to make sure Filatov got to the airport and they could watch him enter the departures lounge.

'Stop fussing, Yuri, it's grand. I said I'd drive you so I'll drive. Sure I'd do it for anyone – well, anyone complicit in an unjust invasion that heaps misery

on innocent people,' added another person, who had offered the US ambassador similar generosity during the 'war on terror'.

Not meaning to rush Filatov, the 4km-long queue of people offering him a free lift insisted there was no

time to pack anything, not even the bullshit statements filled with lies he very clearly reads from when being interviewed about the war on Ukraine.

'The traffic at this hour is terrible. Never mind a car, I've made this catapult. We'll have you home in no time. All the watermelons during testing exploded, but I'm sure you'll be fine,' said an amateur inventor and war criminal expulsion enthusiast.

Elsewhere, a tearful Irish government has been outside the Russian Embassy since 6 a.m. shouting 'We're only sending non-lethal support to Ukraine, so just bear that in mind if you're escalating things' via a megaphone.

STRUGGLING WITH THE COST OF LIVING? HAVE YOU CONSIDERED BECOMING A TD?

THE COMBINATION of inflation, wage stagnation and every conceivable business and service raising their prices has had a devastating effect on the wallets of those Irish people who were already struggling to keep afloat.

However, there is light at the end of the tunnel, as outlined by *WWN*'s money man and consumer expert, Freddy Knobs, who has revealed a simple way to combat cost-of-living struggles:

- Become a TD. I cannot stress this enough, become a TD.
- Need a little extra income in the house? Once you're a TD, just make a family member your parliamentary assistant. That way they're bringing in some extra cash on top of your salary.

- Your Public Representation Allowance could net you anywhere between €16k and €20k in expenses per year. If you're a millennial, just think of the avocado-on-toasts!
- And remember, under the travel and accommodation allowance you can claim for petrol, even on days you're not in Leinster House.
- Then there's the one-off constituency office allowance of €8k. It's hard to keep up with all these allowances, but in short – the cost of living means as much to you now you're a TD as algebra does to a fish.
- Concerned about how you can't afford the basics, like a phone? Not anymore – you can claim €750 for a phone!

- 'What about the 15 per cent rise in house prices this year alone' you ask? Duh, one in four TDs are landlords. This won't just be the last of your worries, it'll be the first of your joys. Think of the passive wealth you'll be accumulating.
- What if you get the boot from the electorate? Don't worry, you still have your pension, and even if you only do three years you'll get a year's worth of severance payments in the region of €50k. Just think of all the electricity and petrol you can buy with that! At least a week's supply.

UKRAINE UPDATE

WOMAN TEARING UP AT BUILDING LIT IN BLUE AND YELLOW TO WELCOME REFUGEES WITH FOLDED ARMS

DUBLIN NATIVE Noleen Andrews became very emotional passing by Leinster House and seeing the landmark lit up in blue and yellow in solidarity with Ukraine, seemingly unaware that her heart will turn to stone once a friend says 'we're taking in too many'.

'As an abstract concept, my heart is broken over Ukraine. But c'mon, actually taking in 20,000 refugees? It's weird, the closer I feel any of them getting to Ireland, my sympathy seems to lessen. This was more of a hashtag support for me,' offered Andrews, who confessed to being an awful softy who cries at anything.

'Don't get me wrong, I'd give them the shirt off my back figuratively, but literally speaking I'm going to immediately harden to these people fleeing war and pre-emptively tell my local TDs they'll have lost my vote if any end up in the constituency.'

Andrews is set to become very open and receptive to phone-in radio shows suggesting that any male Ukrainian refugees making their way to Ireland must be lying criminals out to defile her, having defied an order for all 18-to-60-year-old men to remain in the country to fight.

'As long as they're not kept in Dublin. There's no room in the city,

> **'Stick them in empty rural villages if you must, but not too close to anything'**

let alone the suburb I live in,' said Andrews, not even 50 metres further along the road from Leinster House.

'Stick them in empty rural villages if you must, but not too close to anything,' continued Andrews, as she posted blue-and-yellow heart emojis on a Facebook photo of Leinster House lit up.

'And anyway, we need to help our own. What about the homeless?' Andrews concluded, while flat-out ignoring a homeless woman asking her for help.

EXCLUSIVE

WE TRAVEL TO EAMON RYAN'S GREEN IRELAND OF THE FUTURE

WITH THE COALITION'S Climate Action Plan being published today while Glasgow plays host to the ongoing COP26 conference, everyone's minds have been drawn to focusing on the issue of averting climate disaster.

But what will a greener Ireland look like? We take some peyote with a local farmer and travel to Eamon Ryan's green Ireland of the future to find out:

- All farmers have been retrained as therapists who specialise in comforting bees, helping them process the trauma humans have inflicted on them.
- The dairy herd is no more, and all cows have been replaced by robotic cows that lactate servers to be used in one of the 10,000 data centres Ireland now has.

- Community gardens are flourishing. Today, it's Aoife's turn to hold the nation's lettuce leaf.
- After covering Irish roads in landmines, travel by car has been reduced to zero.
- The last remaining person using turf in their fire is executed in front of thousands in a sold-out 3Arena, which is powered by recycled Guinness farts.
- Irish people have no need for bikes after evolving to grow tyres for legs. However, the public transport system remains unchanged.
- The terror campaign of the radical IFA group has waned after years of tractor-based attacks. However, the Continuity IFA continues to drop hemp-wearing hippies into silage.
- Those who feared that the cost of the government's Climate Action Plan and carbon budgets would

just mean more taxes heaped on the nation were right, as there is an effective tax rate of 99 per cent for anyone who has eaten meat in the last decade.
- Large companies continue to express their disappointment in Irish people, the real drivers of emissions.
- Data centres replace hotels as the number one thing being built in Dublin.
- Homelessness no longer carries any negative connotations, as living out under the stars and never leaving your tent is seen as the perfect way to reduce your carbon footprint.
- Thankfully, in the future, if you're a sitting minister you can sleep when you want, where you want and no one makes fun of you and you don't become a meme.

Bill's Landlord Tips

Presumably, as a landlord, you've already moved all your assets into an offshore special investment vehicle? If not, get on it, because when Sinn Féin are in charge they're going to nationalise your wallet.

Cost Of Living
WEEKLY

Emigration?
Nah, you
love it here

9 MEALS
YOU CAN MAKE
WITH JUST DRY PASTA

Gas & Electricity:
Do you need them both?

You're too thick to understand inflation, so just accept it's your fault

LOCAL NEWS

BREAKING NEWS

LOCAL WOMAN STEERS EVERY CONVERSATION AROUND TO WHEN SHE LIVED ABROAD

TIME AFTER TIME, Waterford woman Margaret Hamilton has proven that there isn't an element of life in Ireland that she can't compare to life in Belgium, where she lived for 18 months some 12 years ago.

Hamilton, now 39, will stop a conversation dead with 'Now, you

see when I was living in Belgium it was much different', which her friends have learned is a sign that they're in for at least 10 minutes of self-indulgent waffle from her.

'Pet care? Better in Belgium. Childcare? Better in Belgium, even though she didn't have any kids at the time, so I don't know how she knows that,' said one of Hamilton's long-suffering friends, who has vowed to never visit Belgium out of sheer principle.

'Road tax, fairer in Belgium. Pint prices, restaurant choice, the taste of the damn chips in McDonald's. Everything is better in Belgium, and boy does she love to remind us. For the love of God, she hasn't been there in over a decade. It could be a nuclear waste ground these days for all she knows, but she'll still maintain you'd get a better blaa in Brussels than you would in Waterford.'

Hamilton's friends can usually get her back down to earth by assuring her that it was a shame she had to leave Belgium because her fella at the time dumped her.

REASSURING HER NEW NEIGHBOURS arriving for the first time at a Dublin city hotel, mother-of-three Deirdre Ryan revealed that they'll get used to the place eventually, even the bit where you're not allowed to mix with hotel guests or use the facilities during the day.

'You'll all get used to it after nine months,' Ms Ryan explained, her head now going side to side as Ukrainian refugees poured past her in the narrow hall of Ireland's latest profiteer of human suffering. 'The hotels must be making a fortune from all this – not that they pay any of that back in respect for their tenants.'

Around 4,500 refugees from Ukraine are currently staying in hotel

Predictions for 2023

Ukrainian refugees will move up one place in Ireland's 'bogeyman' rankings.

'DON'T WORRY, YOU'LL GET USED TO IT AFTER NINE MONTHS' IRISH SINGLE MOTHER TELLS UKRAINIAN STAYING IN HOTEL

accommodation across Ireland, in a move described by the government as only for initial 'short-term stays', a claim Direct Provision refugees in Ireland say shouldn't be taken seriously.

'Don't get your hopes up with this lot,' Mosney resident Yetunde Bolaji stated, adding, 'If the way they treated us is anything to go by, you'll all be shoved into Portakabins in a rural field somewhere for the next 10 years, scraping for tinned tomato soup and rolls, choking on the mouldy rooms,' before then realising Ukrainians are white. 'Oh wait, totally forgot you're the "good refugees", and will be put to work and exploited in low-paying jobs instantly.'

As a kind and generous heads-up to incoming refugees, one father-of-two in emergency accommodation advised Ukrainians to tell immigration officials that they are foreign investment funds looking to buy build-to-rent apartments.

EXCLUSIVE

INSURANCE COMPANY WON'T REST UNTIL IT CLOSES EVERY LAST BUSINESS SELLING CRAIC

IRISH INSURANCE COMPANIES have claimed they are edging closer to winning the war on craic after yet another adventure centre has had to close its doors thanks to yet another extortionate quote, forcing the business out of the market.

'Children's playgrounds, adventure parks, leisure centres – basically, anything that involves even the slightest bit of craic for families will be eradicated by 2025,' a spokesperson for the Irish insurance industry promised today.

So far, the insurance companies' war on craic has taken hundreds of Irish businesses dealing in family fun to the proverbial cleaners, with the latest adventure centre closing

in Bray after being quoted almost four times their premium as last year, crippling the craic for thousands of addicts.

'When you're the only insurance company left in the country able to facilitate insurance for a certain sector then you've got to do the right thing and decimate that sector with totally unreasonable quotes, forcing them to close and thus destroying dozens of jobs in the process,' the insurance industry spokesperson added, while playfully drowning kittens in a bucket for fun. 'There's no better time to fuck over a small-to-medium-sized business than the present – God knows the economy could do with a swift kick in the nuts right now.'

Despite government reforms in new judicial guidelines that slashed awards for personal injury cases coming in early last year, insurance companies are expected to continue acting like members of the Italian mafia regardless, extorting millions from compliant business owners while playing the tired old compensation card.

'Hey, look, don't blame us, blame the judges awarding little Johnny 70 grand for scratching his knee – we're only here to capitalise on insurance scammers by becoming scammers ourselves,' the spokesperson concluded, now masturbating to pictures of businesses he has helped close.

Your Census Time Capsules

'OGGIE OGGIE OGGIE ...'
– Declan (37), Dublin

'PORN, UNDERAGE DRINK, LOOSE CIGARETTES, FLICK KNIVES, HEPATITIS C': WATERFORD BIDS A POIGNANT FAREWELL TO A BELOVED LOCAL SHOP

YET ANOTHER ICONIC BUSINESS in Waterford city closed its doors for the last time yesterday, prompting hundreds if not thousands of locals to come forward and reminisce fondly about the beloved corner shop, J. Rattigan & Sons, and its inimitable owner, James 'Rat Face' Rattigan.

Rattigan, now in his 70s despite looking like a 90-year-old man for the last 40 years, made the decision to close the store this year, citing 'enough is fucking enough' as a reason to bring the shutters down on a storied career that made him the stuff of legend in the locality.

'We always used to go in when we were seven or eight. We'd buy penny sweets and Banshee Bones and single cigarettes and matches,' said one man we spoke to, through his electronic voice box.

'A lot of other shops wouldn't sell loose fags to kids, but Rat Face was sound like that. He knew we didn't have money for a ten pack of Major, so he'd break it up among us. Newsagents these days wouldn't do that for kids. So now you've got kids ordering vapes and fluid over the internet. Not us, though. We got cancer the old-fashioned way!'

'A lot of other shops wouldn't sell loose fags to kids, but Rat Face was sound like that'

Stories like this were plentiful on social media last night, as more and more locals came forward with tear-filled recollections of the shop that 'had it all'.

'Your ma would send you down for a quarter-pound of ham, a bale of briquettes and a newspaper for your da. But it wasn't just groceries, you could buy *The Beano*, a box of Fun Snaps and an army surplus flick knife that Jimmy would have in a box of stuff under the counter,' laughed one local. 'How only that one kid got stabbed to death, I'll never know.'

'It's the shop I learned how to rob in,' sobbed a hardened local drug lord, who owes his start to Rattigan's shop. 'We'd go in and nick anything – tins of sardines, light bulbs, shit we didn't even need. When Jimmy would catch us he'd kick the shit out of us, so we'd come back after hours and spray-paint on the shutters, calling him a paedo and whatnot. He broke a glass jar of beetroot over my head when I was nine. Ah, happier times.'

'I remember my mam would send me down to get her sanitary towels, and as Jimmy would be wrapping them in newspaper he'd ask me if I'd gotten my first period yet, or was I "still only a girl",' said a local woman, who had been convinced at the time not to report this kind of thing, as it was 'only messing'.

Amid further stories, about blood-borne diseases that people picked up from eating sliced luncheon meats cut at the small cold meats counter, or charming tales of Mr Rattigan selling hardcore porn mags to 'any boy that wanted one', the people of Waterford united in their sadness that there 'wouldn't be another shop like Rattigan's' in the locality ever again.

The tiny corner site is expected to be bought by a local vulture fund, which will leave it to sit idle for 10 years before selling it on for twice the value.

TRAVEL

DUBLIN AIRPORT LUGGAGE TURNS UP AT CERN

PASSENGERS who lost their luggage coming through Dublin Airport can breathe a sigh of relief today after scientists at CERN confirmed that hundreds of suitcases were found scattered along the hadron collider and will be returned in due course.

Along with the luggage, several disorientated passengers were also found wandering around the facility before being shuttled to a nearby hospital to be treated for shock.

'Last thing I remember I was queueing for security and the next I'm walking around the tunnel,' said Irishman and Ryanair passenger-to-be, Martin Sterling, who spent three days walking around in circles before being found, 'I was meant to fly to Paris but ended up in Switzerland. I just thought this was normal Ryanair practice.'

Dublin Airport confirmed a chartered flight will now fly to Geneva to collect the hoard of luggage and lost passengers.

'We have no idea how this happened,' a joint statement from Aer Lingus, Ryanair and Dublin Airport read, 'we can only apologise to those passengers affected and charge them three times the tare back from Switzerland.'

A spokesscientist at CERN stated that this isn't the first time lost items have been found at the facility, confirming thousands of odd socks, teaspoons, pens and car keys are regularly discovered at the site.

'WE'D ABSOLUTELY MURDER A FUCKING STEAK RIGHT NOW'

GREYSTONES NATIVES David and Stephen Flynn, aka the Happy Pear, chat to *WWN* about their 14 years on a vegan diet, and how most of their free time is taken up with cravings for a 10-ounce fillet steak and prawn surf 'n' turf drenched in pepper sauce and chips laced in goose fat.

'Aw stop it now, we're famished just thinking about it,' the Happy Pear began, both speaking at the same time, weirdly harmonising with one another. 'We'd absolutely murder a fucking steak right now, preferably rare as fuck, blue and still throbbing.'

The Happy Pear are known for their infectious energy, their hit café in Greystones and of course their delicious vegetarian food range, along with inspirational Instagram content that primarily consists of them sea swimming, doing handstands and recipes for 12,000 different vegan curries.

'I'd eat the hind legs off a donkey at this stage,' both brothers said, emphasising the fact that they really miss eating animals. 'We'd eat you if it wasn't illegal,' they added, now whispering suspiciously to each other as one locked the café front door.

As I made my way nearer the door, the Flynn brothers reassured me that they were only 'pulling my leg', and not to be afraid of their hilarious inside twin jokes.

'It's just these cravings, you know?' they again both said at the same time, drool now visible, eyes manic with hunger. 'Human flesh is a lot like pork,

but you can easily replicate that taste with some yummy Quorn!' they now laughed, one staring at my shoulder while the other eyed my loins.

'Look, I can do a handstand, isn't that gas?' whomever the quirky one is said, now upside down and staring intently at my calf muscle, making a nom nom sound.

As I left the Happy Pear café, David and Stephen bade me farewell, saying I should call in again sometime when it's not so busy, and when there are very few people around.

BREAKING ━━━━━━━━━━━━━━━━━━━━━━━━━━━━

'HALLOWEEN WAS INVENTED IN IRELAND' DOSE STATES FOR 1,000TH TIME

LOCAL MELTER Eoghan Daherty has busted out his favourite bit of Halloween trivia just in time for the spooky season, which also happens to be his only bit of Halloween trivia, and something that he's shared countless times before.

'You know Halloween is an Irish thing, right? We invented that,' said Daherty to his workmates, his kids, a lad on the bus, a Mormon who came to the door, the DPD driver and pretty much everyone he has encountered in the last two weeks.

'Yeah, and we invented witches and Freddy Krueger, and instead of pumpkins, we used O'Neills footballs painted orange. Trick or treating was invented in Macroom. Sparklers represent the 1916 Rising and I think the movie *Halloween* is based on a lad who stabbed a

load of British soldiers in the War of Independence.'

Although Daherty remains shaky on the details surrounding the festival of Samhain, that hasn't stopped him from bringing the subject up whenever he can, in a bid to show the world that he knows something, anything.

'Did you know that Halloween originated in Ireland?' posted the 37-year-old on a Journal.ie article about the lack of abortion services in the north of Ireland, and Sinn Féin's recent abstinence on a vote regarding the matter.

'What the fuck has that got to do with anything?' asked another poster, before being 'treated' to a nine paragraph explanation as to how the Flight of the Earls in 1607 was the inspiration for Stephen King's 1986 horror classic *It*.

BIGGEST REGRET OF WOMAN'S LIFE REMAINS AGREEING TO JOIN SCHOOL PARENTS WHATSAPP GROUP

'I ONCE PUT a winning lotto ticket through the washing machine, and I shit you not, I've bigger regrets about joining this fecking group,' explains Roseanne Fogerty, a recent addition to the 'First Class parents St Bina of the Haunted Hoover National School' WhatsApp group.

'What happened to just throwing your kids into school in the morning and not giving it much thought? Presents, projects, pick-ups, the most mind-numbingly boring thoughts and suggestions. It never fecking stops,' admitted a frazzled Fogerty, who can't

be arsed pretending she's a passionate parent who puts endless thought into the infinitesimal aspects of her children's schooling.

Our interview with Fogerty was then interrupted by several pings from her WhatsApp, with one message reading 'Mrs Carroll's new haircut, oh she looks fab, didn't think she'd pull off the blonde look'.

Beyond idle chit-chat about teachers' appearances (there's usually a separate WhatsApp group for that), the group Fogerty was guilted into joining spends most of its time chronicling the slow expansion of the wet patch on the classroom ceiling, and between 12 and 80 charity bake sales.

'There's less debate on the UN Security Council than there is in this yoke. Do I regret the knife fight in a

dark alleyway in Mexico City when I was backpacking in my college years? Yes. Was defrauding those investors a good thing? No. Setting up a cement quarry and selling mica-stuffed blocks is not my proudest moment either. But I regret joining this godforsaken group more than I do agreeing to spy for the Russians,' concluded Fogerty.

Just as Fogerty thought she was free of the WhatsApp group debating what the end-of-term gift limit for Mrs Caroll should be, it sparked up again with that show-off Teresa Carthy suggesting 80 fucking euro.

Predictions for 2023

Coddle is finally, mercifully, outlawed.

FAMILY

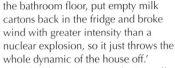

SON RUINS FAMILY'S CHRISTMAS BY COMING HOME FROM LIVING ABROAD

THERE WERE HEARTBREAKING SCENES in the Kelly household as Canadian resident of eight years Conor Kelly made a surprise trip home for Christmas, much to the dismay of his family.

'Nothing against him personally, like, but I just don't like him,' confirmed Conor's younger brother, Eoin, who will now have to sleep in the box room for the next two weeks.

'No, it's great having him home, sure,' conceded mother Patricia, putting on a brave face, 'but he was the one kid who always left towels on

the bathroom floor, put empty milk cartons back in the fridge and broke wind with greater intensity than a nuclear explosion, so it just throws the whole dynamic of the house off.'

'Ugh, Christ, I suppose that's us all being forced out on Stephen's Day for a walk up the mountains,' groused Conor's father, Eoin Sr, who always resented his son's outdoorsy ways.

Of greater concern to the family is the Christmas viewing schedule, which will now have to make room for Harry Potter movies on account of Conor being a complete nerd.

'I'd scribbled a short list and all. We'd Indiana Jones on Christmas Day and a Star Wars – he's fucked that now, he has,' continued Eoin Sr, visibly livid his son would just rock up like this all willy-nilly.

Elsewhere, Conor has been criticised for bringing presents home for everyone, as the family don't deal well with acts of generosity.

'He only did that now to get something out of us. Suppose I'll have to head into town to get him something now, the prick. And me up to my eyeballs as it is,' concluded his mother.

JOBS

'OUR LIVELIHOODS ARE ON THE LINE HERE': KINAHAN DEALERS FEAR JOB LOSSES

A UNION OF DRUG DEALERS are expected to stage a sit-in today in protest of unprecedented job losses across the Kinahan Cartel network after it was announced that international action will be taken against the crime group in the form of US sanctions.

Calling for more clarity around their futures, local gang leaders voiced their concerns, stating that their livelihoods were on the line and that the cartel's HR department hasn't even bothered to address the recent sanctions.

'I'm not even sure if I'd at least a text to one of the burners, but nah, nothin' from anyone,' one worried Kinahan area manager told WWN. 'The only contracts we have are the ones on our heads from rival gangs, and the CEO and others on the board of directors are nowhere to be seen – it's very unprofessional.'

With large families to feed, money still left to launder and stock issues on the cards, many employees now fear they won't even receive a redundancy package from their employer and have begun protesting outside drug dens across Dublin.

'All we're looking for is a severance package,' said 20-year-old protester and drug dealer James Horan outside a stash house this morning as he smoked a rollie while continually spitting on the ground for no reason. 'I've spent most of my teens working hard on my bike dropping off packages here and there, and for what? If I had known this is the way I would have been treated I would never have … actually no, that's bollocks … I probably would, but still – it's bad form from Christy and the lads.'

In an internal email sent late last night from a Dubai-based satellite phone, a cartel spokesman wrote: 'We understand there may be some concerns relating to recent events centred around ongoing sanctions against Kinahan Inc. We are working closely with our international partners in resolving this issue, so rest assured – as long as drug prohibition is in place, no one will ever lose their jobs in this business.'

'SURE STAY OUT' STATES LEGEND OF A WIFE

A LUCKY WATERFORD MAN currently in town for 'a quiet few pints' with the lads has received a text message from his wife with those three little words that every man in a pub wants to read: 'sure stay out'.

'Are you sure?' slurred Francis McWard after ringing his wife to clarify, while ordering his fourth of the proposed 'two or three' pints he had gone out for.

'Listen, if it's as much craic as you've been not-so-subtly hinting at in texts for the past hour, then who am I to insist you come home and help me put these kids to bed?' replied his wife Alice, confirming her status as an absolute peach of a wife in her husband's eyes.

Mrs McWard went on to open up to WWN about how she just wants her husband to have one good night out with his pals, safe in the knowledge that it will put him off wanting to leave the house again until at least May.

'I know full well that giving him the go-ahead to stay out is basically a licence for him to shit his pants,' Alice McWard said while having a cosy night in for herself without her husband insisting they watch Lethal Weapon.

McWard has now re-joined his pals for 'at best, two more pints', which means his wife might see him tomorrow at around five when he wakes up with a hangover that will last for the next three months.

EXCLUSIVE

'YOUR MA'S THE TOWN E-SCOOTER': UPDATING IRISH INSULTS FOR THE MODERN AGE

A TREASURED PART of Irish culture is our ability as a people to eviscerate someone with a verbal barbarity so heinous that they will never psychologically or emotionally recover from it, no matter how much time they spend waiting for a therapist the HSE never assigns them.

But is our flare for insults due for an upgrade? The twenty-first century has seen such a marked change in the way we live and what hobbies and cultural practices we embrace, that perhaps the old turns of phrase don't quite resonate with people in the same way.

With this in mind, *WWN* and linguistic experts at TCD have teamed up to modernise a number of common Irish insults:

- Your ma's the town e-scooter (formerly – Your ma's the town bike).

- Still has his communion money in Bored Ape NFTs (formerly – Still has his communion money in the credit union).
- If there was work in the bed, he'd sleep on the floor of the mould-infested €1,600 box room that's sucking the joy from his life (formerly – If there was work in the bed, he'd sleep on the floor).
- Ye fuckin' gobshite (unchanged).
- He's not the most efficient solar panel on the roof (formerly – He's thick as two planks)
- You're as thick as carbon-neutral manure and only half as useful in the fight against climate change (formerly – You're as thick as cow manure and only half as useful).
- Negative-interest craic (formerly – Minus craic).
- Please don't get offended, but I think you may need to rethink that decision you made (formerly – Cop on to yourself).
- May you melt like the Thwaites Glacier and drown in rising sea levels (formerly – May you melt off the earth like snow off the ditch).
- You're some moany cunt all the same (unchanged).

COVID

COVID-POSITIVE MAN MISSES WINDOW DURING WHICH PEOPLE GAVE A SHIT

IN WHAT HAS BEEN labelled a 'missed opportunity' and a 'crying shame', local man Ferdia Farrell has caught Covid-19 at a time when everyone's concerns and sympathies have long ceased, WWN can report.

Announcing it in his family and friends WhatsApp groups, expecting heart emojis and expressions of concern, just like when others contracted the virus, Farrell was shocked to see his news quickly swept over with little to no acknowledgement.

'When Davey and Conor got it, there was talk of "care packages" being delivered, I sent them follow-up texts, cheer-up Zoom calls were organised – the works,' said Farrell of Delta-era diagnoses friends received.

'And what do I get? My mam completely ignored it, and asked my sisters if they wanted chicken or lamb when they're over for the Sunday roast,' explained an isolating Farrell, whose mother was so indifferent she didn't even suggest a number of holistic remedies, such as sleeping with an onion in your sock.

Farrell's plight was further worsened by exchanges with the HR department in work, who seemed confused on sick days relating to Covid.

'Oh, I don't think we accept doctor's notes for that now, sure everyone had it. Just come in and cough on all of us, sure, be grand,' confirmed Farrell's manager.

Anyone else belatedly catching Covid who is looking for sympathy has been advised to lie about contracting the virus, instead claiming they've stubbed their toe or caught a particularly itchy strain of crabs, which elicits far more empathy these days.

'PEEL HERE' SIGN ON PACKET OF HAM JUST A BLATANT FUCKING LIE

SLICED HAM MANUFACTURERS have been put on final notice for their packaging claims, with a failure to address concerns seeing them facing a violent uprising the likes of which has never been seen in the history of humanity, WWN has learned.

'I'm not saying the person who came up with the "Peel here" and "Easy peel and reseal" labels is evil, but if you told me they were the bastard child of Myra Hindley and Ted Bundy I'd 100 per cent believe you,' shared one frustrated peeler of ham packaging.

Others have speculated on the sick and twisted nature of sliced ham package designers, suggesting they get off on labelling corners on packaging 'Peel here' despite the fact that it would be easier to break into Fort Knox.

'I swear, I was once trying to open a bastarding ham packet in the kitchen and I saw a figure out in the garden. I can't prove it, but it was definitely one of the sickos who designed this abomination, having a dirty auld tug,' shared another customer driven to the point of insanity.

However, it's not all mild inconvenience, as the tragic case of 33-year-old Tony O'Laughlin clearly proves.

O'Laughlin, a divil for a ham sambo, had been in the process of making lunch one day when he became locked in an unforgiving struggle with a packet of Denny ham. Hours of agonising grappling with the packaging ensued before O'Laughlin sadly passed away from starvation, unable to form a functioning sandwich without the ham.

'My beautiful Tony was brought up to respect authority, and when a packet of ham said "Peel here" he listened. He wasn't going to open it with a knife like some brute who cared not for the ongoing freshness of his ham. We've not had so much as an apology from the designers,' shared O'Laughlin's distraught mother.

UKRAINE

BORDER LADS TO SUPPLY UKRAINE WITH 1MN GALLONS OF WASHED DIESEL

DIESEL-LAUNDERING GROUPS from around the border between Ireland and Northern Ireland have made an unprecedented pledge to send vital fuel supplies to the Ukrainian army to help in their fight against the invading Russian forces, playfully adding to 'watch out for the customs lads, they're dipping!'

The move comes as Russia continues to illegally occupy Ukraine, claiming that it has the right to do so because key areas contain many people loyal to the Russian government, something the diesel donators claim to 'not really know much about, but it sounds awful, so it does'.

The first shipment of laundered diesel is expected to set off for Ukraine later today along with a consignment of used vegetable oil, which the diesel launderers advise to 'throw a drop of in with a fill' to help the tank engines run nice and smooth.

'It'll smell like shite but without it, you could fuck up your engine something fierce,' said one lad in a barn on the border, as the first shipment of washed stuff wheeled out.

'As for why we're doing this, well they say that Ireland can't supply

> **'It'll smell like shite but without it, you could fuck up your engine something fierce'**

weapons, as we're a neutral country. And the majority of this barn is in Ireland, apart from that corner over there, which crosses into Fermanagh. So we can't send weapons – not that we have weapons to send, mind you! We eh, got rid of them a long time ago. Anyways, the Ukrainian lads are welcome to a drop of diesel on us, the poor fuckers.'

The diesel trade has also offered Ukraine the toxic sludge left over after laundering diesel, as they were only going to dump it in rural Ireland, and it's bound to be good for fucking up a Russian or two.

BREAKING

A ROOT AND BRANCH review of the Irish Defence Forces' capabilities in the wake of planned Russian naval exercises has confirmed Ireland is helpless if the seagulls, known as the 'pricks of the sky', turn on us.

'Just taking it as a given that we can't even be the irritating fly on the arse of the bear that Russia is, but we're just as poorly resourced if "Operation Birdshit" occurs,' explained an army insider, referencing the hypothetical threat posed by Irish seagulls where they turn more aggressive and coordinate attacks on the Irish public.

A closer inspection of army resources revealed that all its grenades are actually novelty soap bars made to look like grenades, while navy vessels

IRELAND DEFENCELESS IF SEAGULLS TURN ON POPULATION, ADMITS IRISH ARMY

are just strategically placed 12-foot poster pictures of boats attached to floating buoys at sea.

'Right now, if you're out in somewhere like Bray and a seagull takes your ice cream, we can send two lads in the one working jeep we have with the "surface-to-air shooing broom", but if a whole squadron of seagulls mobilise, you're on your own,' confirmed the army source, whose turn it was to have a go of the army's one working rifle on the shooting range.

'And fighting them on their own turf in the skies? Forget about it! The seagull's wingspan of 1.2 metres is far

bigger than any of our kites made to look like air force planes.'

Defence Forces resources took a further hit after the Department of Defence were sent an invoice by an Irish fisherman for 'services rendered in relation to replacing non-existent navy'.

'Our cyber capabilities? Let me just check,' added the source as he wrote a letter to a superior officer by candlelight with a quill.

Elsewhere, the public has stated that maybe it isn't such a good idea for Ireland and its forces to publicly advertise how incapable it is.

BEST ORGANS TO SELL IF YOU'RE LOOKING TO AFFORD COLLEGE IN IRELAND

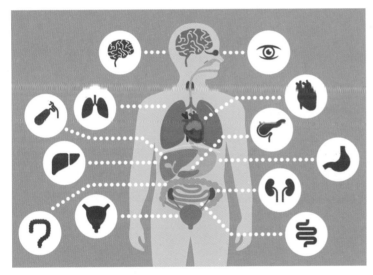

WITH THE *IRISH INDEPENDENT* revealing that college students living away from home are facing living costs of €14,000 for the academic year, *WWN* is here to help students identify the best organs to sell to manage that.

It would be irresponsible of *WWN* to suggest every student set up an OnlyFans, as by and large the Irish are an ugly people, and OnlyFans is only an option for the attractive few. Cash for organs remains your best, least worst option.

Appendix
Worthless. The only way you can make any money out of this pathetic excuse for an organ is by pretending it's a kidney and duping some unsuspecting Chinese businessman online.

Alternatively, you could casually goad your mates into betting you €1,000 to cut your appendix out for shits and giggles.

Lungs
Well, a single lung, you'll need the other one. Well, you really need both, but with a lung fetching €25k it might be worth it. Note: once sold, cease all physical activity and, to conserve energy, choose a post-grad career that requires zero physical exertion.

Liver
Good news – €50k, baby! Bad news, you do need it to continue living. Definitely cut the alcohol out if you sell this bad boy.

Kidneys
God gave you two for a reason, the reason being that if you lived in a country in which successive governments insisted that third-level education was 'free' and rent was 'reasonable' you could sell it so that you barely got by.

Spleen
Honestly, who knows what this thing does? If it was that important you'd know, right? Easy €10k.

Eyes
€14 grand a year, and that's just living costs. And it'll only get more expensive. C'mon, you've seen enough already.

Brain
Well, with the state of Irish third-level education and the jobs market awaiting you once you finish, it's not like you're going to get a chance to use it. €100k.

Sperm or egg
Okay, not an organ, but if you happened to have access to the sperm and egg from a wealthy family, you could sell them online. Once the resulting child is born that family is financially liable for it, and thus the child won't have to worry about the cost of third level once they finish school. This is the official advice from the government too, and it is technically 'priceless'. Just a pity you can't retroactively do this one for yourself.

RELIGION

CHURCH TO PASS GOVERNMENT REQUEST FOR LAND ON TO GOD, THANKS

On This Day

In 1815, Napoleon is defeated at Waterloo. You're humming the song now, aren't you?

18 June

THE CATHOLIC PRIMATE of All Ireland, Eamon Martin, has promised to pass on a letter from Housing Minister Darragh O'Brien, asking to identify Church lands that could be used for housing, to God and will get back to the government when he replies, thanks.

'I'm sure the Almighty Father will be back soon with His thoughts on this, right after He advises us on whether we should use land owned by the Church to cover what it still hasn't paid out as part of sexual abuse redress schemes,' the archbishop stated. Martin said that he is still waiting for a reply on that and other things, adding, 'He's obviously very busy lately with the backlog of prayers, but I'm sure he'll get right on it.'

The Housing Minister wrote to Bishop Martin to identify vacant land units that could be transferred to the state from God's lucrative property portfolio, estimated to be worth in the region of €4 billion in Ireland alone.

'Listen, 56 per cent of these Irish properties are owned by individual priests, so God will need to have a chat with them first before any deal is done,' the primate added. 'And yes, I understand that 20 per cent of all Church properties are listed

> **'God will need to have a chat with them first before any deal is done'**

as houses, thus the interest in them due to the housing crisis, but I think the big man wants to ride it out a bit and get more value for His hard-earned investments on the island.'

Despite the Church committing to a €120 million redress scheme for survivors of sexual and physical abuse nearly 20 years ago, the archbishop defended God's reluctance to sign off on the money, stating that God will probably sort them out when they die.

'I'm sure He'll be the first one to meet them upon their passing and hand them a nice big fat envelope full of cash,' Martin concluded. 'Sure, that kind of money won't bring them any luck.'

UPDATE: God has confirmed that, instead of donating, the Church should use some of its liquid assets to set up a build to rent investment fund instead.

COVID

COMPANY CELEBRATES 18TH MONTH OF BLAMING COVID FOR SHITE CUSTOMER SERVICE

THERE WERE CELEBRATORY SCENES at a sparsely manned call centre today as local enterprise CS Solutions marked its 18th month providing shite consumer service to all five of its contracted companies, *WWN* reports.

Despite continually losing hundreds of calls an hour in a never-ending queue of customer queries, managers Donal Phelan and Teresa Hynes congratulated their absent staff for all their work from home over the past year and a half, and for somehow managing to keep their lucrative business contracts alive.

'I can't believe we're still getting away with this shit,' a group email began, with the subject line 'Holy Fuck We're Still In Business!', 'we couldn't have done it without you guys working from home and continually using the Covid excuse for every single issue raised.

'You guys are a testament to how passive our customer base really are, and hopefully we can continue to use the office restrictions excuse for the foreseeable future.'

Flooded with an array of complaints, ranging from 'No one is answering calls' to 'I'm actually going to burn down your call centre if you don't sort my query', CS Solutions now actively forward all complaints to a humorously labelled 'Black Hole of Calcutta' email address – one of the only new business decisions made at the company since March 2020.

'We can just delete all those horrible emails "by accident" when everyone is back in the office again next year,' Phelan and Hynes insisted, now opening a bottle of €5 champagne bought in Aldi last Christmas. 'Hopefully by then all these eejits ringing in will have forgotten how we never bothered to adapt to the new normal,' they said, before raising a toast. 'Onwards and upwards, guys!'

> ## 'I can't believe we're still getting away with this shit'

My highlight of 2022: Boris Johnson

'It's hard to narrow it down to the favourite scandal I got away with, so I'm just going to say all 4,568 of them.'

Bill's Landlord Tips

Honestly, don't get into the developer game, there's no money to be made in it apart from the profit on top of the hundreds of thousands in state subsidies on every unit.

HERE'S EVERYTHING YOU'LL NEED TO MAKE IT THROUGH DUBLIN CITY AT NIGHT

HUNGOVER WATERFORD WOMAN CALLS FOR ASSISTED DYING

BET INTO HER SITTING ROOM COUCH like a soggy cream cracker, local woman Treena Ryan has called on the government to revisit the idea of assisted dying after downing a half bottle of vodka, six glasses of wine, four Jägerbombs and an extra-spicy kebab tray late last night.

Ryan, who is 37 years old, said she would gladly pass over now if it was legal for someone to assist her in dying, specifically before 5 p.m., when she is due in for a shift at work.

'Just kill me now,' pleaded Ryan, who had originally ventured out for one with the girls but ended up vomiting into a dog poop bin outside her friend's home at 4 a.m. this morning while missing one of her shoes. 'I can only open one eye with the headache and I keep forgetting to breathe. I probably don't have much longer left anyway, so let's just do this now.'

Despite ordering a medium pepperoni pizza with extra cheese and a large bottle of Lucozade, the great-granddaughter of eight showed no signs of recovery, with time now ticking closer to her half-four bus into work.

'Maybe I could just throw myself under it. The pain can't be any worse than this, can it?' she thought, now Googling the average weight of a double-decker bus. 'Jesus Christ, why did I become a member of the Gardaí, huh? Hopefully, I score some Xanax during a stop-and-search later or something – fuck my life.'

SEVERAL RECENT DOOM-MONGERING POSTS surrounding the safety of Dublin city centre have suggested that the nation's capital has been surrendered to roaming mobs of louts, without a single guard to be seen.

Nonsense! The guards are doing a great job, and Dublin is as safe as any other town or village, providing you take the following precautions:

1) Become incredibly skilled in martial arts

Anyone can walk anywhere, providing they can defend themselves. So bone up on some kung fu and you'll be able to stroll around Dublin without a care in the world! Mind you, the last high-profile victim in an assault case in Dublin belonged to the Irish Olympic Tae Kwon Do squad, so there are holes in this theory. Make sure you train to be better than an Olympian, and you should be fine.

2) Become a guard

It's a few years of training, but by becoming a member of An Garda Síochána, you can enjoy hassle-free strolls around the city at any time of day or night. Ne'er-do-wells know that you're not going to go near them, so they'll leave you alone. Mostly. There'll be a few digs here and there, but compared to a normal citizen, it'll be minimal.

3) Surrender your mortal soul to Lord Dracula

It can be scary walking through Dublin at night unless you're the scariest thing there. Become one of Lord Dracula's army of the undead. Allow him to drink your blood in exchange for immortality, and journey beyond death into a realm where you are safe to stroll up O'Connell Street after dark. Just be sure to get indoors before morning; walking around Dublin in the daytime is way more dangerous than at night.

On This Day

2022: God accidentally copies and pastes much of the year 1939 into the present day.

TRAMORE NO SWIM WARNING IN PLACE AFTER HIGH LEVELS OF DUBS FOUND IN WATER

WATERFORD COUNTY COUNCIL is advising people not to swim in the sea in Tramore due to dangerously high levels of Dubs in the water, *WWN* has learned.

The public has been urged not to enter the water on the beach for the next three days until new samples are taken, and the threat has subsided.

'Dubs can cause nausea and vomiting upon contact, with even just the sound of their twang sending people into states of shock,' the council said in a statement. 'If you think you've come into contact with a Dub in the sea, immediately turn your head the other way, put your fingers in your ears and repeatedly yell "na, na, na, na, na" until you're safely out of the water and at least 500 metres away from the Dub. Do not engage with the Dub, as it may hook you into a dreadful conversation about Gaelic football or how cheap it is down here, or they might start slagging "yer ma".'

With temperatures soaring throughout the week, high levels of Dubs have contaminated Irish coastal towns, with no end in sight amid some travel restrictions abroad due to the ongoing Covid-19 pandemic.

'The sooner these vermin can get on a plane and piss off to Spain, the better for places like Tramore and other hard-hit seaside resorts. The bastards are stealing our thunder,' said a man o' war jellyfish, whose whole livelihood and reputation was undermined by the presence of Dubs in the water.

> **'The sooner these vermin can get on a plane and piss off to Spain, the better'**

Tips for Ignoring Climate Change

Get a tattoo – a really bad one, in a really visible spot. People will slag you so much you'll barely have time to dwell on the hell that is roaring over the horizon.

My highlight of 2022: Roy Keane

'Highlight? Are you having a laugh?'

TECHNOLOGY

IT WASN'T AN ENGAGEMENT RING, BUT CHECK OUT THE COOL NEW HEADPHONES SHEILA GOT FROM HER BOYFRIEND

FRIENDS, co-workers and relatives of Waterford woman Sheila Connaughton have all made sure to compliment her on the absolutely sick new noise-cancelling headphones she got for Christmas from her long-term boyfriend, before quickly changing the subject and moving on.

'Wow, they must be so handy for when you're on the bus and you just want to listen to a podcast or something,' stated one of Connaughton's co-workers after the 32-year-old returned to the office without the engagement ring she was sure she would receive this year.

'In the gym, on a walk, at home … it really was a great gift. I only wish my husband, sorry, would have bought me something like that,' offered a friend, who has become skilled in avoiding awkwardness over Connaughton's nine-year relationship with her man.

'It was really thoughtful of him to know that the headphones he bought you last year were perfect, except they didn't have this new advanced bass-enhanced performance mode for optimum audio quality, so he went ahead and got you the latest model 12 months later,' said Sheila's mum, who secretly doesn't like her daughter's boyfriend and will be crushed when the day comes that he gives her an engagement ring instead of a top-of-the-line piece of consumer electronics.

Meanwhile, Connaughton's boyfriend, 36-year-old Martin Whyte, is said to be delighted with the Xbox he received this year and is looking forward to many long years of blissful online gaming with the occasional cup of tea brought to him.

JACK THE LAD FINALLY SETTLES DOWN

INFAMOUS for his brash and cocky ways, the original rowdy buccaneer who prided himself on causing mayhem on nights out with the boys has finally settled down, ending one of the most banter-filled eras of bachelordom on record, WWN can confirm.

'Some man for one man, never thought I'd seem him settle,' confirmed proud parents June and Joseph Ladd, speaking from the wedding reception where, to everyone's shock, Jack has refrained from being a giant dick or an insufferable arse.

'I dunno, he's changed for the worse in my book. Not the same Jack, didn't even get a laugh out of him when I made that crack in my best man speech about his wife not being as good-looking as the stripper at his stag party,' explained friend Richard Head.

Single since the dawn of time and famous for wearing out the patience of absolutely everyone within moments of first meeting them, the turnaround in Jack, whose party tricks included drinking pints from his shoe and starting fights in chippers at 3 a.m., has been credited to his new bride.

'I'd say she must be some divil in the bedroom to get you to commit, huh?' friend Richard joked before being reprimanded by Jack, who demanded that a certain level of respect and civility be maintained at the wedding.

'Honestly, this is some mind fuck altogether. How is this the same lad who did lines off the arse of Thai prostitutes when we were on the Big Banter Bus Tour of 2014? He's had more STDs than there are guests at this wedding,' queried Richard, looking at Jack as though he were a complete stranger.

CRIME

SCAM CALLERS MAKE MILLIONS AFTER CHARGING IRISH PEOPLE BY THE 'GOODBYE'

SCAM CALLERS from around the world have revealed the real reason they have chosen to target Ireland in recent times, stating that Irish phone habits make it incredibly easy to make a huge amount of cash in a very short period.

'Our model relies on a few different things. One, we can make money if people ring us back if we dial their phone but hang up before they answer. Every time,' said our source in the scamming community.

'Irish people just can't resist calling back an unknown number. No other nation in the world gives a fuck, but Irish people have this fear of not knowing who was ringing them that makes them very easy to exploit. After that, all we need to do is keep them on the line and watch the money soar.'

Although our scammer admitted initially using pre-recorded scare tactics about revenue or taxation during the early stages of the scamdemic that continues to plague Ireland, he states that profits soared when he switched to gossip instead.

'Once Irish people heard "revenue", they hung up and changed their number. But if you said in a hushed tone, "Did you hear about the young one up the road?", you could keep them on the line for an hour,' we were told.

'And it was mostly them talking. You just started the ball rolling and then sat back while they added their own gossip. We even made an automated voice saying "No! G'way! Really?" on a loop. We made thousands of euro a day.'

And of course, another automated voice that exploits Irish people's inability to hang up was employed to bilk people even further.

'What we call the "bye bye bye bye bye now" machine is our crown jewel. As long as it keeps saying bye, the target keeps saying bye,' the scammer laughed, before purchasing a yacht with the money earned from scam calling five Irish mothers in one afternoon.

JOBS

NO PAY INCREASE, SAME MISTREATMENT: ALL THE STEPS SOME BUSINESSES ARE TAKING TO FILL VACANCIES

MANY BUSINESSES in the retail, hospitality and services industries are struggling to find staff at this very difficult and precarious time for Irish businesses.

Many debate the reasons and factors behind this, but what are the solutions to this labour shortage crisis? We spoke to a few outspoken business owners who believe they have the answers:

'We find it's very easy to attract staff when you lie about the hourly wage and number of hours they are guaranteed.'
– *John Finelly, Offaly Good Burgers*

'A number of local workers didn't want to work for low wages or under bosses who treat them like shit, so after a lot of soul searching, we decided to keep the wages low and not change a single aspect of our management style.'
– *Eanna Roundtree, Hugs & Mugs Café*

'We pay a liveable wage if you don't take into account expenses like food, clothing and shelter.'
– *Graham Herlihan, Herlihan Fashions*

'Bullying previous staff to the point of causing mental breakdowns usually helps get the positive word out

that Punk Pizza is a great place to work.'
– *Niall Cretin, Punk Pizza*

'It's pretty clear we need young cheap labour, the likes provided by older secondary school students, college students and low-skilled workers, so we took to the local radio to repeatedly insult them and accuse them of being lazy. The applications have been flooding in ever since.'
– *Carmel Drennan, Skyview Hotel*

'Start interviews with something like "You're not one of those pronoun

woke avocado human rights millennium falcons, are you?"'
– *Peter Euro, Euro Shopper*

'It's important, when a non-EU worker with poor English walks in looking for

work, to snap them up and exploit them for everything you can, like a modern-day slave owner, but the nice kind with important political friends.'
– *Martin Heffer, Heffer Meats Factory*

BREAKING NEWS

RURAL PARENTS PREPARING FOR DRIVE TO DUBLIN LIKE IT'S CLIMBING EVEREST

'NOW I'M JUST RINGING you to remind you myself and your father are up in a few days,' rural mother Mairead O'Tofflin said in a phone call to her son Eamon, which was placed not 24 minutes after her husband Noel also rang his son to discuss his route up to Dublin in excruciating detail.

'We'll have the boot full of what we need,' added Mairead, speaking as if she was preparing for an arduous journey normally only undertaken by the likes of Tom Crean or Tenzing Norgay.

'But you needn't worry about us Eamon, we'll be all set,' she added to Eamon, who wasn't worrying about the 1 hour and 15-minute journey to the outskirts of the west Dublin suburb in which he now resides.

Speaking to *WWN* about the fairly straightforward journey his parents are stressing over, Eamon admitted to just 'giving up' after years of trying to tell them that a drive to Dublin isn't the equivalent of bouncing a car on trampolines while on the Death Road in Bolivia. 'They pack sandwiches, flasks of tea, flashlights and a tent in case they need to "stop somewhere for the night". They live outside of Tullamore!'

'They lock the doors on the car once they've left the driveway at home, and they refuse to get out in my driveway until I've checked that "drug gangs haven't placed a bomb underneath the car" when they were stuck in traffic in Dublin.'

For their part, the O'Tofflins have reported they will 'disembark' at 0800 hours tomorrow and ask that anyone passing by a church stop in and light a candle for them

---

INCREDIBLY CHARITABLE Waterford woman Sheila McCarthy has asked for 'no praise' following her generous donation of an entire wardrobe clear-out to a collection for refugees fleeing the war in Ukraine.

The 37-year-old has gone 'above and beyond' in her drive to ensure that Ukrainian citizens who have left their homes have everything they need, including some of her barely worn party dresses, old underwear and a NutriBullet that she doesn't use anymore since she bought a newer, better NutriBullet.

'Please, I'm just doing what anyone with a heart of solid gold would do,' said McCarthy on her ninth Instagram post about the subject.

'I saw a call-out on a local WhatsApp that there would be a collection in the community centre, and that there was an urgent need for warm clothes, baby clothes, food, sanitary products and other essentials. And while I didn't have any of that stuff around the house, I more than made up for it with several bin bags full of busted old shoes, some Christmas pyjama sets that have seen

LOCAL WOMAN KINDLY DONATES ALL HER OLD SHITE TO UKRAINE

better days, this clock that I don't like any more and a pile of kids' jigsaws which still have most of their pieces.'

McCarthy later updated her 87 followers that the people at the collection depots turned away most of her donations, and as such everyone else should boycott the place and support the Russian invasion from this point on.

RELIGION

MAN WHO IS NOT RELIGIOUS AND HATES THE CHURCH STILL GOING TO TICK 'CATHOLIC' ON CENSUS FORM

ONE LOCAL WATERFORD MAN with deep-seated enmity towards the Catholic Church for everything from its covering up of child sexual abuse, operating of an illegal child trafficking racket and condemning people based on their sexual orientation is still somehow going to tick 'Catholic' on the upcoming census.

'I'm agnostic and have no affiliation with the Church at all. The days of their malignant influence in Ireland are over,' explained Ciarán Roundtree, a man whose appearances in church over the last 15 years have been confined to other people's weddings and funerals. And yet.

'You will not find someone more angry and resentful of all the crimes and inhumanity facilitated and

encouraged by the Church on this island,' added Roundtree, despite the fact that when it comes down to it he will tick 'Catholic' since he had a bit of water splashed on his head

when he was 117 days old because a celibate man said he was full of sin.

Roundtree is believed to be one of hundreds of thousands of people who will mark their religion as 'Catholic' despite having no faith, and in the process handing the institution he so resents and mistrusts with an opportunity to claim it is relevant and should be at the centre of all secular decisions on schooling and healthcare.

'Stop, I know, I'm pissed off just thinking about their role in the maternity hospital or how they want a say over the sex education my children receive,' added Roundtree, while flexing the fingers he will use to wildly veer his pen towards the 'Catholic' box at the very last minute on Sunday evening.

POSTMAN HAS NO IDEA HE'S BIGGEST DRUG COURIER IN TOWN

BLISSFULLY UNAWARE of the vast array of contraband he is currently peddling around on his daily route, Waterford postman Davey Holden whistled chirpily as he went door to door, as eager parcel receivers hovered nervously at the other side of their letterbox.

'Hopefully, it's not another "love letter" from customs,' cannabis user Terrace Mark Hannebery thought to himself as the silhouette of the postman approached his frosted glass door, referring to a previous intercepted package of Cali weed he had ordered online last week, which Revenue confiscated and replaced with a letter. 'Poor Davey hasn't a clue what he's dropping through my door, God bless him. Sure, what he doesn't know won't kill him.'

'I'm seeing a lot of these registered "flash drive" parcels lately, and €15 "necklaces", all delivered in the same small box,' the 34-year-old postman pointed out to himself, as yet another overeager recipient opened their door to receive their 'storage device',

looking around suspiciously for unmarked cars before thanking him.

'Ah, good man, Davey boy, fuckin' waiting all week for this to arrive,' thanked number 34 Bayside Drive.

'Tom Jones! Did you get a new flatmate, Joe?' Davey asked innocently, unaware the name was an alias in case Gardaí were flanking the postman down the street.

'Oh, Tom, yeah, that's me cousin, Davey, yeah, he just needed something sent is all,' he smiled, now quickly closing his door while saying goodbye.

'Jaysis, I never see lads so eager to get parcels. I suppose it's like Christmas for people ordering from Wish,' Davey concluded, unaware he had dropped off two grand's worth of crystal MDMA.

POLICING

GARDAÍ UNVEIL NEW GIRAFFE UNIT

AN GARDA SÍOCHÁNA has unveiled a new giraffe unit, which will be rolled out nationwide from today, *WWN* has learned.

Over 1,200 giraffes broken in by expert giraffe trainers will be deployed across Ireland, giving Gardaí a better view over ditches, gates and walls in crime hotspots.

'They look great, don't they?' a Garda spokesperson said, unveiling a sample mounted giraffe in Waterford today. 'We've even mounted little cameras on their heads and can see for miles around. There are so many related crimes that can be thwarted by a Garda from the comfort of their giraffe.'

> **'There are so many related crimes that can be thwarted by a Garda from the comfort of their giraffe'**

'Crowd control, protests, Temple Bar, messing on the top decks of buses – this will change policing for the better. From this height, we can also see people dumping their drugs on the sly that bit better too.'

The €3 billion roll-out is now expected to cut crime by 0.03 per cent, with hundreds of Gardaí already applying to join the new Garda Giraffe Unit.

'Now they see it, every Garda wants a giraffe, and we believe this will be a stunning success,' the Garda spokesman added. 'Imagine breaking into a farm and seeing a giraffe's head

running towards you like stilt-mounted chaos. How we didn't think of this before is beyond me.'

However, some animal rights campaigners have lambasted the new unit, claiming that taking giraffes out of their natural habitat for this purpose is cruel and doesn't make any sense.

'Seriously, what the actual fuck are they at?' one small-minded opposer pointed out. 'Think of all the overhead electrical cables in rural Ireland, and the fact that giraffes are notoriously clumsy bastards with zero use to anyone apart from trimming leaves and branches that are hard to reach.'

WWN'S OLD IRISH MYTHS

OLD IRISH MYTHS #317267: THE METROLINK

LAST WEEK in *WWN*'s Old Irish Myths series we covered the famous 'Ulster Cycle'. This week it's the turn of the oft-mentioned, never seen mythical illusion known as 'the MetroLink'.

As always, we speak to lecturer in folklore Dr Jennifer Alwin, who has kindly lent us her expertise once more:

'While most great bedtime stories have no basis in fact, what's curious about the MetroLink is that still to this day many people assert that it is in fact real. This makes it a fascinating myth, which stands out from other tales such as the Salmon of Knowledge and what have you,' offers Dr Alwin.

'I think the MetroLink is such a great myth because it lends itself to a nice

> **'I think the MetroLink is such a great myth because it lends itself to a nice escape for the reader or the person being told the tale'**

escape for the reader or the person being told the tale. Who doesn't want to retreat into a world where the 500,000 plus residents of a city can get around locations in a timely fashion thanks to some joined-up thinking and sensible long-term planning executed by capable people?

'Of course, as the fable goes, anyone who says the word "MetroLink" subjects themselves to the instant onset of madness and horrifying senseless visions of this serpentine creature slithering its way from Charlemont to the airport,' continues Dr Alwin.

An earlier version of the myth had the MetroLink extending to Sandyford, but then Minister for Housing Eoghan Murphy led opposition to a single road closure in his constituency, scuppering solutions to capacity issues with transport links.

'Those afflicted by the visions lose all sense of time and believe the year 2031 is the same as 2002, when the prophecy of the MetroLink materialising was first foretold. In the most haunting version of the myth, the public cry tears of euros into the great stream of the river Taxpayer, which never actually reaches the ocean.'

Dr Alwin also said that, in one version of the myth, locals go mad waiting for its arrival, and this part is believed to have influenced Samuel Beckett's famous play *Waiting for Godot*, which was provisionally titled 'Waiting for the DART Underground'.

'Of course in the story the doubters, the unbelievers, are harangued by the mythical figure called the Great Bullshitter, who pours scorn on those who are so negative, and they are blamed for wishing the MetroLink out of existence. The Great Bullshitter has gone by many names in recorded versions of the myth, including Bertie, Brian, Enda, Leo, Micheál and yet more to come,' concluded Dr Alwin.

POLICING

LOCAL MAN OKAY WITH SHOOTING AFTER HEARING VICTIM WAS 'KNOWN TO GARDAÍ'

THE ADDITION OF THE PHRASE 'the victim was known to Gardaí' at the end of a horrific news report surrounding a shooting in Cork today has come as a relief to Waterford man Miles Canlon, who came very near to actually being upset about the incident.

'I'd heard on the news that a man about my age, with two kids just like I have, was shot to death outside his house, and it put a chill up my spine. Then the news informed me that he

was "known to Gardaí" and I thought, ah sure that's grand,' stated 37-year-old Canlon.

'I had thought "my God, what if that was me?", but the last line of the bulletin let me know that there was no cause for worry. In fact, I'm feeling better about it now, if I'm honest. Now, I can just go about my day as if it never happened, without feeling bad for this guy, his friends, his family or anyone to do with him. Cheers, news!'

Meanwhile, Cork cops have been informed that there's 'no panic' when it comes to solving the case, as the nation is more than happy to let people who are 'known to Gardaí' shoot and kill each other all day long.

'Big shout-out to our friends in the media for making that phrase work so hard for us over the years. It really has helped put a good spin on how we've failed to prevent the deaths of so many young men and women,' said our source in the force.

UTILISING ALL THE MUSCLES in her neck and shoulders, retail worker Leanne Fisher cast her head skywards and took two steps backwards to demonstrate in the most dramatic fashion to a customer that she wasn't slyly trying to learn his PIN prior to mugging him for his card at some point in the future.

The art of services industry personnel dramatically making a big show of how you're not secretly part of some big defrauding cabal was thought to be a dying skill with the onset of contactless payments, but Fisher is still flying the flag.

'I appreciate the gesture, it does make me feel safe as a customer, but the backflip over the counter and blindfolding herself was a tad much,' confirmed one customer.

'Look away, by all means, I know what stress-heads arsehole customers can be if they accuse you of looking at their pin, but such actions do come at a cost,' shared a former retail worker who was diagnosed with giraffe neck from years of doing the same. 'My head is permanently looking away to the side because of it, and I had to settle for a civil service job ignoring complaints.'

Confronted about why she felt she needed to commit Meryl Streep

RETAIL WORKER MAKES OVERLY DRAMATIC SHOW OF NOT LOOKING AT YOU ENTERING YOUR PIN

levels of overacting when it came to customer payment, Fisher was candid: 'I actually have a horrific phobia of fingers. Hideous wrinkly

sausages, ugh, makes me want to puke. You're all manky mangled-handed stabby-stabby index-fingered fuckers.'

EDUCATION

SUCCESSFUL PEOPLE WHO DIDN'T DO WELL IN THE LEAVING CERT SHARE THEIR ADVICE

WITH THE NATIONAL NEWSPAPERS full of young Leaving Cert students gloating about their results, *WWN* has taken the time, and a large chunk of its financial resources, to interview past pupils who didn't make the grade but went on to succeed regardless.

Michael Fassbender
'As long as you've got a huge throbbing member, the world is your oyster … except of course if you're a woman. I guess then it's big tits for them, right?'

Joseph Kony
'When I got just 95 points in the Leaving Cert I was furious at the Irish school system. Fellow students laughed and jeered at me, so I left for a new start in Uganda. Now I take students hostage for a living and have never looked

'As long as you've got a huge throbbing member, the world is your oyster'

back. Always believe in yourself.'

Professor Luke O'Neill
'I only received 750 points in the Leaving Cert and didn't get the course I wanted. I decided to just go for my second choice of biochemistry at Trinity. I hated every single moment of my career, but look at me now: famous, miserable, yet immensely wealthy, motherfuckers!'

The Monk
'Don't mind that aul' exam crap, I didn't even finish

bleedin' school and look at me now, wha'?'

Jim Corr
'The Leaving Cert is designed to keep idiots in line with the corrupt agenda of the military-industrial complex and their new world order. If I had my way, school teachers and books would be replaced by a TV streaming alternative YouTube documentaries in a blacked-out room laced with lead paint to protect children from 5G radiation.'

'Don't mind that aul' exam crap, I didn't even finish bleedin' school'

Shane MacGowan
'Arghhhough am erghhhh my bashhhing is marrrgh.'

Minister for Education Norma Foley
'Fuck school.'

Michael Flatley
'Aw begora to be sure to be sure. I remember me father Michael senior always saying to me, "Michael, me boyo, if you don't pass the Leaving, you can always dance with the ladies. But just remember, it's up here for thinking and down there for dancing." At the time I thought he was pointing to his legs for the dancing part, which I took literally.'

The Cliffs of Moher
'My teachers said I'd amount to nothing, but then after a few hundred million years of geological this and that, I got into tourism and never looked back.'

Simon Coveney
'I deleted my Leaving Cert results to make space … because I was hacked … something like that anyway.'

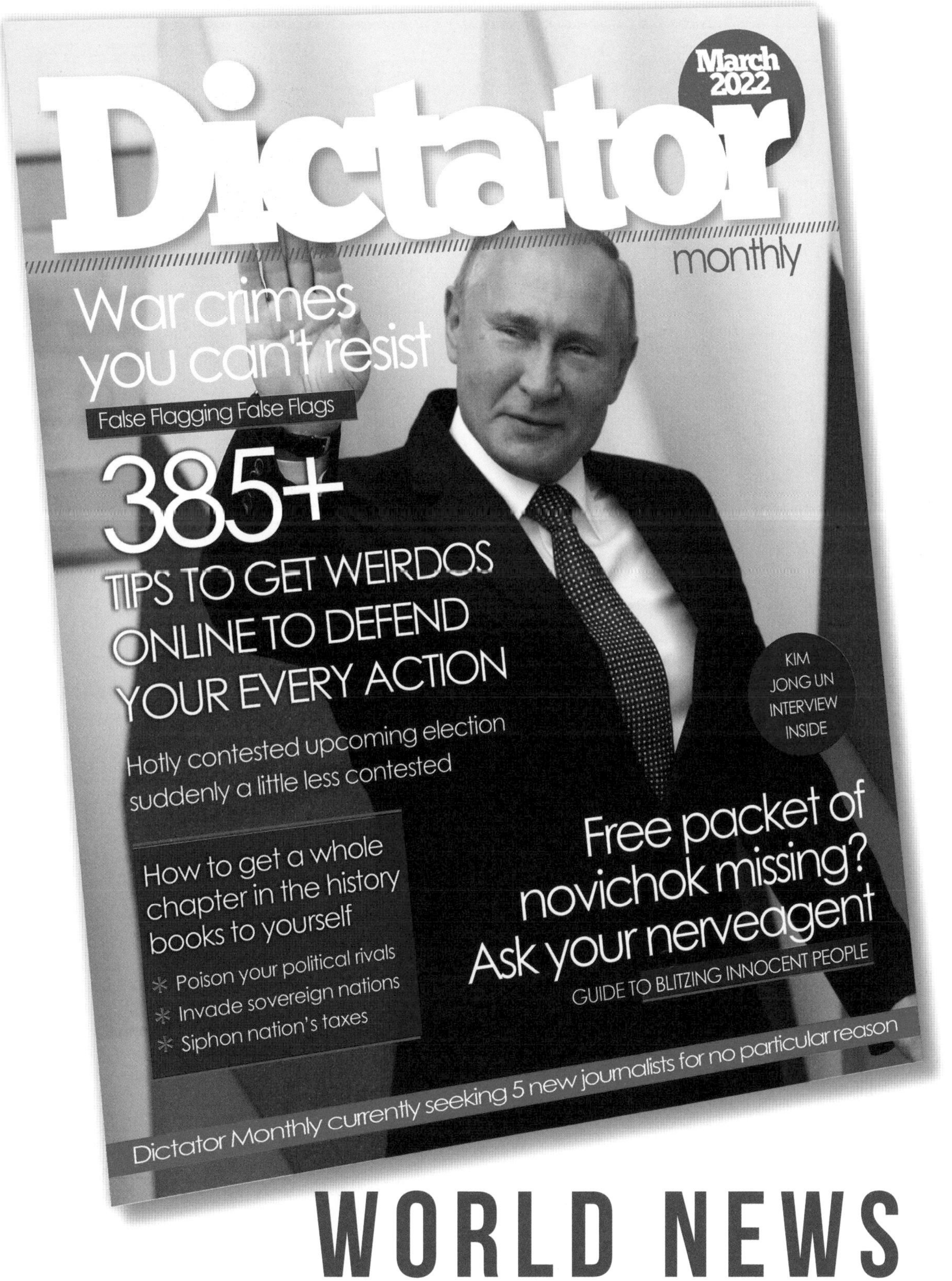

Dictator

monthly

March 2022

War crimes you can't resist

False Flagging False Flags

385+

TIPS TO GET WEIRDOS ONLINE TO DEFEND YOUR EVERY ACTION

Hotly contested upcoming election suddenly a little less contested

KIM JONG UN INTERVIEW INSIDE

How to get a whole chapter in the history books to yourself

* Poison your political rivals
* Invade sovereign nations
* Siphon nation's taxes

Free packet of novichok missing? Ask your nerveagent

GUIDE TO BLITZING INNOCENT PEOPLE

Dictator Monthly currently seeking 5 new journalists for no particular reason

WORLD NEWS

UK ROYALTY

'I STARTED FROM THE BOTTOM AND HAD TO WORK FOR EVERYTHING I'VE GOT'

IN A RARE PUBLIC INTERVIEW, Queen Elizabeth II of England shares her secret to pulling herself up by the bootstraps and, despite coming from nothing, working hard to achieve it all.

'Nobody gave one anything in life, isn't it? So you must beg my pardon if I don't shed a tear for those who take up complaining as their nine-to-five.

'My hustle was pre-Insta, no easy product endorsements for one, no freebies, no try-on hauls, no 20 per cent using the discount code "Lizzie20". People don't know how easy they have it, isn't it?

'One had to fabricate it until one materialised it. And even now, people doubt one, say one was handed everything on a plate. One was never given handouts, only people casting doubts. Best believe.

'Ignore the haters and don't get drawn into the drama. One never spoke on things, one never did the equivalent of a YouTube MUA apology video. Apologise for what? One's ambition? One's hard work? Never.

'One must grind it 24/7 and have that 25/8 mentality. Don't stop, won't stop. Sure, pyramid schemes and MLM scams are big now, but when one presided over the biggest pyramid scheme ever – convincing people to fund one's lifestyle with their hard-earned tax money – people said one was crazy. But one believed, and one achieved.

'It's that simple. One wished one had Twitch, YouTube, Patreon,

OnlyFans, Instagram and TikTok in one's day. Instead one only had the wireless and the Queen's speech. But one still used what little one had to build what you see before you today.

'Stay humble. Stay hungry.'

UH-OH: YOUR FAVOURITE CELEBRITY IS TRENDING

OH NO: You just went on Twitter and noticed that one of your favourite celebrities is listed as 'trending', and what's worse – they're trending worldwide.

There are only three possibilities:

1) Sexual abuse allegations

Just ask any fan how they felt after noticing their idol was trending worldwide, to get an idea of what will go through your head when you realise your favourite singer, actor or personality has hit the headlines for less-than-savoury reasons. There it is, laid in front of the whole world to see; the celeb you have expressed a liking for has turned out to be a dirty bastard, making the last few decades of your fandom look pretty dodgy. You're a fan of a sexual predator. That's the kind of thing that sticks.

2) They're dead

There's mercy in death. You can grieve death, and you can share stories in death. People come together in death.

If your favourite celeb is trending because they're dead, it might actually be a relief. You were a fan, they died and nobody looks stupid here. Unless of course, a load of allegations come out about them after their death, as is known to happen. Maybe they were a dickhead behind it all? Kinda makes you look like a dickhead too, to be honest. You can get into a Twitter beef about it all being 'a long time ago' and 'having a bit of respect for the dead', but you're just digging a deeper hole for yourself.

3) They're releasing a collaboration with Tekashi 6ix9ine

You didn't need this. Nobody needed this.

'IT'S OKAY PUTIN IS DOING BAD THINGS BECAUSE OTHER NATIONS ALSO DID BAD THINGS ONCE'

'Do you have any idea how silly you sound advocating for an end to senseless slaughter?'

AS PART of the '*WWN Voices*' series we offer a platform to people we really shouldn't. Today is the turn of Fergal Defflin, who can't believe your hysteria over Putin's war in Ukraine when other countries do other bad things too.

'It's okay to feel a little stupid, to feel like an imbecile of gargantuan proportions for thinking you can insist Ukrainians' suffering is manifestly unjust. And before you even try, I'm not buying your counterargument that it's possible to care about multiple conflicts, past and present, and those caught in its crosshairs at the same time.

'I don't think you fully get the wider context and the imperial impulses of that other country the time they did that thing, so maybe think about that before you harp on about "war crimes" this 'n' that. You sound ridiculous.

'Remember Afghanistan? No, not the Soviet invasion, the other ones.

'I didn't hear you say this about the Battle of Megiddo back in 1479 BC either, huh? Not a peep from you about the actions of the King of Kadesh. Hmmm, interesting.

'If I had a euro for every time another country did something similar to what

Putin is doing I'd have enough money to buy up all the advertising hoardings on your bus route into work, on which I would emblazon "But what about the other atrocities?" It kind of makes your assertion that Putin's actions are abhorrent a little trite, doesn't it?

'And this isn't even the first murder-war-crime-palooza Putin's been on. He did the same in that other place, which is why it's a bit rich that you're making out like dead women and children is such a bad thing all of a sudden when it's happened elsewhere before.

'Do you have any idea how silly you sound advocating for an end to senseless slaughter when other countries, regions, towns and peoples are subjected to the evil whims of regimes that claim to live on the moral high ground, guided by superior ideologies?

'Punish Putin? Sanction him? Put him on trial? And what about all the other crimes committed by the hand of other governments that lead to immeasurable suffering too? What about them?

'Oh, you think they're bad too? Ha! See, I finally got you to admit how silly … wait, what was my point again? Oh yeah, you're thoroughly embarrassing yourself with your flagrant appeal to the concept of basic humanity. Do me a favour and type "Agent Orange" or "Belgium in the Congo" into Google there. Honestly, you're going to feel a right idiot for your hysterics, you naïve summer child.'

RELIGION

'JUST TAKE IT WE HAVE MASS GRAVES IN EVERY COUNTRY', VATICAN RESPONDS TO LATEST CHILD PIT

FED UP WITH BEING CALLED out every time a new mass grave full of dead children is discovered in the backyard of one of its institutions, the Vatican has released a one-for-all statement going forward, *WWN* reports.

'Just take it we have mass graves in every country that we wormed our way into under the guise of "helping the vulnerable",' the statement began. 'Obviously, building schools to groom communities into our religion for our own financial gain got the better of us, and some strays got dumped aside, but look, you weren't all complaining when we literally beat Catholicism into you, so yeah, mass graves are a bit of a thing with us, so get used to it.'

The statement comes after an indigenous community in Canada identified nearly 100 'potential' graves at a residential school site, months after the discovery of more than a thousand children's remains in sites run by various religious sects as part

of a Canadian government system, something the Canadian taxpayer has so far paid $116.8 million in compensation to the First Nation, Inuit and Métis survivors.

'Did the Vatican manage to accumulate over €15 billion in stored-up wealth over the past few centuries by means of infiltrating poor countries and transforming their communities into God-fearing tax-free donating praying machines? Yes. Will we financially now compensate those still affected by the abuse and death today? Absolutely not. We'll leave that to the taxpayers of whatever country we converted,' the very brief statement concluded, much to no one's surprise.

YOUTUBE OPENS FIRST-EVER VIDEO LIBRARY FOR PEOPLE LOOKING TO DO THEIR OWN RESEARCH

VIDEO-STREAMING PLATFORM YouTube has unveiled its first ever public video library in Dublin in a bid to facilitate a surging number of people choosing to 'do their own research', *WWN* can report.

The three-storey modern-style building will house walk-in streaming booths with access to YouTube's vast array of independently produced, unresearched and unregulated video content for those wishing to 'inform themselves'.

'I used to spend most days sitting on me hoop smoking reefer, but now I'm going to spend all my time smoking reefer, sitting on me hoop researching alternative news channels that churn out unverified content oozing anti-Semitic ideology,' shared a former fuel injection technician turned conspiracy

theorist, welcoming the new library. 'Finally, people with lower IQ levels are starting to wake up!'

The need for truth in a world full of misinformation has seen queues for the new library from the early hours of this morning, with the so-called 'activist' and 'journalist' Gemma O'Doherty cutting the red ribbon to mark the opening today.

'George Soros is a Nazi collaborator plotting a destructive revolution in America, and wants to control your children using microchips in vaccines

Predictions for 2023

Parisian police will be hired to provide security at the 2023 Oscars.

while he feeds on the freshly tortured adrenal glands of Catholic infants who were kidnapped by Muslim fundamentalists,' a manic O'Doherty screamed while cutting the ribbon, before being met by cheers from the crowd, who then began shouting 'paedo scum off our streets' for no apparent reason.

YouTube – who, unlike Facebook, has so far managed to evade global enquiries into its algorithms, which have been delivering conspiracy theorists with questionable content since 2005 – has vowed to continue its torrent of lies while the offending video uploaders continue to earn 20 cent per video advert delivered by Google's ad network.

'We're making way too much money here to stop now,' Google defended.

WAR CRIMES

'WHOA LET'S NOT GO CRAZY CALLING FOR EVERY WAR CRIMINAL TO STAND TRIAL'

AS THE HARROWING DETAILS of war crimes in Ukraine continue to emerge, the vast majority of people reaffirmed their support for the ICC and holding war criminals to account, something old pals George W. Bush and Tony Blair completely agree with.

'War criminals of every kind must be brought to justice, but obviously, I'd encourage you to really think about your definition of "war criminal",' enthused a sweating Bush.

'Honestly, it's crazy, some people apply this term in a very broad way to any normal person, like your postman or your nana or a former head of state who oversaw a war in which 3 per cent of the population died,' added Bush.

Blair, asking Bush for permission to speak, held a similarly strong view on people being held to account for wanton murder and destruction.

'Just to piggyback, war crimes in Russia need to be prosecuted, but let's not go crazy with that sentiment – keep justice-seeking to this conflict only. This is like when that one person said, "I'd like a doughnut", but now you can't move for doughnut shops – next thing you know it's Oreo-frosted war-crime trials with salted caramel filling for everyone,' added Blair, going off on a tangent.

Bush then carefully noted that he was unsure why *WWN* was asking him specifically about these things, as it was irrelevant due to the US not signing up to the ICC.

'Plus, if you want to talk about being punished for actions; I had a shoe thrown at me once, so if anything, I've served my time.'

UKRAINIAN PRESIDENT Volodymyr Zelenskyy has been very quiet about where he got the money for all his new arms, prompting suspicion that US President Joe Biden has pulled a classic grandparent move of tucking a few quid into his back pocket and swearing him to secrecy.

'Now did Grampa Joe give you the money for those surface-to-air missile defence systems? We're not mad, we just want to know,' Zelenskyy was asked today by the Russian government, while President Biden winked and mouthed the words 'say nothing'.

Zelenskyy stayed true to his deal with the US, however, and bounded off with a mischievous smile on his face to distribute his cool new military hardware to his friends on the frontline, while the Russians had a quiet word with old man Biden about how he can't keep giving money to Ukraine.

'Look, Joe, we know you want to be like this kindly old grandad to

'SAY NOTHING NOW': BIDEN SLIPS UKRAINE $33BN IN CLASSIC GRANDPA MOVE

Ukraine, but you have to understand that we're trying to subjugate these people at the minute and you're kinda mucking it all up,' a delegate for Vladimir Putin said in a stern address to the White House today.

'You know he's just going to use that money to get into trouble, and that's something we have to deal with, not you. It's all well and good to be the favourite grandparent handing over $33 billion in aid, but you're not going to be there when he's shooting down our planes or blowing up our tanks. So please, for everyone's sake, just stay out of it.'

Biden has shrugged off the pleas from Russia, citing 'Ah, it's only a few coppers for the young lad' as an excuse.

BREAKING NEWS

On This Day

9 November

1989: The fall of the Berlin Wall led to a huge overhaul in Germany's wall safety regulations.

TERRORISTS EYEING UP THAT NEW WORLD TRADE CENTER LIKE IT'S DISNEYLAND

INTERNATIONAL TERRORIST ORGANISATIONS have admitted that 9/11 will never be topped in their lifetime, even if that new One World Trade Center tower in New York is 'like an arse in the air begging to be smacked'.

The musings came as shadowy anti-capitalist groups from around the world met this week at the Annual Terrorism Summit in Davos, where it was agreed that further attacks on America would be pointless, as the Americans were doing a good enough job of attacking each other as it was.

'If we tried to storm the Capitol building we wouldn't get past the first pillar before being shot down by some white lad toting an AR-15,' said one terrorism bankroller from a Middle Eastern nation, definitely not Saudi Arabia.

'And there's no sense in us trying to do 9/11 part deux. It'd be like any sequel; nobody is really interested after all these years, and it'd never be as good as the original anyways.'

Meanwhile, the US has stated that there's nowhere on the planet that it needs to invade for oil anymore, and as such will not just sit back and let itself get attacked again.

THREE-YEAR-OLD HAS ALREADY LIVED THROUGH ENOUGH HISTORY, THANKS

EXHAUSTED AND UNABLE to deal with the stress of switching on the TV or catching a glimpse of a news app push notification on her mother's phone she's using to watch YouTube videos, three-year-old Jess Mannigan has pleaded with those currently creating history to please 'cut it out'.

'Honestly, that's my limit. I don't know if this was going on before I was born, but it's … A LOT. Do you guys ever take a day off?' asked Mannigan, pleading directly with everyone from the Taliban, Saudi Arabia, Putin and the people who advise Kanye West on his Instagram updates.

With her 36 months on this planet largely dominated by wars, climate change, a pandemic, ongoing Brexit nonsense and Jason Momoa and Lisa Bonet breaking up before getting back together again, Mannigan has asked for the unceasing accumulation of era-defining historical events to ease off a bit, as she's just trying to play with some Duplo here.

'Eighteen episodes of Paw Patrol in a row is my only break from this shit. I barely get any joy out of drawing on the walls with crayons anymore. If this is life, book me a one-way ticket back into the womb,' added a tired Mannigan, and it's not even nap time yet.

'And hey, if it's taking a toll on me, I can only imagine what my fellow three-year-olds in Yemen must be feeling,' concluded the Waterford-based tyke before sighing wearily after another Russian diplomat mentioned

how Russia wouldn't hesitate to use nuclear weapons.

Elsewhere, there was little sign from today's evildoers that they intended to stop creating the sort of human misery that will end up as a particularly sobering question on history tests years from now.

EXCLUSIVE

EXCLUSIVE

ALTERNATIVE NAMES FOR EU DEFENCE FORCE THAT DON'T MAKE IT SOUND LIKE WE'RE JOINING A BLATANT ARMY

TASKED WITH CLOAKING the fact that the government is willing to conscript Ireland into the EU Defence Force without so much as a referendum or any consultation with the Irish public, the Department of Defence and the EU have coined several new names that make it sound like we're not joining an active army.

After consulting a focus group of professional copywriters, here are all the non-army-type names for the EU Defence Force that they believe sound a lot less army:

Not a Territorial Oppressor
This sums up what they're aiming to achieve nicely, and doesn't have any negative connotations relating to war. They could abbreviate this down to the letters NATO … ah fuck, just realised it sounds like … yeah.

EU Democracy Department
Getting there. Labelling this military outfit a department really gives it an 'official' and almost corporate air. Maybe instead of camo, troops could wear expensive suits, and when the time for war comes, they could just sit down for meetings with their counterparts and settle disputes over a liquid lunch and some lamb sliders. Yum.

Friends of Europe
This is great, as the name suggests a warm, friendly atmosphere, but if you're not friends of Europe then it makes it quite clear that you're enemies. The DoD believe everyone

will want to be friends if this name is chosen – a keeper.

Conscripted Teens
Actually, this sounds a lot like a Pornhub category. Not sure about this one. Also, the word 'conscription' is very warlike. Yeah, back to the ocean floor with you, Fungie. Next!

Pew Pew Bang Bang
Okay, this might be dumbing it down way too much. We get the cutesy cloaked references and the meme potential, but it still spells out army.

Money Pit
Considering the billions of euros of Irish taxpayers' money that Simon Coveney is so willing to spend on

an unnecessary arm of an EU war machine, we believe Money Pit perfectly sums up exactly what's going on here – a European branch of the military-industrial complex that has already ravaged the world 10 times over. Yeah, we really like this one. Fitting, and it's not like we need the money for other struggling government departments anyway.

SPACE

BILLIONAIRES VOW TO END WORLD HUNGER BY LAUNCHING STARVING PEOPLE INTO SPACE

CALLED TO TASK on their egotistical space race amid an ever-growing divide between rich and poor, the world's billionaires have agreed to join forces and end world hunger once and for all, WWN can report.

The conglomerate of tech, science and financial billionaires announced this week that they are planning to develop one-way trips to space from strategic locations around the globe, and will launch tens of millions of starving people off the planet, eradicating hunger for good.

'We have already begun constructing launch pads across the African continent,' Tesla CEO and founder Elon Musk told a packed press conference yesterday afternoon. 'We're going to call this Project StarvLink, and hope to shoot half a million third worlders into the stars by 2023.'

StarvLink's collective of billionaires has humbly asked the world not to thank them for the project, which is funded by lucrative government contracts, with many stating that they just want to do this for the greater good of mankind.

'Imagine going from being starving in a desert with thousands of people,

> **'The world can thank us later, but for now, let us focus on getting the poor off the planet'**

to being blasted off into space with thousands of starving people. I'm starting to well up thinking about how generous we all are in doing this,' said a teary-eyed Jeff Bezos, simultaneously high-fiving Richard Branson. 'That moment when they look back at Earth and realise the amount of vegetation, mineral resources and vast utopian cities lighting up the dark skies will surely bring it all home to them – equality is only for the rich.'

With an estimated 690 million people currently classed as undernourished and desperate for food, StarvLink is expected to take four years to eradicate world hunger.

'The world can thank us later, but for now, let us focus on getting the poor off the planet,' the billionaires stated, sparking a lengthy round of applause by themselves, for themselves.

On This Day

AD 980: The Battle of Tara, a fight involving only Taras, occurs. Clumps of hair flying everywhere.

8 March

CLIMATE TO IDENTIFY AS BANK IN HOPES PEOPLE WILL SAVE IT

A NEW INITIATIVE that will reclassify Earth's climate as a commercial bank so it can avail of a quick-acting bailout from governments is expected to get the green light next year, saving the climate from proverbially going bust, *WWN* has learned.

Much like the 2009 bank bailout that saw Irish citizens fork out €41.7 billion to save six commercial banks from defaulting, the climate will soon become listed as a financial institution

and will demand that citizens here stabilise it or face even worse consequences than a financial crash.

'People have got to ask themselves which is worse, your money disappearing from your account, or the world disappearing from your life and ending it,' argued the head of the campaign to reclassify the climate, Dr Gerald Hashhold. 'Obviously, this concept is aimed more at the people in power, who actually call the shots, but once we have them on board, I'm sure this idea will be plain sailing.'

The move, which would involve the climate somehow floated on the world's stock exchanges, will see it run like a multibillion euro financial institution, affording it an importance it was previously denied, with every citizen in the world given equal shares

in the climate to start in the hopes that more invest, with lucrative bonuses for shareholders if it starts improving.

Since it was announced, hundreds of huge multinationals have already shown interest in the climate stock, and have vowed to protect it at all costs.

'Whatever we do, we've got to save the climate bank no matter what,' IMF CEO Kristalina Georgieva told a press conference, flanked by dozens of world leaders and very panicked and sweaty-looking bank officials. 'We can't let the climate bank go bust, and must act now, now, now, now!'

Thanks to the change, the climate is now expected to make a full recovery in just three short years, a staggering 30 years ahead of schedule.

Bill's Landlord Tips

Don't make any attempt to convince a tenant to stay; if they want to leave, let them. Stop acting like there isn't an endless supply of these people. Harden up!

COMMUNION WAFER ORIGINALLY BROKEN BY JESUS SELLS FOR £200MN AT AUCTION

CHRISTIE'S AUCTION HOUSE in London has confirmed that it sold the original communion wafer broken by Jesus Christ for a staggering £200 million at an online auction earlier today, *WWN* has learned.

The 2,000-year-old wafer, which was originally broken by Jesus during his last-ever supper in Jerusalem, is hosted in its original gold monstrance and was sold to an unknown Russian billionaire for a record sum.

'It's even branded with Jesus' signature symbol of the cross,' one collector told *WWN*. 'Jesus would have only made a handful of these before being crucified, and people would have swapped and exchanged them like Pokémon cards back in the day. Fuck knows why he made the things.'

It is understood that the communion wafer is also stamped 'Last Supper', with the date AD 33 on it in small print, the last in a long line of wafers marking Jesus' infamous supper parties.

'Christ loved his suppers, and made a different batch of wafers for each one,' explained another collector, who claims to have the first-ever supper wafer in his collection. 'Apparently,

the best wafer is actually from the sixth supper, which was meant to have been mental, with Jesus turning water into wine for three days straight.'

The body of Christ was originally trademarked and patented by Jesus when he was just 27, before being bought out by the Vatican in AD 453 for a record-breaking 4,000 gold coins, and is now estimated to be worth over €3 billion in today's money.

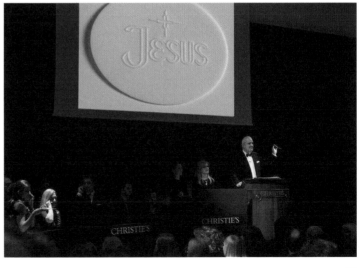

TECHNOLOGY

HUMAN CARBON TAX METRES WILL CHECK INDIVIDUAL ARSE EMISSIONS

CARBON EMISSION METRES installed in a person's backside are set to get the go-ahead next year to help monitor humans' individual output and tax them according to how much methane they produce, *WWN* has learned.

The flatulence metres are expected to cost each Irish citizen €300, with a bi-monthly bill ranging anywhere from

€100 to €500, depending on how much gas the individual passes in the given period.

'Human arse emissions contribute to around 5 per cent of the world's greenhouse gasses, and we believe this metering system will help reduce that by half over the coming decade,' Green Party leader and absolute genius Eamon Ryan explains. 'Ireland will be the first-ever country to trial this exciting new tool.'

The arse metre design allows it to sit discreetly between the bum cheeks, connecting directly to the anus to avoid any leaks, and will be implemented from 1 January 2023.

'I barely even notice I have a methane metre up my hole,' said one person who took part in the initial government six-month trial. 'It does tend to make your flatulence sound like when you let the air out of a balloon while stretching the blow part tightly, kind of a high-pitched whistle noise, but you get used to that after a while.'

Fines of up to €1,000 are expected to be issued to people trying to game the new arse metre system, something the government said will be treated with the utmost severity.

'Arse metre cheats cheat us all,' Tánaiste Leo Varadkar warned would-be offenders. 'Sure, you can squeeze a straw up in there to bypass some methane, but the only person you're cheating is yourself.'

FEARS ARE IN NO WAY GROWING for the fate of US military aid to Israel in the wake of its forces killing Al Jazeera journalist Shireen Abu Aqla, *WWN* understands.

With calls for a formal investigation, a push for a UN enquiry and serious condemnation from Western leaders; experts expect that all to be ignored and US military aid to be ramped up.

'You keep this up or kill any more Palestinian-American journalists and we're warning you, you might get more fighter jets,' a stern US Congress told Israeli PM Naftali Bennett.

'It would be remiss of us not to warn you, this type of behaviour will only result in a strong lack of condemnation, closer economic ties and help with identifying anyone criticising this murder online,' the White House said in a hastily issued statement.

With an Al Jazeera colleague of Abu Aqla's confirming that they were shot at by Israeli soldiers without warning and that there was no Palestinian military resistance present, it has never been clearer that Israeli forces trying to cover up their misdeeds will face the full force of a blank US chequebook.

ISRAEL IN DANGER OF HAVING US MILITARY AID INCREASED AFTER KILLING OF JOURNALIST

'We're working on some sonic bombs, and bullets that explode inside the body like a grenade, you're gonna love those. Hold off killing any more innocent unarmed people until then. It'll be much easier to do it with the new tech,' confirmed US

military officials, who appealed for a return to one-sided slaughter after recent weeks saw 17 Israelis and 26 Palestinians killed.

In an official statement, the Israeli government condemned Abu Aqla 'for lunging at an innocent bullet'.

TRUMP

TRUMP AMONG PUTIN'S ASSETS BEING FROZEN

FOLLOWING A RAFT of sanctions by the EU, America, Canada and other nations on Russia's regime, Vladimir Putin is set to personally feel the pinch as his own overseas wealth is targeted.

'Aside from any assets like boats and houses abroad we can link to Putin, other assets have been frozen in an effort to prove that his invasion of Ukraine will not be tolerated,'

confirmed one official charged with placing former US President Donald Trump into a block of ice.

While cryogenic technology is in its infancy, the official confirmed that keeping Trump in ice for an indeterminate period of time would result in absolutely no change in the current levels of brain activity.

'This is a very comprehensive set of sanctions, so Putin will suffer personally. Priceless assets will now be out of his reach,' added the official, luring Trump into

> **'Losing money? Doesn't matter to Putin, he can just steal from his people once more'**

the large freezer with the aid of a fishing rod and a picture of a topless Putin riding a horse.

Experts believe that, while Putin, a man on only a €100,000 salary, might miss the yachts he somehow magically owns, it is the loss of his beloved lapdog that will hit him the hardest and potentially turn the tide in this developing war.

'Losing money doesn't matter to Putin, he can just steal from his people once more, but the loss of his whining, undermining, division-sowing, Putin-kowtowing, borscht-for-brains, not-quite-sane Trump – that's a one-of-a-kind treasure,' explained one political expert.

EXCLUSIVE

I SAYS TO HIM, 'YURY, YE BETTER NOT GET IN OUR WAY NOW, OR THERE'LL BE FUCKING SLAPS'

WITH NEWS OF AN AGREEMENT between Irish fishermen and the Russian government over controversial naval exercises off the southwest coast of Ireland, *WWN* speaks to Irish fisherman Kevin Mackay, who, along with his fishing peers, single-handedly defused an international incident.

'Ah, Yury's not the worsht of them now in fairness, God love him. Shure I could tell he's all fart and no shite,' Mackay opened up today, speaking from his trawler about his encounter with the Russian Ambassador to Ireland, Yury Filatov.

'Shure didn't he lash out a bottle of vodka, not a patch on the Aldi stuff, but shure, and us batin' into a few shots and some pickled green yokes before we even got shtarted, whisht, he's a right character altogether. He doesn't look like he skips dinners either, if you get me, would eat the hind legs off the lamb of God.'

Initially, fishermen were angry at the potential disruption to their traditional fishing grounds, and this week hinted at their intention to peacefully disrupt the Russian plans by fishing as normal in the area.

'I pulled him up on it, I did,' Mackay explains. 'I says to him, "Shtop the lights, Yury, you'll be getting more slaps than a stripper's arse on an Irish stag if ye try anything," I said. Sure, then he says to me, "Kevin," he says, "we're only teshtin' the bloody missiles is all." He said, "We'll make sure not to blow ye up – how's that?", and I says back to

him, "Yury, you're some fucking man for one man. You've enough cheek for two arses." And that was the general gist of it now – fair balls to him.'

Despite strong opposition from the government, with Minister for Foreign Affairs Simon Coveney previously telling Russia it wasn't welcome, the fishermen agreed to let the global superpower carry out their drills.

'Simon who?' Mackay said. 'Fucking simple Simon more like. Sure, all he had to do was ask Yury the craic instead of going off spouting shite to the papers and licking America's hole. Better off necking a few shots and coming to an agreement instead of that aul' childish muck.'

Following the successful agreement between the two sides, Mackay said he will now travel to 'the Ukraine' with a few of the lads to help sort out problems there.

'Yury said he'll come along for the craic too, and we might even meet their president lad that walks funny,' Mackay stated.

AFGHANISTAN

'JUST GIVE US THE SAUDI ARABIA TREATMENT', TALIBAN ASKS WORLD

THE TALIBAN HAS VOWED to secure Afghanistan and promise they will uphold human rights according to Sharia law and have asked the Western nations of the world to just treat them like they would any other tyrant regime, like Saudi Arabia, for instance, *WWN* has learned.

'Public executions, poor record on women's rights, roles in terror attacks on US soil – when you think about it, we're no worse than your good friends in Saudi,' Taliban leader Mullah Abdul Ghani Baradar stated. 'We even have millions of dollars' worth of US military hardware. We're the exact same pack of cunts you're used

to dealing with – fuck it, put us on the UN Human Rights Council while you're at it.'

The leader's comments come after the Taliban triumphantly marched into Kabul's international airport on Tuesday, hours after the final US troop withdrawal that ended America's longest and most pointless war, but hopefully not their last.

'We'll probably focus on Iran or Venezuela for a bit, waste a couple more trillion on destabilising them before pulling out and creating a dangerous insurgent vacuum for the rest of the world to clean up,' a spokesperson for US foreign affairs

explained, before contemplating the Taliban's bid to treat them like Saudis. 'It's a great point, and yes, we'll probably cosy up to them for a bit and help them fight this new ISIS-K thing we concocted … for a small fee of course. It's all gravy, baby.'

Meanwhile, the Taliban has made an open request for user manuals for US tanks, Black Hawks, Apaches and those big armoured trucks with surface-to-air missiles. If anyone has them please post them to Kabul, thanks.

NOW ALSO A GOOD TIME TO CUT LINKS WITH COUNTRY THAT HAS 1MN UIGHURS IN PRISON CAMP

AS BUSINESSES and individuals with links to Russian state bodies, businesses and oligarchs dramatically cut ties following sanctions by a number of nations, experts have pointed out that, while it has come a decade or so late, the trend of disentangling yourself from authoritarian states and de facto dictators doesn't need to stop there.

'Like many people, I was shocked to learn overnight that the Vladimir Putin I posed in photos with on a business trip to Moscow three years ago is the same Vladimir Putin in the news today. If I had known …' trailed off one CEO of a food manufacturer, who will absolutely shit his pants when

he realises the contracts his company has in China are fraught with moral complications too.

'We stand with the people of Ukraine, but not so close that our Russian benefactors get the wrong idea and think we're directly criticising the Putin regime,' confirmed a third-

level institute that has taken this opportunity to pause and reflect on the huge Chinese investment it has received and decided, no, internment of a Muslim minority is actually fine.

'The government has been clear from the start, we are working in concert with our international partners, and these sanctions will hit Russia hard,' confirmed a deputy leader of a country, while also lobbying that those very sanctions would not affect a Russian-owned company in Limerick.

'Whoa, whoa, I think everyone has to calm down. How do we know the Uighurs aren't in China's version of Disney World and are just so happy there they've forgotten to get in touch?' asked one influencer who has a collab with a Chinese tech gadget company going live any day now.

UK ROYALTY

THE QUEEN is reportedly devastated at having to melt down one of her ornate and bejewelled crowns to pay for her son Andrew's 'definitely not a hush payment' hush payment, *WWN* understands.

Andrew had reached an out-of-court settlement with his accuser before asking the Queen if she could increase his pocket money to get the British taxpayer to pay the settlement, which prompted the Queen to melt down the crown pictured above and sell it to her nearest Cash4Crowns outlet.

For those unfamiliar with legal terms, an 'out-of-court settlement' is often used by famous and powerful people to avoid going to court, with one notable example being infamous sex offender Jeffrey Epstein.

The crown itself is worth precisely £12 million and was gifted to the Queen on the occasion of Her Majesty's wooden jubilee by Count Orifice DuPont Inclement Weatherall IV of Alexandringham.

It is a highly contentious piece as, strictly speaking, the crown, previously on display at the V&A, was never technically the Queen's to receive, and by 'gifted' British royal historians

HERE'S THE CROWN THE QUEEN HAS TO MELT DOWN TO PAY ANDREW'S £12MN HUSH PAYMENT

mean 'stolen during an unprovoked and bloody massacre'.

Sources inside the palace say they heard raised voices between Andrew and the Queen late into the night, with the Queen remarking, 'This is the last time I melt down a crown in the Royal fireplace just to keep you out of sodding jail, you lecherous, handsy, octopus-limbed

idiot', and 'You're running our meal ticket, Andrew. These idiot plebs fund everything, and we have them convinced they should be thankful. Fuck up again and it's tunnel time.'

Elsewhere, the *Daily Mail* has halted all reporting online and printing of its physical newspapers until such a time as it can conclusively prove that this is all somehow that bitch Markle's fault.

MAN DISGUSTED TO FIND NO RECEPTION ON EVEREST

THE NATURAL AND MAN-MADE WONDERS of this Earth are only as good as their phone reception, according to a new survey, which found that most people cannot enjoy the spectacles this world has to offer if they can't live-stream it at the same time.

'I would have thought that because Mount Everest was closer to space, I'd at least get a few bars, but nothing,' fumed one furious adventurer, who had to wait until he'd descended the mountain before he could upload a selfie.

'The pyramids of Giza could be greatly improved by the addition of a 5G mast. I could barely connect to Twitter at all,' said one distraught influencer, who felt she had wasted her entire trip to Egypt.

'What's the point of scuba-diving along the Great Barrier Reef if the sea water is just going to break your phone? There's just no thought put into it,' added another, while giving the nation of Australia two stars on Tripadvisor.

'Say what you want about Temple Bar, at least you can get Wi-Fi,' said

one relatively happy punter. 'I was on that Great Wall of China once, not a lick of Wi-Fi at all. For those of you keeping score: that's McDonald's in Temple Bar one, the largest man-made structure in history nil.'

SPACE

ISS PELTED BY ROCKS DURING DUBLIN FLY BY

My highlight of 2022: Snoop Dogg

'Turning 357 years old.'

CREW MEMBERS of the International Space Station have been advised to 'keep the windows up and not hang around' when flying over Dublin, following a spate of upper-atmospheric anti-social behaviour, *WWN* can report.

Damage to the side of the orbiting craft has been put down to rocks, used batteries and eggs that have been launched from the Dublin region at the ISS craft, presumably after youths in the area became bored with pelting trains, fire engines and ambulances.

It's believed that the new trouble may have started after one astronaut on board the ISS posted a pic on social media of Dublin from 400km up with a heartfelt message. This antagonised some locals, who thought he was 'starting' on them.

'Take a picture of this, ye space prick,' roared one young lad this evening, sending a half-filled bottle of Boost energy drink into the heavens using a rudimentary launching device made up of two e-scooters running at full whack.

'Fuck off out of it, you cosmic dickheads,' chanted a crowd of assembled youths, as they gathered another salvo of debris to be sent spaceward using a load of fireworks they'd bought off a lad in town.

The current antagonism towards the ISS is the second time that NASA had to deal with unruly Irish kids, following an incident a few years ago when Cmdr Chris Hadfield posted from space about how much he loved Ireland, prompting large gangs to demand that he 'say it to their fuckin' faces' when he got back to Earth.

> **'Fuck off out of it, you cosmic dickheads'**

Tips for Ignoring Climate Change

Even if the sea rises by two metres, the Cliffs of Moher will still be very, very tall. You'll barely even notice it there.

PUTIN

WORLD ASKS TO SKIP TO PART WHEN SCRUFFY, GAUNT PUTIN IS PULLED FROM HIDING HOLE

MIRRORING THE FATE of his former dictator peers, there have been renewed calls made from the world to just skip to the part when a scruffy, gaunt-faced Vladimir Putin is dragged from a Russian hiding hole and dealt with in the usual fashion, *WWN* can confirm.

'It's probably best to avoid all the in-between death and suffering and just do a Gaddafi on him, or a Saddam, or, if he so desires, a Hitler,' proposed just about everybody now sick of his shit, while making a gun trigger motion to their head.

'It's not like anyone will miss him, apart from a

> ## 'It's not like anyone will miss him, apart from a few million brainwashed Russians'

few million brainwashed Russians and your mental mate sending you conspiracy theories ... oh yeah, and Oliver Stone.'

With tens of thousands of both Russian and Ukrainian troops killed, along with countless civilians, many

believe the time has already passed for the Russian leader to be trialled for war crimes at the Hague, stating a complete all-out mission to remove Putin would suffice, before he gets a chance at his 6,000 nuclear warheads.

'What the fuck are we waiting for?' asked other

people, more worried about the price of oil and gas than anything else. 'The man is obviously unhinged, and I don't have time to assess the wider geopolitical fallout from all-out world war – not when filling up my car feels like being robbed at gunpoint. Just get it done.'

US REPUBLICANS DOUBLE-CHECKING OVERTURNING *ROE V WADE* DOESN'T AFFECT ABORTIONS FOR THEIR MISTRESSES

A LAST-MINUTE potential stumbling block to US states overturning *Roe v Wade* on foot of a leaked Supreme Court opinion has been identified by a large number of US Republicans, *WWN* understands.

'Before we take steps to outlaw abortion, criminalise the taking of the morning-after pill, any of that great stuff, we're just seeking clarity … this wouldn't apply to our mistresses, would it?' queried one visibly worried Republican senator, who had a follow-up question about his babysitter as well.

Having blocked an attempt by Democrats to safeguard the right to abortion by making the 1973 Supreme Court decision law, Republicans have been searching for more detail on what a post-*Roe v Wade* America will look like.

'Abortion is an ungodly sin that will never be forgiven and we must punish it, no matter the circumstances – rape or threat to the life of the mother. Having said all that, I find it just feels better having sex with my mistress when I'm not wearing a condom, so I just need guarantees here, special dispensation, you know?' offered another Republican, who had additional questions about whether a college intern or housemaid qualifies as a mistress too.

'Potentially giving a woman suffering a miscarriage a criminal record and therefore making it illegal for her to vote sounds just peachy, I'm proud we're going further than Sharia law on this, but what if my daughter is one of those women?' added one Republican governor. 'I fear there

needs to be a more severe punishment. Have we considered the death penalty? My daughter hasn't talked to me in years, and I'd like to teach her a lesson.'

Elsewhere, the most popular Google searches in the US in the last week have been revealed:

- 'Canadian abortion clinics map'
- 'How to break it to my boyfriend he's getting a vasectomy?'
- 'Is Handmaid's Tale fiction?'
- 'Am I a bad person for voting for the "force rape victims to have babies" party?'
- 'There's got to be at least one thing the Taliban and Republican politicians disagree on?'

YEMEN PLEADS WITH WORLD TO DONATE EVEN A SINGLE FUCK

DEEMED BY THE UN to be 'the worst humanitarian crisis in the world', the current situation in Yemen has prompted its desperate population to appeal to the world to give a fuck, just one fuck, if that's possible.

'By the end of the year, almost 19 million of us will face starvation. We've had nearly a decade of war and famine. Can some of you please give a fuck about us?' said one Yemeni woman we spoke to, currently feeding her family one meagre meal a day as the Russian invasion of Ukraine puts extra pressure on supply chains and fuel prices.

'What will kill us first, the starvation or the Saudi-backed army? The lack of hospitals and medical supplies or the lack of a future due to a near-complete halt to all education? Who knows. We need help, supplies, food, money. Please give what you can. But if you can't give any of that, at least give a shit. Put a flag somewhere, post about it on your computer. Show you give even one lonesome, solitary fuck about us.'

Despite the pleas, many around the world have stated that they're sorry, but they gave all their fucks to Ukraine and they're fresh out at the minute.

'I can't be expected to care about two things at once,' stated one non-fuck-giver we spoke to.

AFGHANISTAN

TALIBAN STAGE MOST UNWELCOME COMEBACK SINCE WESTLIFE

PROMISING all the old hits as well as a few new tunes, the Taliban have announced a comeback tour of Afghanistan that is said to be about as necessary or needed as Westlife's upcoming 'Stadiums in the Summer Tour'.

'Honestly, who needed this? Who wanted it? Who asked for it? So much unnecessary suffering, for no reason, no reason whatsoever. And as for the Taliban, they can fuck off too,' said *WWN*'s music and Middle Eastern politics correspondent, looking at the bleak future ahead.

'In truth, both of these things were predicted and could have been prevented. The US were adamant that they had stamped out the Taliban once and for all, and Westlife went on a farewell tour. The dogs in the street could have told you what was going to happen next: both would be quiet for a few years then flare up again, possibly worse than ever.'

With the Taliban capturing their 10th Afghan province capital as they advance around the country with their eyes on the capital, Kabul,

many people fear a return to the brutal Taliban regime of the past – although not as many people as those who fear the reintroduction of Brian McFadden to Westlife, the band he left behind in 2004.

'Things are bad right now, but they can always get worse,' warned our correspondent.

'Just promise me one thing: no matter what happens, don't send me out there to cover it. I have a wife and young child, I don't want to have to leave them, possibly never to return, or if I do return, perhaps return a changed man, ruined by the horrors I've seen. I don't mind going to Kabul, but not that Pairc Uí Chaoimh Westlife gig, please, I beg you.'

NATION CAN'T HELP BUT TAKE A SMALL BIT OF PRIDE IN SUCCESS OF KINAHAN CARTEL

THE ANNOUNCEMENT by US drug enforcement agencies that a local drug gang ranks 'up there with the Yakuza or the Russian mafia' in terms of size and power has prompted a tiny bit of COYBIG energy in Irish hearts today.

At a briefing attended by the DEA, the US Department of Homeland Security, Europol, the UK National Crime Agency, Thunderbirds, the Famous Five, the Mighty Morphin Power Rangers and An Garda Síochána, the breadth of the billion-dollar Kinahan drug empire was laid bare for all to see, prompting mixed reactions back home.

'I know the road to success in the drug game is paved with mayhem, pain and death. But still, you have to kinda hand it to them,' said one man we spoke to on the streets of Waterford.

'Could they give me a few quid, could they? Ha ha! Ah, I'm only messing. But seriously, dreadful carry on. Mind you, I kinda don't want them to be caught? Is that bad? It's just been years since we've been at the top of anything. We haven't won the Eurovision since 1996, give us something,' added another.

'It's a relief that the Americans are after them now. It doesn't make our

efforts over the last few years look so bad in hindsight,' a patrolling guard told us in the Kinahans' ancestral home of Tallaght.

Meanwhile, a bounty of $15 million has been offered for information leading to the arrest of the Kinahan family, pushing them past the realms of drug barons and straight into supervillain territory.

Why Pac-Man shouldn't be judged for his pill addiction   MARCH 2022

PC GAMER

700+
Politically correct insults to hurl at online players

'THEY MADE ME RUN INTO WALLS JUST TO HEAR ME MOAN': LARA CROFT OPENS UP

ENTERTAINMENT

TELEVISION

THE CROWN REVEALS FIRST LOOK AT NEW GERRY ADAMS, MARTIN MCGUINNESS AND BERTIE AHERN

HOT ON THE HEELS of the producers of hit Netflix drama *The Crown* revealing the new images of their Charles and Diana, played by Dominic West and Elizabeth Debicki, more exclusive set photos have made their way onto entertainment sites.

The new series charts the personal drama of the royal family through the 1990s but as with all seasons of the prestige drama, other geopolitical events are very much at the forefront.

Three figures who will feature heavily are Gerry Adams, Martin McGuinness and Bertie Ahern, and in true *The Crown* casting, the actors bear an uncanny resemblance to the real-life figures they play, as accuracy is everything to the show's producers:

Martin McGuinness
While admitting he has struggled to perfect the accent, Harry Styles more than passes for McGuinness here in a period-appropriate costume from the set of *The Crown*.

Bertie Ahern
The physically demanding role of Bertie Ahern will be played by Superman himself, Henry Cavill, seen here in an exclusive pic from the set of *The Crown* during the initial Good Friday Agreement negotiations. Not seen in shot: the lack of a bank account.

Gerry Adams
In this exclusive image, a topless Gerry Adams, played by Chris Hemsworth, is seen being interviewed on ITV News, but famously with his voice dubbed by an English person.

SOCIAL MEDIA

ANNOYING FAMILY ON TIKTOK THINK THEY'RE THE FLEMINGS

LOCAL AUTHORITIES and the Gardaí have been inundated with calls from the public, begging them to intervene in the case of one family on TikTok who clearly think they're the next Flemings.

'Doctors might say you can't die from cringing at people's videos, but I have,' confirmed one TikTok user after stumbling upon the Mannigan family, who are operating under the misapprehension that they are a gas family altogether, constantly engaging in hilarious craic.

'We do be awful gas sometimes,' said father Thomas Mannigan, whose family now film themselves 24/7 ahead of what they expect will be worldwide social media fame.

'Sure didn't the wife spill some water the other day and the kids did this "spilling water dance". Well, I made them do it. We were fake laughing for hours, so we were,' added Thomas, who has printed T-shirt merchandise of his family online at MannigansShenanigans.com, which is a solid name in terms of brand building in fairness.

For their part, Gardaí say they can't intervene unless a crime is being committed, which prompted onlookers to suggest that surely driving people slowly insane counts.

'They did a video there and they were all wearing odd socks and acting like they were madder than a hornet's nest stuck up a bull's hole – they need to be stopped,' confirmed a petition signed by 200,000 TikTok users.

Advice to simply 'stop looking at them' has been dismissed by the public, who labelled such suggestions as 'absolutely useless, as everybody knows it's impossible not to gawk at a car crash'.

APPLE AIRPODS USER SPENDS MAJORITY OF LIFE TRYING TO LOCATE APPLE AIRPODS

Predictions for 2023

The Bank of Mum & Dad applies for a bailout.

'YOU HAVEN'T SEEN them, have ya?' remarked Apple AirPods owner Gavin Malley, now resorting to tearing up the floorboards in his home in search of the elusive audio aids, which go missing at least 40 times a day.

'Fuck sake, I swear I had them a second ago there on the table,' added Malley, running his hands over his ears just in case he hadn't realised he was wearing them the whole time.

Malley is believed to be just one of 100 per cent of AirPods owners whose life is now solely dedicated to searching for the constantly missing phone accessory, with many forced to quit jobs, renege on social engagements and generally retreat from society in order to partake in constant searches.

'They're the fuckin' David Blaine of earphones, always staging elaborate fuckin' disappearing acts,' added a

frustrated Malley, arse up in the air as he poked his head underneath the couch he had already checked five times to no avail.

'Oh but they're great though, so handy. Wouldn't be caught dead with the old plebphones – that's what I call the ones with wires. Ugh, talk about a nightmare, all that tangling,' added Malley, slowly going insane as he realised he had now misplaced the charging chase.

'Best €179 I ever spent,' continued Malley, breaking down in tears before screaming, 'Yes I've tried the Find My Phone app thingy already!'

EXCLUSIVE

'WE'RE GRAND': YEMEN URGES BONO TO NOT EVEN THINK ABOUT IT

QUICKLY INTERVENING before anyone could arrange an impromptu underground gig for them, the people of Yemen issued a joint statement to Irish singer and U2 frontman Bono, stating that they're grand for any future visits.

'No, no, don't mind us at all at all, we're grand here. Seriously, don't you bother your little head about us,' the official statement read, emphasising the point that Yemen doesn't need any

songs sung there, thanks. 'The days of lifting our hopes are gone anyway, and to be brutally honest you'd be nearly eight years late at this stage so it would look forced – best keep that craic for your own kind, we guess.'

This plea from the Yemeni people comes after both Bono and The Edge performed in an underground metro station that is being used as a bomb shelter after being invited to perform by Ukrainian President Volodymyr Zelenskyy as a 'show of solidarity' with the Ukrainian people.

> **'Can you please make sure those celebrities bring food instead of songs with them?**

'It's great to see all the world leaders, their wives and popular rock bands flocking to Kyiv for photo shoots, it's really brave of them and doesn't look one bit opportunistic,' the Yemeni people added, 'but if you guys were ever to insist on sending us such "gifts", can you please make sure those celebrities bring food instead of songs with them? There's 17.4 million of us classed as food insecure and another 1.6 million of us are on the brink of total starvation, and we can't eat music.'

TELEVISION

'I COULDN'T DOCK A SMARTPHONE'

'SERIOUSLY, I don't know how the hell I've docked hundreds of luxury yachts, I haven't a clue what I'm doing,' *Below Deck*'s Captain Lee Rosbach tells *WWN* in an exclusive one-on-one interview, following on from the success of the hugely popular reality show.

We caught up with Captain Lee in Monaco ahead of filming for the latest series, just as he was docking yet another multimillion-dollar superyacht.

'Right, that's it … no, wait, the other right, ah, for fuck's sake Josh, we're going to hit the ah, balls.' Lee shouted, now blaming everyone else but himself before turning to this reporter. 'Ah, that will buff out, I'll just blame the deck crew – to be honest, I couldn't dock a smartphone, lol.'

Captain Lee has been at the *Below Deck* helm for eight seasons now and puts his long-running success down to good old-fashioned delegation.

'Most of the time I just sit in the bridge listening to Kris Kristofferson tracks, smoking rollie pollie hash I picked up in Morocco,' the Captain said, detailing the stress of running one of the world's most sought-after charters. 'Shit, can you pass me the other bong there, this one's gacked up to the max and needs a good clean,' he added, now calling on his latest chief stew to give it a good clean. 'I don't care if the engine room is on fire, Emily, my bubbler needs steaming.'

Lounging back on his swivel chair, and taking time to spin around while making a 'wheeee' sound, Captain Lee rubbished rumours that he may depart from the popular show next year.

'Ha-ha, me fuck, have you seen my pay cheque?' he jested, now frantically rubbing out a hot nodge burn on his pants. 'Shit, man, I need to lay off the pre-breakfast whiskeys. The way I'm going I won't have any pants left for the next charter.'

AS PART OF *WWN*'s opinion series, we give a platform to those who don't deserve it. This week is the turn of Dublin man Tim Kelly,  who goes out of his way to promote television shows that have been suddenly cancelled and left without any conclusion.

'It was an accident at first. I began watching the Starz show *Boss* starring Kelsey Grammer and recommended it to a work colleague, Darragh, but then when it was cancelled without warning after season two, I noticed Darragh would go out of his way not to talk to me – he was obviously livid. And then I knew I was onto something great.

'I went on to research some of the most disappointing cancelled shows ever produced, and I compiled a nice juicy list that I carry around with me everywhere I go now for the right occasion and prick to recommend them to. *Boss* was infuriating, but it was only two seasons long – I needed something that really dragged out and would take weeks to watch before realising

'I LIKE RECOMMENDING CANCELLED TV SHOWS TO PEOPLE I HATE'

the story just suddenly ends in limbo. So I began with *Stargate Atlantis* – six seasons and ends so abruptly that it causes mental health issues in people.

'My first victim was my local shopkeeper, Dave, who would try to short-change me every chance he got. I gave up calling him out on it years ago, so for me, he was a perfect target to offload a hundred 43-minute episodes of sci-fi.

'Dave was so excited during the watching of it that he didn't even short-change me once. He was just happy to have a connection and something to talk about other than the weather. I still smile when I remember his irate call at 2 a.m. one morning, going crazy that there weren't any more episodes to the show. I've never heard so many curse words in my life. It was a nice fuck you to him before I changed local shop. I believe he soon

lost his mind after it, which is fair enough, but I don't feel guilty – all that stolen change added up and Dave had to pay it back somehow.

'I've probably ruined many lives doing this and would suggest keeping this for the most prickish of pricks. I guess if I were to pick my top favourite cancelled TV shows to irk people with, it would be, *Stargate Atlantis*, *Heroes*, *Hannibal*, *Rome*, *The OA*, *Lois & Clark: The New Adventures of Superman* and of course *Angel*, which will leave you wanting to physically murder someone, it ends so abruptly. Hopefully, you too can use my research for your own pleasure.

'Enjoy, you cunt.'

Cost of Living Tips

Put yourself up for adoption.

CINEMA

FILM FANS STARVED for something more than endless superhero movies and blockbuster schlock can find entertaining and emotionally satisfying experiences by browsing the 'world cinema' section of streaming sites, without fear that it's just old Godzilla movies and borderline porn.

'Back in the day of video shops you would have one tiny "world cinema" aisle populated almost entirely by either ultraviolent Japanese movies or continental filth,' explained Arthur Cannahan, one of Waterford's foremost movie buffs. 'And that was all deadly, don't get me wrong, but now we can appreciate that there are excellent dramas, thrillers, romances and a couple of horror movies that

WORLD CINEMA MORE THAN JUST VIOLENCE AND RIDING, STUDY SHOWS

will scar you for the rest of your life in ways you never imagined possible in there too, if you so desire.'

The rise in people opening up to foreign movies may be linked to greater acceptance of subtitles, which Cannahan believes comes from new TV shows and films being practically inaudible even on high-end TVs.

'Sound mixes these days are just deafening action noises combined with whispered dialogue, so everyone watches with the subtitles on now anyway,' said Cannahan, watching his ninth consecutive hour of anime.

'So people are used to it, and they don't mind it when it comes to Bollywood or Hong Kong cinema. It also means we enjoy the movie more because we have to watch it to read

the subtitles, as opposed to being on our phone the whole time.'

Cannahan went on to recommend 27 Croatian movies that he insists are absolute masterpieces, which we will take his word for.

THINGS ELON MUSK SHOULD SPEND $44BN ON

THE WILL THEY WON'T THEY business saga of 2022: Elon Musk buying Twitter. The vastly wealthy owner of a vastly outsized fortune and ego once mentioned being open to donating $6 billion to aid the eradication of world hunger, but focused his efforts this year on nabbing the angry opinion library that is Twitter for $44 billion.

Could this money be better spent? Absolutely, and here's how:

- Nerfs for everyone. Nerfs are great fun, but do you know what's more fun than one Nerf? Eight billion people with eight billion Nerfs facing off in the largest game of Nerf ever.
- Musk previously touted tickets for a one-way trip to his vision of a colonised Mars, which would cost

people $500,000. But he could use his Twitter price tag money to send people to Mars for free. It could be turned into a competition, with people nominating others for the honour. Crunching the numbers, that's about 88,000 interfering mother-in-laws residing on Mars.

- While there's no price on obtaining self-control, it should be easy enough for Musk, a frequent embarrassment and pathetic troll on Twitter, to pay someone to hammer his hands any time he attempts to tweet.
- Some of the $44 billion could be put aside to pay people to literally massage Musk's ego.
- Actually, wait, the self-proclaimed champion of free speech did make a former SpaceX employee sign an NDA, silencing her after he allegedly took his penis out and asked her for an erotic massage in exchange for buying her a horse. So maybe the money could go towards more NDAs. Or on lessons on how not to do that.

CINEMA

'MAKING FISTS WITH YOUR TOES' FROM *DIE HARD* REVEALED TO BE TOTAL HORSESHIT

IT BRINGS US NO PLEASURE to tell you that, after nearly 30 years of experimentation, we can conclude that the 'make fists with your toes on carpet' advice given to John McClane in the movie *Die Hard* as a means to lessen the effects of jetlag simply does not work.

Our researchers have tried the method after every single flight they've made in the decades since seeing the action classic, and have concluded that at best it does nothing and at worst it gives you little carpet burns on your toes.

Other aspects of the Bruce Willis blockbuster that turn out to be false include:

- Getting out of an elevator via a panel in the roof is impossible, as no such panel exists. Believe us, if there were panels in the roofs of elevators, we'd be up and down in those

all the time with the lads. We'd be having cans on the roof of the thing.
- Bare feet are almost instantly debilitating, and one cannot just run about the place like John McClane does in the movie. Just like McClane, we too were once invited to our wife's Christmas work party and ended up

limping around with no shoes on by the end of it.
- There is no way McClane could have thrown a dead body from a roof onto the bonnet of a police car from that distance with that accuracy. Just trust us on this one.
- In the movie, Sgt Al Powell eats Twinkies like they're actually a nice thing and not the greasy heartburn machines that they are in real life.
- Staying with Powell, part of his backstory reveals that he once accidentally shot and killed a child who had a toy gun. We are expected to feel sympathy for this, which is nonsense. Powell, however, was not sacked from the force after this, which in fairness is completely accurate.

The above article contains spoilers for *Die Hard*, by the way.

Classifieds

Wingman

Passenger-seat driver needed urgently in Waterford area. Needs to be able to relay unnecessary information to me, such as when I'm 'alright this side'. Radio-fiddling skills a must.

CELEBRITIES

LADY GAGA TO LIVE ON BLASKET ISLANDS FOR 18 MONTHS IN PREPARATION FOR UPCOMING ROLE AS PEIG SAYERS

HAVING MISSED OUT on the Best Actress Oscar for her role in 2021's *House of Gucci*, Lady Gaga has thrown herself into intensive preparation for her next film, where she will play Irish author Peig Sayers in what is being described as 'potentially the most joyless movie of all time'.

Lady Gaga, who already claims Irish heritage (her stage name is derived from her real name, Lady Gannon-Garvey), is delighted to portray a character as iconic as Peig and is working hard on getting into character by inflicting as much misery on herself as possible.

'Lady Gaga insists we only refer to her as Peig. She wakes up each morning and deliberately stubs her toe on the bed. Then she takes a cold shower and wipes her arse with a nettle before sitting down for a breakfast of pipe-smoke and seawater,' said a spokesperson for the Blasket Islands, where Gaga will live for the next 18 months before filming begins.

'Gone are the meat dresses and the glamour. She wears nothing except itchy wool and goat hair blankets now. It'll be interesting to see how this translates to the screen. Remember, she did all this prep for *House of Gucci* as well, and ended up sounding like one of the Dolmio puppets, so fingers crossed this will be at least as funny as that.'

Peig: Bitter Fury will hit screens in 2023, and is directed by Michael Bay.

MUSIC

WE PRINTED THIS ARTICLE SLAGGING K-POP IN THE BOOK BECAUSE WE DIDN'T DARE ANGER THE FANS ONLINE

THE WRATH AND FURY of K-pop 'stans', coupled with their never-offline existence, has led to many online publications – including this one – swearing off ever opening up about how their music 'just isn't for us'.

Korean popular music, or K-pop for short, has exploded in popularity over the last number of years and carries a fanbase that makes Beatlemania look like a solemn novena in comparison.

This army of mostly young, incredibly quick-tempered music fans has been known to attack any website that so much as suggests that K-pop is just 'bleeps and bloops', with a severity that makes piranhas look like paraplegic hamsters.

Many websites have already had to pull the plug on their operations after incurring the wrath of the fans, and as such *WWN* have opted to save any anti-K-pop rhetoric for our printed edition, which, thanks to book technology, does not have a comments section, a downvote button or angry emoji.

We'll not belabour the point but will just say that it all sounds like a Casio being thrown down a flight of stairs, and leave it at that.

For the safety of our team and their families, please do not photograph this page and send it to any K-pop fans you may know, as our lives and livelihoods depend on it.

PLOT DETAILS HAVE BEGUN to emerge about *Toy Story 5*, the latest instalment in the 30-year-old franchise that many describe as 'the only kid movies that are okay for adults to watch in the cinema without people thinking they're nonces'.

Here's what we've heard:

- The plot will revolve around Buzz Lightyear and the gang being put up for sale on eBay to raise a few quid and ease the family's struggles during the cost-of-living crisis. 'I always cry at these things, but God damn this one hits home,' admitted our Pixar source.

TOY STORY 5 TO FOCUS ON GANG GETTING SOLD ON EBAY

- Although the core group of characters remain, many of them will require new voice artists, as much of the cast has now passed away. As such, parents are being advised to get ahead of any questions their children may have about 'why Mr Potato Head sounds weird now'.
- One (currently unnamed) toy has an unfortunate scene where it gets mauled and humped by the family dog, which involved the CGI team having to apply motion-capture dots onto a real-life dog penis to get the thrusting 'just right'.
- Tom Hanks has agreed to reprise his role as Sheriff Woody after losing his entire career fortune on NFTs.

- Bo Peep will also return in the movie, and yes it's still creepy to think of her like that, you pervert.

Toy Story 5 will be making grown adults cry like little children in theatres next summer.

THE FUCKIN' CHEEK: FIVE CELEBRITIES WHO DARED TALK SHIT ABOUT IRELAND

IRELAND IS KNOWN as the land of a thousand welcomes, but if anyone dares to slander or malign our fair island, then our doors are shut to you forever! We don't care how famous you are! Just ask these five smartholes who are no longer welcome on these fair isles:

1) Kanye West
Rap god Kanye West infamously visited Portlaoise on honeymoon with his then-wife Kim Kardashian in 2014, before putting the town on blast in his next album on the track 'Fuck The Midlands'. Don't let the M9 hit you on the arse on the way out, ye bollocks!

2) Arnold Schwarzenegger
The Austrian oak visited Ireland to open a branch of Planet Hollywood in 1997, but refused to take a customary snap drinking a pint of Guinness for some reason. You'll be back Arnie? We don't fucking think so.

3) Tom Cruise
The two worst things to ever happen to Ireland are the failure of the potato crop, and Tom Cruise's Irish accent in *Far and Away*. The star's brogue caused so much ridicule that the nation promised Cruise they'd give him 'reason to run' if he ever came about the place again.

4) Angelina Jolie
Noted humanitarian Jolie cited Ireland's Direct Provision system as 'one of the worst in the world' when it comes to depriving migrants of their human rights. Eh, c'mere Anj. That's as may be, but you don't need to say it out loud, like. If we can ignore it, you can too.

5) The Queen
There's never been any love lost between the people of Ireland and the monarchy of the UK, but for HRH Elizabeth to visit Ireland and not even swing by the Barack Obama Plaza for a Supermac's and a photo op? You're dead to us Liz, DEAD.

Your Census Time Capsules

'Bray is technically South Dublin, so be sure to say I'm from Dublin, okay?' – Agatha (47), Wicklow

CELEBRITY LEGAL

WOMAN KNOWS MORE ABOUT DEPP/HEARD TRIAL THAN SHE DOES HER OWN CHILDREN

SUCH IS THE CLOSE ATTENTION with which local woman Norah Cartigan has been following the Johnny Depp defamation trial that she can recall every single question posed by lawyers, and knows the exhibits introduced into evidence off by heart.

'Conor? He's my middle one, I think, why?' answered Cartigan, nose

deep in the celeb magazine rack at her local shop, when asked by a shopkeeper.

Having amassed an encyclopaedic knowledge of Johnny Depp and Amber Heard's movements over several years, it is believed Cartigan has no extra capacity or inclination to retain information about her children.

'Ailbhe likes camogie or painting, or some shit like that. She's only 12 or 10 or 7 maybe, it's not like they're real interests. What is this, *Mastermind*?' dismissed Cartigan, as she was rudely interrupted from gorging on her Instagram feed, which has fed her nothing but *Depp v Heard* videos for the last six weeks.

Talking with friends, Cartigan breezed past questions relating to all aspects of her own life to talk exclusively about the trial.

'Conor broke his arm at football? Oh, sorry to hear that. What do you mean he's my child? Did you not hear what I said about Amber Heard pooing in Johnny Depp's bed?' said Cartigan, ploughing through her friend's attempts to get her attention.

On This Day

In 1947, Cork first began to question this whole 'real capital of Ireland' thing.

25-YEAR-OLD FEELS LIKE A WITHERED OLD HAG WATCHING *EUPHORIA*

SETTLING IN to watch the season two opener of the Zendaya-starring HBO hit show about teenagers doing the sex, drugs and mental disintegration dance, Róisín Dollins is fully aware that she's an ancient basic bitch of a

hag who is nowhere near cool enough to consume the show.

'What if some teenagers passed by the window and saw I was watching it? They'd point and laugh, saying, "Look at this pensioner trying to be

down with the kids",' thought the 25-year-old, who can't believe the things the young folk in *Euphoria* do be getting up to.

'God, she's taking it all off and her not even switching the lights off first so yer man can't see her jiggly bits,' added Dollins, who had never considered herself a prude but now thinks she might just be a sixteenth-century puritan Calvinist compared to these HBO teenagers.

Dollins, ageing before her eyes as she continually has to look up drug and sex terms from *Euphoria* she's never heard before, is giving serious consideration to calling off this whole *Euphoria* business, even if it's all the much cooler and younger women in work talk about.

'It's too much. What next, a sex thing called "the horny octopus"? A drug you snort via the anus? There's already one of them? Jesus, more penises!' concluded Dollins, finally able to admit that marginally younger people scare her half to death.

Putting down her hot cocoa and emerging from beneath a giant blanket on her couch, Dollins reached for the remote and finally admitted she's an *Emily in Paris* loser.

MUSIC

A LONDON HIGH COURT has suggested that singer-songwriter Ed Sheeran should simply admit he didn't write the song 'Shape of You' if he wants to clear his good name, *WWN* has learned.

Sheeran and two of his 'Shape of You' co-authors are involved in a legal row with two songwriters who claim his number one hit rips off parts of their 2015 track 'Oh Why', something Sheeran and co. deny.

'Seriously, you actually want to stake a claim to this?' the High Court judge asked the plaintiffs, his face grimacing as both tracks were played to the court. 'I get there may be a financial element to your case, but wow, both songs are equally irritating to listen to, and if anything, you all should be at the Hague for crimes against humanity.'

Taking to the stand, Mr Sheeran hummed musical scales and melodies

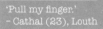

Your Census Time Capsules

'Pull my finger.'
– Cathal (23), Louth

COURT ADVISES ED SHEERAN TO ADMIT HE STOLE SONGS IF HE WANTS TO 'CLEAR HIS GOOD NAME'

as he was questioned over how 'Shape of You' was written, forcing the judge to once again hastily intervene.

'Great, now it's stuck in my head, cheers,' said an increasingly irritated judge, covering his ears. 'Mr Sheeran, you don't have to do this. If you claim "Shape of You", where does it end? "Bad Habits" too? Are you saying this under duress? I'm sorry, I just can't buy someone would admit to this unless their family was kidnapped.'

Calling a two-hour recess and insisting some Pink Floyd, anything, be played in court to help remove the 'ear worm', the judge instructed, 'Put

on the song "Money" there. It's why we're all here, and it actually qualifies as music.'

'You know, Ed, you should have probably called it "The State of You",' the judge concluded, staring directly at Sheeran in disgust.

GARDAÍ REOPEN COLD CASE ON MISSING THIRD JOHNNY

GARDAÍ IN TIPPERARY have confirmed they will reopen a historic cold case into the missing Johnny Mafflin, the third wheel of the famous comedy duo the 2 Johnnies, *WWN* has learned.

Mafflin, who was known by many in the industry as a bit of a dry shite who wouldn't know a punchline if it punched him in the face, was an ever-present in the 3 Johnnies comedy group before suddenly going missing after a community hall gig in Oola one night, something that conveniently occurred right before the 2 Johnnies shot to fame.

'Sure, Johnny Mafflin wasn't particularly chirpy or outgoing, and he was renowned for always leaving the pub when it was his turn to get a round in, but he did have clout when

it came to the business end of things,' offered Sergeant Sean McCreedy, who confirmed the last known note written by Mafflin read 'GAA songs/videos + podcasting + RTÉ gigs = world domination'.

'Now, I'm not suggesting for a second that when RTÉ came shaking their huge bag of cash – presuming that's what RTÉ do, work off a bag-o-cash system of luring in performers – that some fellas began to think three didn't divide into two so good, if you know what I mean?' Sergeant McCreedy added, at pains to suggest he wasn't heavily insinuating anything suspicious happened to the third Johnny, despite repeatedly raising his eyebrows in a suggestive fashion and nudging this reporter with his elbow several times.

Meanwhile, McCreedy promised to explore a line of inquiry, which suggests that Mafflin is propping up a bar in South Tipp somewhere alongside a lad playing a poker machine who swears he got down to the final seven for Boyzone back in the day.

MUSIC

LOCAL MAN PATRICK KELLY STANDS BY FIRST COUSIN R

COUNTY WATERFORD MAN Patrick Kelly has defended his American cousin R. Kelly as the R&B star stands accused of racketeering, sexual abuse and bribery at a court in Brooklyn, New York this week, *WWN* reports.

'A Kelly wouldn't be at that craic at all at all,' 43-year-old Patrick began, who was visiting Waterford city via bus from local village Portlaw today to 'do the messages'. 'Now I could be wrong, but he'd be Bridey Kelly's young fella third removed, and if that's the case there's not a hope Bridey would raise a scutt like that, may God have mercy on her.'

Insisting on the 54-year-old's innocence, Patrick stated that if there was a 'bad bastard' in the family, he'd know about it – like the time

> **'Me father Gerry Kelly courted me mother when she was 14'**

his grand-uncle T.J. was arrested for lamping rabbits on Tadhg Phelan's farm one morning.

'The mother would be first on the phone to me if one of the family were shaming us like that,' he insisted, now reading a newspaper article on R. Kelly's court case. 'Whisht, he's some tan on him now in fairness, but a fine-looking man all the same … if he's a true Kelly he has nothing to worry about,' he continued, reading through R. Kelly's horrific litany of crimes against young women.

'Sex with a 17-year-old, another one 19. I don't get what he did wrong. Sure me father Gerry Kelly courted me mother when she was 14,' the Portlaw man added, scratching his head at the news article. 'It says here "prosecutors described Mr Kelly as a man who

used lies, manipulation, threats and physical abuse to dominate his victims". Sure jaysis the whole family would all be in jail if that's the case, what? How else are ya supposed to get a woman at all, hah?'

Realising the severity of the charges against the singer, Patrick Kelly stopped for a moment before concluding, 'Ah fuck, sure that's not Bridey's lad at all … sure isn't Rory doing tarmacadam in Australia and hasn't a fucking note in his head. He couldn't sing the alphabet. But I tell ya one thing, it goes to show how women can ruin a man.'

Tips for Ignoring Climate Change

Data centres require huge amounts of energy to keep cool, so best live near one and leave the doors open so you get a nice breeze when it gets too hot.

TELEVISION

ITV CONFIRM *LOVE ISLAND* CANCELLED THIS YEAR, VILLA GIVEN TO UKRAINIAN REFUGEES

A LAST-MINUTE CANCELLATION of ITV's ratings behemoth *Love Island* has shocked dating show fans to their core, *WWN* can reveal.

Despite the recent launch of a marketing campaign heralding the show's imminent return, production managers of the hit show confirmed the news in a statement earlier today, revealing that the villa will be given to Ukrainian refugees instead.

'Honestly, given world events, it doesn't sit right with us to give this much-needed accommodation to two dozen narcissists desperate to secure collabs with fast fashion firms and dodgy cosmetic outfits offering Botox for internal organs,' began the well-reasoned statement.

'Faced with editing hundreds of hours of "my type on paper" discussions around a swimming pool … we just can't,' added producers, giving up months of paid work to instead donate the accommodation to refugees fleeing a warzone.

Young *Love Island* hopefuls who had their bags packed and were all ready to carry out thousands of hours of inane and inarticulate

conversations for the entertainment of couch-bound viewers are reportedly considering legal action over the decision, but will have a hard time winning over the public.

'Where am I supposed to go and pretend I don't know what geography or an egg is now? My agent's already arranged the guy I was going to pretend to fall in love with, and my team had our "yes she flies off the handle but toxic online bullying is wrong, she's actually a sweetheart" character arc sorted out,' sobbed one irate would-be Islander.

The show's producers apologised to viewers for the late notice but thankfully didn't rule out turning the refugees' stay at the villa into an exploitative reality show for the amusement of the public.

BREAKING

'EVEN THOUGH FEW know his name, he left a mark on the Irish music industry that will live on forever,' sobbed a distressed Bono, speaking in tribute to the late Ian Callan, the Longford man who was the first to add pro-Republican slogans to the song 'The Fields of Athenry'.

The U2 frontman was just one of several to praise Callan, who passed away at his home earlier this week following a long battle with hoarseness of the throat, believed to have been caused by his insistence on being the loudest person to yell 'Sinn Féin' and 'IRA' whenever the song was played in

TRIBUTES FLOOD IN FOLLOWING DEATH OF LAD WHO FIRST ADDED 'SINN FÉIN' BIT TO 'THE FIELDS OF ATHENRY'

pubs, clubs, 21sts, wedding receptions or Hunger Strike commemorations.

Callan was the first innovator to realise that the mournful, famine-set song had the perfect spacing in the chorus to drop in bits of his own, and after finding that 'Sinn Féin' and 'IRA' worked so well, crafted the perfect phrase to follow the poignant line about 'watching the freebirds fly'.

'Once you get used to someone shouting "hey baby watch them soldiers die" at that part, you wonder why it wasn't in the song all along,' said one Irish music historian, taking us through the history of the song.

'Written by Pete St John in 1979, first recorded by Danny Doyle that same

year, made famous by Paddy Reilly in 1982, and perfected in 1985 by Ian Callan in the residents' bar at the afters of a cousin's wedding. A pioneer, we shall not see his like again.'

Waterford Whispers News

VOL 1, 20156136   WATERFORD, TUESDAY, 16 JANUARY, 1921   2p

Provisional Government Looking Forward to Never-ending Peace

FOLLOWING the signing of the Anglo-Irish treaty last month in London, the new Provisional Government has welcomed the new Free State at a special handover ceremony in Dublin Castle today, stating that Ireland can now look forward to never-ending peace and tranquillity, WWN reports.

Speaking from Dublin Castle this afternoon, the last Lord Lieutenant of Ireland formally handed over power to the new Provisional Government, marking an end to centuries of violence and bloodshed.

'I'm just glad it's all over now and everyone can get back to normality,' said Treaty signatory Michael Collins, 'it's gas to think we were all fighting over this place a few years ago. I'm looking forward now to a little break in Cork, putting the feet up and doing absolutely nothing for a few weeks or so before tearing into this whole newly formed Republic craic.'

Cursing flatpack instructions, fellow signatory Arthur Griffith echoed Collins' exhilaration, stating that he'll be glad now when the place gets a nice Irish makeover.

'I can't find part D34, whoever made these instructions must have written the Treaty itself, they're so vague,' Griffith stated, scratching his head as to what an Allen key is, 'I suppose we'll have a few moaners giving out that we didn't take the six counties, but 26 out of 32 ain't bad – I'm sure all this negativity will blow over in the end.'

LIST OF CELEBRITIES NOT PICTURED WITH EPSTEIN, PUTIN OR SAUDI ROYALTY GETTING SHORTER BY THE DAY

PR FIRMS have advised their celebrity clients that, while they will do their absolute best when it comes to old photos of them hugging some of the world's most despised human beings, they're 'not miracle workers', and some of this dirt 'might just have to stick'.

'We're coming hot off a year where pictures just kept cropping up of people partying with either Jeffrey Epstein or Ghislaine Maxwell, and that was Jedi-mind-trick levels of getting the public to forget or forgive,' said one public relations consultant we spoke to, with clients from across the worlds of music, movies and sport.

'So that was hard, but thankfully it was mostly world leaders, ex-presidents, things like that. But now, with Putin waging war in the Ukraine, we're at it again. He's in pictures with everyone! Sure, there are the usual suspects, like your McGregors and your Seagals. But there are also pictures of Putin all pals with Paul McCartney! And Leonardo DiCaprio, the Pope, the Queen … everyone wants to hush it all up, but there's only so many of us, and there's only so many hours in the day.'

Further headaches are due for already-stressed PR staff, as many celebrities also admitted that images are floating around of them getting jiggy with a collection of Saudi Arabian royals and Emirati princes, apparently the next big 'no-no' on the horizon due to some human rights abuses or 'other such nonsense'.

'Richie Kavanagh, that's who I'm going to be left with as a client, Richie Kavanagh, the only celebrity not pictured with a paedophile billionaire, a mad dictator or a bunch of blood-crazed oil billionaires who carry out executions by the gross,' sighed our contact, while frantically emailing celebrities, pleading with them to delete their Instagram accounts ASAP.

NEW STREAMING SERVICE WATCHES EVERY NEW TV SHOW ON YOUR BEHALF FOR €4.99 A MONTH

A NEW STREAMING SERVICE WATCH4ME has launched today with the promise of helping overwhelmed culture vultures cope with the endless flood of new recommendations and releases on streaming platforms, *WWN* can report.

For just €4.99 a month WATCH4ME will consume all the TV and movies from top streaming platforms, like

Disney+, Netflix, Apple and TG4, on your behalf, thus eradicating all the time-consuming, anxiety-drenched pressure that comes with trying to keep up to date.

'Oh, this is perfect for me and my boyfriend. If we had WATCH4ME we'd get back hours of our lives every night by cutting out "what do you want to watch" discussions/meltdowns alone,' confirmed Darragh Griffin, one of the platform's newest customers.

Not only will WATCH4ME watch the 440 hours of TV that culture sites tell you are 'unmissable', but the platform also provides little blurbs for when the friend who bullies you into watching their favourite shows asks you questions.

'It's amazing, now whenever my friend Eabha tells me to watch *Bridgerton* I can use the WATCH4ME cue cards to say "Stop, I can't! What is Penelope at?" and "Your man is some ride" and she's none the wiser,' added WATCH4ME superfan Helen Brogan.

Speaking at the launch of the service, WATCH4ME CEO Victoria Clements spoke of further innovations being explored by the company:

'We're not quite there yet, but we hope to one day use clones to take your place in these conversations about the latest grisly murder documentary about unspeakable violence that Carol in the office insists is "great craic". These clones could also be used for other purposes, such as to make small talk on the sideline with other parents at your children's football matches.'

BREAKING

SORRY UKRAINE, BUT WILL SMITH SLAPPED CHRIS ROCK SO WE'RE A LITTLE DISTRACTED TODAY

APOLOGIES have been extended to Ukrainian civilians currently on the receiving end of the most heinous and inhumane war crimes, but Will Smith just fucking slapped Chris Rock across the face – we kid you not!

'All high-minded opinion pieces, all TikTok explainers, all 150-tweet Twitter threads and all comment section arguments will solely be focusing on the Smith Slap today. I mean did you see how Rock took it like a champ, although some are saying it's fake,' said the world, just running on pure controversy-generated adrenaline.

Similar apologies have been made to the conflicts in Syria, Yemen, Ethiopia and elsewhere, but all meme-making abilities of the internet have now been fully diverted to Will Smith's reaction to a joke about his wife's bald head.

'A brief break will be taken to share the heart-warming footage of Lady Gaga and Liza Minnelli, and maybe if we have time we'll mention that *Coda* won best picture, but honestly it's just one of those crazy days. Ukraine won't make the cut, but you're going to love our "What Smith's Slap Tells Us About Toxic Masculinity" article,' sections of the media and online publishing

'Did you see how Rock took it like a champ'

game told Ukraine, hoping they'd understand.

Ukrainian government officials were advised to hold off on pleas for further military and humanitarian aid or highlighting of war crimes until everyone has gotten over the Oscars slap, as there were a lot of *Fresh Prince of Bel Air*-based dad jokes to get through.

Elsewhere, Chris Rock has confirmed that he feels like the most under-attack comedian alive today following the altercation, which took place on live TV. Volodymyr Zelenskyy was not available for comment, as he was quite busy.

MUSIC

MISSING IRISH SINGER-SONGWRITER FOUND UP HIS OWN HOLE

A LOCAL SINGER-SONGWRITER who has been missing since 2019 has been found safely up his own hole, *WWN* can confirm.

Rescuers freed Waterford musician Mark Rogerson, famed for his whiny, self-indulgent material, from the confines of his bowels after becoming lodged up there for the past three years.

It is understood that the 37-year-old's arsehole just opened up one day, curling in on itself, and quickly engulfed Rogerson, his backing singers and his entire clique of better-than-you mirth fans.

'The whole 10-piece band were up there when we found Mark whimpering his latest contribution to song,' rescuer David Larch told *WWN*. 'They were all so consumed by their own self-importance that they had no idea they were trapped in the lead singer's lower colon for the last 37 months.'

The rescue operation was launched when fans failed to see Rogerson's name in the small font part of the Electric Picnic line-up, prompting several doses to contact emergency services.

'I dunno what we'd do without Mark's unique melancholy style,' stated long-time fan, vegan and unemployed Arts student Carla Dunne. 'I can't wait to now don my knitted poncho and fawn over Mark's misery-based songs centred around his dysfunctional relationships with women who were simply sick of his self-deprecating bullshit and constant need for reassurance.'

So far this year over 23 Irish singer-songwriters have been rescued from their own holes.

LIKE A SLOW-MOTION CAR CRASH made entirely out of tattoos and vomit-inducing PDAs, news of Kourtney Kardashian's engagement to Travis Barker has prompted millions of women who went through their own bad boy phase to partake in the largest intervention ever committed in the history of 'we tried to warn you'.

'Sure, your mom is like super pissed and you get a kick out of it, but girl, it's time to stop – it's not funny anymore,' confirmed one well-meaning and wise 16-year-old who went through her bad boy phase this summer by dating a leather jacket-wearing teenager who carried a copy of *Catcher in the Rye* with him everywhere.

'Kourtney, it's not too late. Don't waste years pretending to be into Fugazi. He might seem edgier than a dodecahedron but it will only lead you to matching tattoos and laser removal sessions,' thousands of other women said, speaking directly of their own experiences of living through a bad boy phase that they deny ever happened when reminded of it by friends and family.

MILLIONS OF WOMEN WHO WENT THROUGH 'BAD BOY' PHASE APPEAL TO KOURTNEY KARDASHIAN TO SEE SENSE

Some 99 per cent of women who reported dating a bad boy with a heart of gold who understood them on a deeper level than anyone else revealed that in hindsight the relationship mainly consisted of making out nonstop and hanging out on bridges as their boyfriend said 'hey watch me spit on these cars as they go by'.

'Sure, a bad boy will do romantic things like make a candle that smells exactly like your orgasm, but he'll also do things you'll look back on and say "wait a minute",' added the I Dated A Bad Boy Support Group.

Elsewhere, parents everywhere have explicitly stated that you are banned from hanging out with Machine Gun Kelly and Megan Fox, as they are a bad influence.

TELEVISION

RTÉ ADVISED THAT NOT EVERY CELEBRITY'S KID IS OWED A JOB

THE NATIONAL BROADCASTER'S HABIT of handing out high-profile gigs to the offspring of the Irish celebrity pool has been criticised in a new report titled '1,789 reasons why the country aren't going to pay another cent in licence fees'.

Singling out no one in particular, the report shows that Ireland has reached the peak of how much nepotism it can tolerate from RTÉ, while adding that if Director General Dee Forbes thinks she can cry about not being able to keep the service running then maybe she needs to consider stepping aside, as long as her replacement isn't some cousin of Ryan Tubridy.

'The Irish people are tired of seeing the same 14 surnames cropping up over and over again,' said a spokesperson for the Anti-Nepotism Association of Ireland, a group that also speaks out about prominent business owners giving

cushy managerial posts to their doofus kids.

'And while nobody is suggesting that any specific kids aren't talented or don't belong on TV, it'd be nice to think that they didn't just get their spot based on a belief that "if you liked their Mam, then you'll love her son!" All we're asking

is that when it comes to the few positions that RTÉ has to offer, with the talented pool of actors and presenters in this country, there's at least some sort of audition process.'

The report comes amid backlash against RTÉ's new summer line-up, which includes a show apiece for each of Miriam O'Callaghan's 18 kids.

SIMON COWELL'S FACE CELEBRATES FIRST BIRTHDAY

A MILESTONE in Celebland today as Simon Cowell's face was pictured celebrating its first birthday in an exclusive LA eatery, *WWN* can reveal.

Paying someone who has full control of the muscles in their face to blow out the candles for him, Cowell was presumably happy beneath the face he wasn't born with as he rang in its first birthday.

'It's not clear if this will be the only birthday of Simon's new face. He's known to upgrade it any time he gets a new car, which is roughly every year,' shared one insider.

'Simon can't believe how quickly the time has gone, and maybe after another facelift or a bit of Botox his face might be able to emote that, but I think the surgeons charge by the emotion,' added the insider.

While it is not clear if Cowell specifically asked face upgrade specialists to make him look like a manic cocaine-addled forest-dwelling goblin who hasn't slept since 1993, there's no doubt that anyone's first anniversary is worth celebrating in style.

'It's not just his face's first birthday, it's the three-month anniversary of his

new hair, which – I shouldn't say this – he got from a guy who plucks the hair off newborn skunks and then sews it into a wig. Whatever ethical questions may have arisen from that are swept away when you see how good he looks,' the source said of the former *X Factor* judge's host body.

Tips for Ignoring Climate Change

When you see a Healy-Rae worrying, that's when you should worry. For now, you're grand.

RADIO

MAVERICK RADIO HOSTS ASK LISTENERS IF THEY KEEP KETCHUP IN THE FRIDGE OR PRESS

GROUNDBREAKING morning disc jockeys Niall Galvin and Tracey Fields were said to be bombarded by tens of texts this morning after sparking listeners' interest with a common everyday conundrum, *WWN* can report.

'It just came to me this morning when I found the ketchup on the table and put it in the fridge in front of my boyfriend who then asked me what the hell I was doing,' Tracey Fields said,

explaining how she came up with the never-thought-of-before question. 'It was mad because he said it should go in the press, so then I said I'd put it to my listeners, and by Jesus, I wasn't expecting the class responses we got.'

The local radio station reported a flood of at least seven texts relating to the ketchup phenomenon, forcing the station's CEO Rupert Holmes to chime in.

'It's gone viral!' Holmes confirmed, who also said there were three people on Twitter now retweeting their tweet. 'It's just relatable content that everybody gets, so I guess that's why there was such a huge response to it.'

The morning radio hosts, who go by *The Niall and Tracey Show*, believe they may now be in line for an IMRO award this year and have promised that their 15 minutes of fame are not over yet.

'Wait till we ask them if they keep the foil on the butter tomorrow at 6 a.m.,' co-host Niall Galvin teased, the pair now chuffed with their newly found relevance bait. 'Sure the pair of us are gas out, so we are.'

On This Day

In 1605, Guy Fawkes launches the Anonymous movement.

4 November

JOE ROGAN OR JOE DUFFY: WHO IS DOING MORE HARM?

ONE IS A HIGHLY PAID, highly influential broadcaster with a slavish, almost maniacally devoted listenership who won't question anything their hero spouts. The other is Joe Rogan. But which of these men is doing the most harm to our society? Let's investigate.

Just as Spotify consider *The Joe Rogan Experience* a cornerstone of their platform, more than justifying

Rogan's $100 million deal with the streaming service, so too does RTÉ look at *Liveline* with Joe Duffy as 'great value' for the €400k per year that the veteran broadcaster receives. And to justify those price tags, both platforms demand the same thing: a constant flow of rabble-baiting rhetoric that keeps listeners angry, divided and, above all else, tuned in.

'Joe Rogan casually throws out information about Ivermectin, enraging liberals and emboldening conspiracy nuts. Joe Duffy does the same, except instead he gets people to ring in about the sex scenes in *Normal People*,' an industry insider explained to us today.

'While Rogan's output is certainly colouring people's opinions when

it comes to more outlandish, fantastical things like New World Orders and the like, Duffy is doing it on a much more parochial, curtain-twitching level.

'It's hard to say what harms society more, the guy telling you that vaccinations are part of a plan to control our minds with 5G, or the guy telling you in a matter-of-fact manner that you're going to get fined from now on if they find old batteries in your recycling bin.'

Regardless of the damage either Joe may be doing to society, it seems both will remain a key part of our cultural landscape for as long as there's an audience for straight-talking, no-nonsense white men who 'tell it like it is'.

Bill's Landlord Tips

Cold water is incredibly refreshing and has been shown to provide a number of health benefits, so consider these things before you run crying to your landlord to fix the boiler.

VAGUE

NOV 22

BEAUTY TIPS
THAT COULD WORK,
OR COULD NOT

WAIT, WHAT DO I KNOW
HER FROM AGAIN? IS SHE
A MODEL OR AN ACTRESS?

'SURE, YOU KNOW YOURSELF'
– SAOIRSE RONAN

'SURE, LET ME
CHECK FIRST'
– CONFIRMING
SOCIAL ENGAGEMENTS

THE SECRET TO
A HEALTHY DIET?
WE'RE NOT SURE

7 OUTFITS THAT MAY OR
MAY NOT SUIT YOUR SHAPE

'PERHAPS?'
– BEYONCÉ
REVEALS
NOTHING
INSIDE

LIFESTYLE

CHILDREN

'HE'S DEFINITELY A LITTLE SHIT': JUDGING KIDS EXITING SCHOOL WHILE YOU WAIT FOR YOUR PERFECT LITTLE ANGEL

JUDGING CHILDREN leaving school is a great way of passing the time while you wait for your precious little angel, so here's a handy guide to speculating on the character of school kids for your personal enjoyment.

Locating potential upstarts from a young age is a very natural parental instinct, and you should not feel any shame in pinpointing little shits from 100 yards away.

Overly animated, shaved-headed, overweight red-cheeked boys wearing filthy uniforms are prime for profiling, especially when their pyjama-wearing mother, billowing plumes of blue cigarette smoke from their '01 Toyota Corolla, littered with years of built-up happy meals, is double-parked outside.

No wonder Tanya isn't paying attention in school these days, she's probably too busy being distracted by this destructive little scutt. Like, where is the father? Make a note for the next teacher meeting to make sure her kid is not sitting anywhere near yours.

Wait a minute, is that child wearing a headscarf? Of course, you've no issue with different religions, but surely allowing displays of beliefs into St Joseph's National School will spark demands from your school uniform-abiding daughter, like 'I want a scarf too'.

You didn't buy two pleated skirts for another pupil to come in and wear whatever she bloody well-liked. What next, trousers for schoolgirls? Please. You don't want Tanya to start that 'they' business. No wonder the world's gone cracked.

That young lad is very tall for his age. He could push you around if he wanted, never mind anyone in his class or the teachers. Do they even check birth certs in school these days? He could be one of those predators. Always smiling too. Very polite and very suss. Scary, when you think about it. Keep an eye on that one.

Oh, here we go, a young one lighting up a cigarette. Not a fucking care in the world. Parents probably never at home. Her whole life ahead of her filled with drug and alcohol abuse. Probably end up as a prostitute on the street. Tanya! Get that poison out of your mouth, now!

WORK

'HYBRID WORKING' CERTAINLY SEEMS A LOT LIKE 'FULL TIME IN OFFICE'

THE NEW 'FIVE DAYS ON, two days off' hybrid working scheme currently being trialled in a Waterford office sure seems very familiar to staff, many of whom believe that this is just a full-time return to the office without any post-Covid evolution whatsoever.

'Incorrect, not at all, this is a revolutionary new way of working,' said bosses at McMillan & Whelan, in an all-staff mail to their employees.

'We listened to all our employees during the pandemic, and you all said that working from home was great, you loved it, you didn't miss the office whatsoever, and that the data shows you were as productive as you ever were.'

'That's why we brought in this whole new workweek that only requires you to be at your desk from the hours of half eight to half five every day, leaving you the weekend to do any unpaid extracurricular bits and pieces we may need you to do, from the comfort of your own home. The best of both worlds.'

Puzzled employees enquired how spending up to three hours a day commuting to the office to do the same work that they were easily doing at home could possibly be called 'hybrid working' but were quickly reminded about how many people were unemployed at the moment and would love jobs like theirs, and how those new employees probably wouldn't bitch about it so much.

JUST TAKING THE DOG out for a 'quick walk' are you? Think again. Experts have revealed that the duration of a round-the-block stroll with your pet could take as long as 75 minutes, depending on how many random patches your pooch takes an interest in.

'There's a lot of pet owners who think they walk their dog when in fact their dog walks them,' explained Dr Peter G. Chumm, canine expert.

'You can beg and plead with them to keep pace all you want, but if they take the notion to investigate a patch

NOT SO FAST THERE PAL, DOG HASN'T SNIFFED THIS PARTICULAR PUDDLE OF PISS JUST YET

of grass or a lamp post, a shovel wouldn't move them. All this before your dog stops upon sight of another dog, again refusing to move until it

gets a sniff of that butt. You're helpless in these situations. I hope you brought a podcast.'

Dr Chumm went on to add that canine behaviour today revolves entirely around playing their humans for absolute chumps, in order to get as much of a good life as they can.

'They're way more like cats than we ever thought,' said the doctor, while his dog chewed up all his notes.

'You think your dog is a fussy eater, but he just knows he'll get a slice of turkey from the fridge when you're making yourself a sandwich. He's not chewing your stuff out of anxiety, he's doing it out of spite for you going to the pub and leaving him at home. I swear, these lads should count their blessings that they're so cute.'

WWN would like to reassure readers that if your dog eats this book, you can always buy another one.

SEX

THE STINGING PAIN of a UTI is barely registering with local woman Jessica Coffley, as it remains dulled by the fact that she earned the infection via a regular diet of riding.

'Let's not even think about the fact that UTIs are usually caused by bacteria from poo entering the urinary tract, because eww, and let's just celebrate your girl Jess for having the best sex of her life,' confirmed Coffley, to anyone who would listen.

Bringing up her UTI unprompted and then answering the question of how she thinks she got it before anyone actually asked, Coffley is also suffering from aching of the face from all the smug smiling she's doing.

LOCAL WOMAN DELIGHTED SHE'S HAVING ENOUGH SEX TO WARRANT UTI

'Met him on a dating app, yeah, oh he's some appetite. No, we haven't put a label on it, but we've put the springs in my mattress to the test,' confirmed Coffley, whose last bout of cystitis came at a particularly fallow period, and was shamefully not caused by regular intercourse.

Glugging on several litres of water and knocking back the cranberry juice like it was a happy hour cocktail, Coffley is determined to get over her UTI as quickly as possible so she can get another one, repeating the cycle of being delighted with herself and lording it over her friends who have seen less action than the Irish army.

'Oh, you haven't got a UTI in years, Sarah? After switching birth control

and always peeing immediately after sex? Okay, sure, tell yourself whatever you want to make yourself feel better about being as active as a dormant volcano,' concluded Coffley when offered UTI-combatting advice by a friend.

BOSS INCENSED BY EMPLOYEE WHO KEEPS LEAVING WORK ON TIME AS OUTLINED IN THEIR CONTRACT

ONE VULNERABLE BOSS is on the verge of a mental breakdown after a belligerent employee insists on only working the hours required by his contract.

'I'm at my fucking wits' end with this asshole,' confirmed stressed-out boss Neil Findley, as employee Mark Pallew routinely leaves work at 5.30 p.m. on the dot.

'It's like Q4 revenue means nothing to him – selfish beyond all comprehension,' Findley added of an employee who performs well and manages to complete his tasks in the allotted time, something that only arouses further suspicion.

'I'm out the door with customers. I've the rest of the team guilted into

working 'til 7 p.m. most evenings – I'm in no rush to hire extra staff – and this ingrate won't dig me out of a hole of my own making. Hands down the worst employee I've ever had,' Findley said out loud, although Pallew couldn't hear him as he'd headed home an hour ago.

The nightmare scenario is reportedly repeating itself in businesses across

the country, as employees drunk on power remind employers that slave labour isn't the pervading working environment of 2022.

'And don't get me started on HR, I feel so unsupported,' the boss said of his failed attempts to orchestrate a bullying campaign against Pallew that would amount to constructive dismissal.

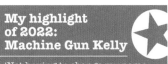

FRIENDS

MAN ALWAYS THERE FOR FRIENDS DURING THE EASIEST TIMES

EASYGOING MATE (and all-around friend when it's convenient for him) Seán Temple has made himself available for socialising with several friends again now they seem over serious issues like depression, fruitless job hunting, the death of a loved one or a break-up.

'Howiye, gents, the Four Horsemen of the Açockalypse are back in action, wahey!' Temple cheerily declared to his friends when entering his local pub, the only socialising venue he will attend.

Liam, Chris and Gavin, who have acted as confidants and support systems for one another over several years, can only rely on Temple to turn up when there's a drink and absolutely no sharing of feelings or true inner thoughts on the menu, a practice which has garnered Temple something of a reputation as a 'good times friend'.

'Did yiz hear the one about the blind nun who became a pornstar? Ah, fuck it I've forgotten the punchline, something to do with not seeing the second coming,' barked Temple, shattering the contemplative silence with which his friends greeted news of Liam's father's cancer diagnosis.

'Youse are shite craic altogether. It's always sad-face serious with you lot. Can't we just get trashed and enjoy a surface-level-only friendship, sustained by excessive alcohol consumption like normal Irish lads?' continued Temple, snaking off to the bar in search of less demanding friends.

Coming back later to inform the lads that he was heading into town with his new bar friends, Temple told the men to give him a shout for five-a-side next week, funny memes and videos of people falling over and for absolutely nothing else.

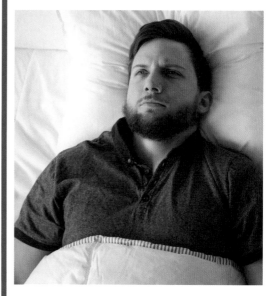

'I SHOULD PROBABLY CHECK': DAD HAVING LIE-IN WONDERING IF KIDS STILL ALIVE

AWAKENING TO A DEAD Saturday-morning silence, dad of two Ger Gleeson pondered if his two darling kids were still sleeping soundly or had indeed passed in the night and now lay lifeless in their rooms.

'Surely Jane would have checked on them on her way to work this morning,' thought Gleeson, who was far too comfortable and cosy to get up and check himself. 'I should probably get up and see, but Jesus that floor is freezing, and if I wake them up then that's my whole lie-in fucked.'

Holding his breath now to enhance his hearing, Gleeson became more and more suspicious of his children's current state of being. Panic was now gripping him, but still not enough to check.

'I'll give them another 15 minutes, and if I don't hear a peep, then I'll definitely get up,' he continued, before getting caught down a TikTok hole for the next hour and 18 minutes.

'Ah fuck, they must be still asleep. They couldn't be … you know, dead?' he fought with himself. 'What if they are and then the Gardaí ask me why I didn't check on them when I woke two hours ago? They'll think I killed them!' he continued. 'Okay, I'll watch one episode of *Ozark* and then go in.'

Three episodes in, a loud bang was heard, and a cry from the other room.

'Thank fuck for that,' Gleeson exhaled, before shouting through the walls, 'Stop messing in there, guys, Daddy is trying to get some rest!'

DRINKING

'NEVER AGAIN ON A SCHOOL NIGHT': 13-YEAR-OLD VOWS TO STOP DRINKING MIDWEEK

SLOUCHING over his school desk while trying to nurse the mother of all hangovers, 13-year-old Waterford teen Tony Phelan vowed to never again drink on a school night, *WWN* reports.

Citing a banging headache, upset gut and still kind of being drunk,

Phelan told fellow classmates it's never worth it the next day.

'Oh, it was great craic necking 12 cans down the canal with the lads, smoking bongs and taking bumps, but I don't know how I'll get through double Maths with Ms Corrigan when I smell

like Bulmer's Lane in Clonmel,' the now groaning teen exclaimed, head like a burst boot and pale as the 5 per cent coke he was snorting at 2 a.m. this morning. 'I could have called in sick, but that would have meant staying at home with my drunk parents, and they're zero craic when they're pucking the heads off each other.'

Downing three whole cans of Monster, Phelan picked up a bit following a lunchtime joint, two Valium, several consecutively smoked cigarettes and a packet of king-size Meanies.

'That's better now,' he smiled, head now back to its usual buzzy stage, like being wrapped in a ball of cotton wool. 'I'll need the cure tonight, I tell ya,' he shouted, before asking the rest of the class, 'Who's on for a few tins later?'

Your Census Time Capsules

'Bono is a pox.'
– Mark (56), Monaghan

'THERE'S UKRAINIAN YOUNG ONES STAYING IN THE HOTEL DOWN THE ROAD, ALL STUNNERS I HEARD'

BREAKING NEWS coming in from local man Paddy Rotchford today suggests there's a 'rake of young ones from Ukraine' after moving into the town yesterday afternoon.

'All stunners I heard,' Rotchford added, before going on to divulge more important information. 'All the husbands left fighting in Ukraine then, sure they'll probably never see them again, the poor craturs.'

The divorced 47-year-old delivered his report out the driver-side window of his car while on his way to do yet another reconnaissance mission, the fourth such lap of the hotel block today.

'Ah, you could tell them a mile away – not a pick on them now, not like our ones here,' the full-time

skulker revealed, unaware of how desperately shallow he sounded, before further chipping away at his character. 'They'll be lonely in those little rooms now, I tell ya, and it

won't be long till they start moving on with their lives and settling down here – you'd feel sorry for them now all the same, but jaysis, there are a few crackers there now that will be whisked up.'

Spending €5 on some charity shop clothes, Rotchford is expected to kindly drop down a bag of clothes at the hotel on his next lap, hoping to personally deliver the bag and receive some well-earned praise from the new arrivals.

'I bought a lovely summer dress there for €2 and high heels,' he said, now brandishing the Lidl bag of second-hand garments. 'This would suit that little tanned blonde one I saw smoking outside the hotel this morning – it's nice to give back.'

BEAUTY

GOODBYE THE BRAZILIAN, HELLO A DETAILED MAP OF WESTEROS

WAX TECHNICIANS in Ireland have appealed for time off to improve their skills as more and more customers request increasingly elaborate pubic hair designs.

'I haven't done a Brazilian in over a year,' said one waxer, before clarifying she meant the pubic hair adornment rather than a person hailing from the South American country.

'If it's not someone coming in looking for a detailed map of Westeros, it's those fecking head-the-balls from Cork looking for the Beara Peninsula. These things take more time and training,' a stressed-out beaver-weaver explained.

The change in waxing trends comes as more high-profile influencer types take to social media to boast of ever more elaborate decorations down there.

'Me rug's in the style of the Claret Jug. For all your waxing wishes get 20 per cent off with the code LOWRY20,' said golfing ace Shane Lowry in his latest Instagram post.

Trends come and go, and interest in them waxes and wanes, however, this is of little consolation to the waxers subjected to highly complex requests.

'Oh you've got to be shitting me,' said one technician before quitting on the spot after a client asked for the Sistine Chapel ceiling.

> ## 'Me rug's in the style of the Claret Jug'

PARENTING

COUPLE WHO DON'T WANT KIDS TO BREAK IT TO THEM TONIGHT

'WE'RE ALWAYS BEING ASKED about it. A day doesn't go by when someone doesn't pressure us, but kids are not for us. We're happy with our lifestyle and the money it will save us,' confirmed local couple Michael and Fionnuala Harrington.

More and more couples in their family-starting years are reporting their reluctance to have children owing to the cost of childcare, inability to get on the property ladder and the general cost of living, with the Harringtons being no different.

'David, our youngest at eight, will take it the hardest, I'd say,' Fionnuala explained, relieved that her disposable income will be freed up now that the decision has been made not to have kids.

'Ciara will be a harder sell on this,' Michael admitted of their 17-year-old daughter. 'Look, people are always judging couples who say they don't want kids, but it's time they started honestly listening and accepting it's just not something we want.'

Pre-emptively reaching out to friends and family, the couple explained their decision, but insisted that they did intend to entertain well-meaning comments, like 'Well,

you say that now', 'You're still young, things change', 'What do you mean you don't want kids, are ya having fertility issues, is it?' and the old reliable 'Sure I said the same before I had mine'.

'They don't mean any harm, but the decision is made. Yes, they'll be in tears, but David and Ciara will just have to accept our wishes,' the delighted couple said, packing their children's suitcases.

'Lie-ins, restaurants that aren't McDonald's, spa weekends, a new car, new clothes – it's all ahead of us now,' the high-fiving couple concluded.

E-SCOOTERS: DID THE WALK OF SHAME JUST GET EASIER?

WHILE IRELAND HAS WORKED hard at discarding the culture of shame the Catholic Church imposed on society, the 'walk of shame' after a one-night stand can still prove to be an anxious, shame-drenched experience for some.

Enter: the e-scooter.

The e-scooter is already revolutionising the walk of shame in major cities across Europe, and it's time the same happened here.

Pressure is growing on the Department of Transport to extend the Bike to Work scheme to cover scooters specifically for the bleary-eyed, panicked, rush-home-after-you-were-somehow-charmed-by-a-bogger-in-Coppers-in-boot-cut-

jeans-and-brown-shoes section of the population.

For those of the walk of shame persuasion, time really is of the essence. The speed capabilities of the e-scooter could bring an end to people trudging through crowds of early risers and families off to sports training or playgrounds.

The e-scooter is also better for the environment than struggling to figure out where you are and being ripped off by a taxi taking you the long way home.

This is a no-brainer. This is the future. Get in on the ground floor before there are no e-scooters to be had!

BEAUTY

DESPITE LOOKING nothing like her latest carousel of social media pictures, Dorothy Woods believes that she has gotten away with the fact that she's a 45-year-old mother-of-three and not some out-of-proportion cartoon character that in no way resembles any current human being living on planet Earth.

'She knows everyone knows she doesn't look anything like that, right?' put one concerned friend, scrolling through her account in disbelief. 'I can't find any mention in her posts to say this is a filter. She can't be chancing her arm here and thinking

Tips for Ignoring Climate Change

Climate change isn't real. There, you read it published in a book – now you can quote it and say you've done your research.

LOCAL WOMAN UNDER THE IMPRESSION FACE FILTER IS FOOLING EVERYONE

people believe her eyes are that big and face that impeccably flawless, can she?'

Posing for another picture with her teenage daughter, the recently divorced Woods posted yet another filtered image, this time with the words 'hard to believe this one is 18 now', in the hopes of receiving some age-related commentary from friends and family members.

'Ah fuck, she's doing the whole age fishing thing now and using the filter,' another friend chimed in, too afraid to call her out, as she 'knows how Dorothy gets' when prodded. 'She's really going for it this time,' she added, while posting the comment, 'Looking

Cost of Living Tips

Become a TD and vote for a pay rise for yourself, and more expenses.

stunning as usual girls, xxx', before showing everyone at work how one of her friends is using phone filters to make herself look younger.

Defending her use of phone filters, Woods stated that it's cheaper than surgery and that she also has a fetish for cartoon characters and is hoping to attract a man who resembles Prince Charming from Shrek.

'Fuck it, I'd settle for Shrek himself at this stage,' she concluded.

PARENTING

A PARENT'S WORST NIGHTMARE: THE CULCHIE BOYFRIEND

YOU CAN WORK HARD at raising your children right, but for city dwellers and townies everywhere there is a scenario they fear more than anything when it comes to their kids: the day they bring a culchie home.

Such a nightmare scenario has engulfed one suburban home in a leafy Dublin area as parents John and Fiona McAniff have been informed by their youngest, Ciara, that she has taken up with a young man from a rural backwater.

'The language will be a big adjustment for him, have you considered that Ciara?' bleated Fiona, already catastrophising.

Ciara reminded her parents that her Longford-hailing boyfriend Martin McCreedy does in fact speak English and that stereotypes can be both hurtful and unhelpful.

'Have you thought this through, Ciara? Have you taught him how to use the Luas? You know I heard of a culchie who fell down the gap between the DART and the platform and that was the end of him. You'll be like a full-time culchie carer,' continued Fiona, failing to hear Ciara inform her that Martin has lived in Dublin for eight years.

Finding no delicate way to phrase it, Ciara's parents explicitly stated that McCreedy's family had a completely different culture and value set and weren't necessarily compatible with civil city life.

'We've never been a coleslaw household, and if he's expecting bacon and cabbage every time he's over, he's deluded. We only get the *Sunday Times* of a weekend, I don't think we get the *Farmers Journal* in

Dublin, Ciara. Ciara!' Fiona added, while John wisely stayed out of the line of fire.

'What's your poor dad going to talk to him about? He knows f-all about fertilizer and slurry. He's never watched the *Late Late* country special either! Honestly, Ciara, would you get back with Jamie?' Fiona said of Ciara's last boyfriend, who dumped her after turning cheating into an Olympic sport.

LOCAL WOMAN HAS KID AS PROFILE PIC

SOCIAL MEDIA PROFILE PICTURES have evolved into bafflingly cryptic hints about people's lives instead of being a picture of their own damn face, according to a recent survey among Facebook's 783 active users.

'We see here an account for a woman named Martina Fergus, 47, from Waterford, yet her profile picture is that of an 8-year-old boy for some strange reason,' said Dr Melmut

Cannahil, currently working on the self-funded project.

'We have a scientific term for this – "weird as fuck". It makes no sense. It's like when young lads have a picture of a car as their profile pic. Except cars are badass, so you can see why you'd want them to represent you. But your child? What does that tell me, other than "I have a child". Like are you single here, or what? What are my chances here? I don't mind that you have a kid, I just want to see what you look like.'

Reaching out to Ms Fergus, we learned that she changed her profile picture to that of her kids in an effort to ward off weirdo men and oddball stalkers, something the good doctor had many problems with.

'First of all, I'm not a weirdo, I'm just divorced, okay?' said Dr Cannahil, who currently works from his mam's house.

Cannahil would not answer questions on just what exactly he was a doctor of.

SOCIAL MEDIA

SOCIAL MEDIA

HAVING TRIED EVERYTHING ELSE, LOCAL LAD TO ATTEMPT HUMOROUS TINDER PROFILE

THEY SAY GOD loves a trier, and if that's true then perhaps he might swipe right on the Tinder of Waterford man Dominic McCullen, because Christ knows nobody else is.

The 27-year-old McCullen has done everything to attract female attention on his dating profile, from including a picture of him posing with five of his mates all sloshed out of their faces at Body & Soul, to including a graphic description of his penis and what he's capable of with it in lieu of his interests and hobbies, and still no takers.

'What do these damn bitches want?' fumed McCullen, seeing no matches despite swiping right on every single profile he sees.

'I've said it out straight here, if there's anyone looking for a quick ride and they're within bus distance of Waterford city, I'm their man. And nothing. I've put up a pic of me wearing mirrored sunglasses while in the seat of a car – nothing. I've put up a picture of Sadio Mané smashing in his 100th goal for Liverpool – nothing. Looks like I'm just going to change plans and put up a funny profile with a load of jokes and cry-laughing emojis. If that doesn't work, then it's just proof that the Déise is full of lesbians.'

McCullen left to Google 'funny things to say on Tinder to guarantee the ride', as he couldn't think of any himself.

HEN WHATSAPP GROUP AVERAGING 40,000 MESSAGES AN HOUR

THE CLANDESTINE HEN-PLANNING WhatsApp group plotting the perfect weekend for bride-to-be Laura Dowling is currently averaging 40,000 messages an hour and risks crashing servers belonging to the world's biggest tech companies.

'Ah Jesus, here we go again, just buy some straws in the shape of penises and be done with it, girls!' screamed WhatsApp tech support worker Ailbhe Gready as she monitored the most prolific WhatsApp group on the planet.

As of today, the group is being dominated by suggestions for fun activities from individuals who haven't responded to any previous messages authored by maid of honour Jane Healy, with the offending group members only chiming in after all activities had been finalised and paid for.

'We were a month deciding the theme, don't bring me back to those dark days,' offered Healy, now tormented by sudden and immediate group silence when asking the hen group if anyone has dietary requirements for the fancy meal out on day two of the hen, which will be run like a precise military invasion.

'I've never met this Siobhán one who Laura's friends with from college, but I'm ready to burst her. Matching pyjamas are fine, a great suggestion even, but pyjamas with only Siobhán and Laura's faces on them? Give it over,' said Healy, ready to spontaneously combust from the stress.

UPDATE: Organisational problems have been incurred after an overwhelming deluge of thumbs up emojis to questions and requests from Healy that absolutely cannot be answered with just a thumbs up emoji were sent.

Bill's Landlord Tips

Always make the tenant feel that they work for you by reminding them to cut the grass every two weeks.

SOCIAL MEDIA

PRAY FOR JOHN! HE'S JUST BROUGHT UP VIOLENCE AGAINST WOMEN IN THE LADS' WHATSAPP

HAVING SPENT SOME TIME listening to the women in his life in recent weeks, John O'Hanley has taken the commendable if a bit insane decision to begin a conversation about violence against women in the lads' WhatsApp, *WWN* has learned.

Observing a seemingly never-ending parade of distressing headlines relating to violence against women, O'Hanley agonised over drafting a conversation-starting message in the notes app on his phone to place into the BoozeBantsBoobs group, which has most recently been discussing Transfer Deadline Day.

'I suppose it is a systemic problem, and there is a need for society as a whole to move on these issues, not saying it's easy or straightforward or anything but,' said O'Hanley with the sort of open optimism that suggests he's as naïve as a newborn.

'There, and send,' remarked O'Hanley as blood rushed to his cheeks and his stomach felt like it was put on a spin wash.

Closely eyeing the group, he spied 'is writing' appearing multiple times as responses failed to materialise.

'Well, it is early afternoon, the lads would be in work, not exactly supposed to be on the phone,' reasoned O'Hanley as he contemplated a future of being labelled 'a fucking eejit' or having 'grown a vagina'.

Now in the full thrust of panic and regret, O'Hanley hovered over the 'delete for everyone' button on his message before realising it was pointless, as everyone had already read it.

'Aaron Ramsey to Rangers? Never liked the cunt, now I know why,' responded Gav, in the first correspondence since O'Hanley poured out, 'Lads, I think we need to examine how we talk about women going forward, and before you pile on, I'm not accusing anyone of anything so don't pull that "not all men" shite, we're not some incel forum. Like Liam, that hassle your sister had on the bus that time, I'm saying if I was there, would I have spoken up, y'know?'

'See Rihanna's ruined now,' followed the next message, leading O'Hanley to the blissful realisation that his mates weren't going to savage or ridicule him, but simply ignore any attempt to bring up the subject.

HOLIDAYS

WHAT TO PACK FOR ONE NIGHT IN A HOTEL, A GUIDE BY YOUR GIRLFRIEND

SO YOU AND YOUR PARTNER have planned a brief but well-earned getaway, what joy! As luck would have it, your girlfriend has succeeded where everyone else has failed and produced this indispensable guide for all the essentials, like toothbrush, toothpaste and phone charger. For the rest, we'll hand you over to your other half:

- Iron and ironing board. If you think I'm letting you iron a shirt with their poor excuse for an iron, you've got to be kidding. D'ya not remember last time? Your shirt had more wrinkles than Brendan O'Carroll's scrotum.
- Don't just pack a shirt – if we end up in a fancy place for dinner you'll need a blazer. And leave room in

the second suitcase for my backup dresses, romper and pants suit.
- Did I mention the phone charger? Good. And bring the toaster, we'll bring our own bread too, the bread at hotel breakfasts is drier than the Sahara. Fuck it, bring a box of Barry's teabags; can't stand that English breakfast muck.
- Bring your laptop too, they won't have Netflix on the hotel TV, but that's because you went for a three-star (a decision we'll address at a later date). And the iPad too in case the laptop goes kaput.
- They have a pool in this place, so bring your togs but not those red ones   you're on full display in them and I don't want you embarrassing us. My eight bikinis will fit in my

third backup handbag, which will be in the trailer we'll attach to the car
- Oh yeah, you've to hire a trailer, there's feck-all room in the jeep.

WOMAN JUST GOING TO GO THROUGH BOYFRIEND'S PHONE ONE MORE TIME, SOLVES TRUST ISSUES FOREVER

SIFTING THROUGH TEXT messages, WhatsApp messages, Instagram DMs and photos on her boyfriend's phone one final time, local Dublin woman Hannah Colvin believes she has finally brought an end to her ongoing insecurities and trust issues.

'I honestly can't see myself staring at his phone on the coffee table when he's in the shower and being tempted to have a quick look,' confirmed Colvin, confident that this is the last of it now, having got it out of her system.

Explaining heartache and betrayal in other relationships as a motivating factor for now formerly daily investigations, Colvin has admitted to feeling pretty silly.

'I was checking every day expecting to find something, some woman talking seductively to him for example, but

it's a relief now to say I'll never do that again,' confirmed Colvin, before reminding herself that her boyfriend John has football tonight and usually showers when he gets home so his phone will be free to look through then.

'I wasn't addressing any of the underlying issues that make me feel this way, but that's all changed going forward,' added Colvin, reminding herself to double-check all recent Instagram activity of John's female friends, even the ones living in Canada, just on the off chance.

'We've never been stronger, me and John. I've never felt so at ease,' Colvin said, debilitating distrust and anxiety coursing through her veins with the potency of pure heroin.

Colvin's progress was suddenly undone after catching half a glimpse

of a message from someone called 'Football Lads Group' on WhatsApp who seemed to have sent John a picture of David Beckham in a sarong with the words 'remember this lol'.

'Remember what? Remember when they were shacking up with each other? Behind my back?' a serene Colvin asked herself repeatedly in a torturous fashion.

DRINKING

BENEFITS OF DRINKING ONE BOTTLE OF WINE EVERY NIGHT

BY NOW, everyone knows that wine is the healthiest drink you can consume in large quantities, and is nine times more beneficial than water, with calls from those in the health and wellness community to include both white and red wine taps in every home in the country.

Thanks to ongoing research, we now know a range of benefits of drinking at least one bottle of wine every single night, which we've compiled below:

- Due to its high alcohol content, wine can help you get drunk quicker, and is a great option as a pre-going-out drink with friends you want to chastise later in the night for not sticking up for you when you're refused entry to your favourite pub by a bouncer.
- Wine helps regulate blood sugar by infusing your blood with sugar, which is ideal for hangovers the next day; just drink another bottle of wine and your hangover quickly disappears.
- Wine is the perfect beverage for just sitting at home peacefully and relaxing with your family before your partner irks you by pointing out that you're scaring the children with your shouting, and what the actual fuck would they know anyway?
- Quickly skulling the first three-quarters of the bottle has been proven to help you mull over the final glass and persuade you to open bottle number two and later sleep-piss in the wardrobe at 3 a.m. because your brain is too fried to remember where the bathroom is.
- Wine is low in cholesterol and also great for lowering your IQ.
- Drinking one bottle of wine every night has been proven to give you buckets of confidence the next day and is ideal for motorists and daily commuters who just want to rage the fuck out at other motorists for simply driving their cars slightly differently to you.
- Children of parents who drink one or two bottles of wine every night are 20 times more inclined to stay in their rooms all evening until it's time to go to bed.
- Drinking a bottle of white wine straight after drinking a bottle of red cancels out all effects of the red wine and most memories in-between.
- Doctors suggest drinking a litre of wine every night for a good night's sleep apnoea.
- Wine is also a great way of suppressing emotions and problems, so by drinking a bottle every night of the week you will never have to deal with deep-seated trauma ever again.
- Drinking a double whiskey chaser with every glass of wine can boost your serotonin levels by 100 per cent and give you superhuman strength when Gardaí try to forcibly remove you from your home for your family's safety.
- Wine is rich in antioxidants, which is great because it is packed full of toxins like alcohol and sugar.

BREAKING

LICK ARSE STILL WEARING MASK

A LITTLE GOODY TWO SHOES lick arse is persisting with wearing a facemask in the supermarket despite such restrictions having been lifted weeks ago, *WWN* can confirm.

'I'd say she's a bit of a dose now in fairness,' one shopper commented, now throwing filthy looks at the person in question as she sanitised her hands for the second time while walking around the store. 'Urgh, for God's sake, does anyone do that anymore? Absolutely mortified for her now.'

Wiping down the shopping cart with wipes, the woman also appeared to be still social distancing and spacing herself two metres from

fellow shoppers, like it was March 2020 all over again.

'Some people are just sheep,' said another shopper. 'She'll probably start making baa sounds now in a minute.'

Unaware of the judgements and general disdain for her adherence to health and safety, the woman told *WWN* she just wanted to keep her family safe, as Covid 'hasn't gone away'.

'I care for my mother with COPD, and my daughter has problems with her immune system, so I guess limiting their chances of getting the virus makes me do it,' explained the lick arse, who probably regularly washes her hands like a lunatic too, come to think of it. 'Ah, yeah, of course, I wash my hands after leaving here. My family are still at risk, but yeah, you just laugh at me for protecting them,' she added, finally realising how ridiculous she looks.

CONFUSION AND DISAPPOINTMENT AFTER LOCAL MAN ASKS DATE IF SHE WANTS TO DO A LINE WITH HIM

THE SOARING RATES OF COCAINE USAGE in every city, town, village and townland in Ireland is causing huge confusion among the dating population, according to a new survey that shows the meaning of 'doing a line' has tipped in favour of drug-taking.

'I was out on a Tinder meet-up with a lad and he asked me if I wanted to do a steady line with him, and I said fuck yeah, deadly,' said one Waterford lady we spoke to, following what she described as 'the worst date of her life'.

'Love a line, so I do. I assumed it was coke, but I'd take a line of anything to liven up this crap night out. And then what happens? Not only

does this sap not produce a bag, but he starts going on about when would I like to meet his parents? And then he has us on Facebook as being "in a relationship"? I was like, ah here, can we not just get coked off our faces like normal people?'

With cocaine becoming more popular than Coors as the confidence-boosting stimulant of choice when attempting to woo a potential lover (or at least get a good feel of them before the bouncers throw you out), experts fear that 'doing a line' in the old-fashioned sense of the phrase may be on the verge of extinction.

'It's funny, I was doing a line with a lady for years until I started doing lines, if you get me,' sighed

linguistics professor Ian Hartlemann, explaining the shift in phraseology happening today.

'But then I just kept doing a bunch of lines and nothing seemed to worry me after that – well, besides where my next coke was coming from. I'm sorry, what are you here to discuss again? I got distracted.'

Meanwhile, bars around Ireland are to stock only Pepsi from now on instead of Coke, again to keep confusion to a minimum.

PARENTING

DAD PROUDLY FINISHES JOB THAT DIDN'T NEED DOING

WATERFORD DAD-OF-THREE Mark Sewell has re-joined his family indoors for the first time in over six weeks, having taken himself to the garden in early July to 'do a few bits', *WWN* can report.

'Good to have that done,' said Sewell, sitting with his family for a rare lunch together.

'Took a bit longer than I thought, but when you really get into a job,

you lose track of time. Anyway, how is everyone here? Áine, you've gotten very tall altogether! Sorry I missed your birthday, by the way.'

Meanwhile, Sewell's wife Carolyn has admitted that she's been looking out at the garden for almost a month now and cannot see what exactly her husband has been doing all this time or offer any suggestion as to why he felt it was so urgent when there are a hundred more pressing jobs lined up for him.

'Whatever the hell he was at outside, it wasn't as important as helping me get the kids ready for back to school or fixing the rattle in the washing machine or any of any number of other tasks,' sighed Mrs Sewell, who is well used to this kind of thing.

'But this is how it is. He'll get it in his head that the house is going to fall if he doesn't pull a bit of ivy around the side, or replace a shelf with a smaller shelf or something like that. To be honest, I get more done with him out of the house, so I leave him to it.'

Mr Sewell was unavailable for further comment, as he has already embarked on a new project, and has set off to blow 100 quid in the hardware shop on a tool he'll use twice in his whole life.

> **Predictions for 2023**
>
> In an unusual departure in tone, Sally Rooney reveals that her next book will be a horror set in entitled *Intersectional Feminist Communist Vampires From Mars.*

EXCITEMENT OF TRUCK DRIVER SEEING OTHER TRUCK DRIVER SPARKS HEADLIGHT-FLASHING FRENZY

ASTONISHMENT at the fact that a similar-looking vehicle was travelling the opposite way on a road in the same country of origin has sparked an uncontrollable headlight-flashing frenzy on the M9 today, *WWN* can report.

In what was meant to be just another casual haulage trip to Dublin, Waterford city truck driver Damien Thomas recalls the incident in stunning detail.

'Seriously, what are the chances?' the son-of-two opened up, the emotion still fresh in his quivering voice. 'It was like two ships sailing in the night, unaware of the vast scale of the universe, yet drawn together in some kind of cosmic destiny, disintegrating the probability of chance and all known logic and reason.'

The chance encounter began while Thomas was driving over a slight hill, descending the M9 motorway past Mullinavat.

'I squinted at first, not believing what I was seeing,' he recalls. 'It was a 2019 Hino 500 beating it up the hill towards me on the other side of the road,' he added, shaking his head in disbelief. 'It even had the roof headlights – like mine – spray wafting from its tires on the wet road like an angel emerging from the clouds …

and there it was, a bright white light blasting towards me, calling me to respond.'

It is understood that at that moment the Waterford truck driver engaged his counterpart with some headlights of his own.

'There was something in the comradeship, that feeling of oneness. We were essentially at one with one another like everything made sense at that exact moment in time and space, but time didn't exist and space was a fabrication of our collective consciousness experiencing itself momentarily in a passing acknowledgement of togetherness,' Thomas said, describing the incident, before concluding, 'Now, it was either that or he was flashing me over the backdoor of my truck being wide open and flapping in the wind, but it was a moment nonetheless.'

LOCAL MAN HAUNTED BY CROSS TRAINER OF CHRISTMAS PAST

A DUBLIN MAN has called on local priests to exorcise his home in a bid to rid his spare room of a recurring entity that has been haunting him for the past 11 months, *WWN* can report.

Martin Giles first recalled the spirit in the early part of this year but didn't take any notice of it at the time.

'I awoke one night to see it at the end of my bed with some towels hanging off of it and jumped right up out of bed with the fright,' recalls Giles, who used the machine once on New Year's Day. 'I just put it down to the light playing tricks on me and went back to sleep, but then in the last few weeks it just started getting worse.'

In one instance, the 45-year-old stubbed his toe off the cross trainer while going to the toilet early one morning, leaving Giles speaking in tongues.

'Martin began cursing and shouting incoherently at the machine like a madman possessed,' wife Tabitha said, recalling the terrifying incident. 'The cross trainer just kind of loomed over him, almost taunting Martin for not using it.'

> **'Sometimes when I walk upstairs the door to the room creaks open to reveal the trainer peering out'**

Although they moved the exercise machine into the spare room, it continued to haunt the couple.

'Sometimes when I walk upstairs the door to the room creaks open to reveal the trainer peering out, almost calling me in to use it, like a siren to a sailor,' added Martin Giles, who admitted to purchasing more gym equipment ahead of his next New Year's fitness resolution. 'My fear now is being haunted by the treadmill of Christmas present or the kettlebell of Christmas future.'

HEALTH

HEALTH FUCKED NO MATTER WHAT YOU DO, FINDS STUDY

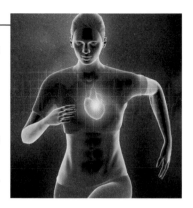

SENIOR HEALTH OFFICIALS have recommended that everyone should crack into the gin and the quarter pounders as soon and as often as possible, 'for all the difference it makes' in the grand scheme of things.

The announcement comes following research that suggests that exercising may cause high levels of calcium in coronary arteries, leading to a greater risk of 'the same damn heart attacks that exercising was supposed to prevent'.

'Damned if you do, damned if you don't, isn't it?' posed one doctor we spoke to, who was chain-smoking fags while necking Pernod straight from the bottle, because why not.

'One week we tell people, "don't eat fatty foods". Then it's "oh, some are good for you". "Don't drink alcohol", then "well, some is beneficial in moderation". Don't vape, don't smoke, don't take those pills, do take these pills, walk a lot but not too much, stay fit but don't get injured … Listen, I hate to break it to you, but we're all going in the fucking ground. Do whatever you want.'

Meanwhile, a breakthrough revelation that occurred to our doctor friend while off his face may be the answer to living the lifestyle you want without fear of heart problems.

'Stents for everyone!' he roared, pissed as a fart.

'Why are we giving people stents after they've had heart attacks? Stick 'em in every fucker that wants them. Stent them heart tubes open, then you can run, walk, fuck, eat, drink and bungee jump as much as you damn well like. Stents, ya bastards!'

The doctor then asked us if we knew anyone who sold coke, before remembering he had 'a whole buncha morphine' back in the clinic.

𝔚aterford 𝔚hispers 𝔑ews

VOL 1, 452789   WATERFORD, TUESDAY, 11 JULY, 1922   2p

Michael Collins Spotted Shifting Lad in The George

IRISH revolutionary Michael Collins wasn't available for comment today after rumours were spread linking him to shifting another man in The George last weekend, WWN can report.

Third-party details handed down to this fine publication alleged the 31-year-old Chairman of the Provisional Government of the Irish Free State was caught eating the face off of a homosexual at the questionable bar on Saturday night, sparking fears he could be arrested on charges under the Offences Against the Person Act 1861.

'I heard he was aiding the tumescence of another man's seed sower,' an anonymous source we're quoting without doing any further investigation confirmed, 'they probably sodomised each other afterwards and made animal sacrifices to Satan.'

Collins, who has long been suspected of being a prostate milker, has neither denied nor confirmed the allegations, sparking fears that he is indeed a chimney sweeper, because if he wasn't he'd definitely be going around the place denying it.

'They don't call him the big fellow for nothing,' another speculator we spoke to speculated, 'I'd say he has to wrap the thing around his leg and tuck it into his socks it's that long – those lads love that.'

Meanwhile, Eamon de Valera is also yet to comment after he was spotted in Temple Bar giving out about the price of pints.

'Dev was shouting about how Yanks are always being overcharged in Temple Bar and vowing to never drink there again,' an eyewitness confirmed, 'yet there he was an hour later, hoofing down a kebab outside the place singing rebel songs.'

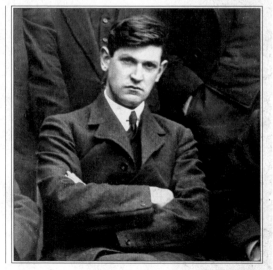

PARENTING

FUEL HIKES, REFUGEES, WAR – IS THIS THE GOLDEN AGE OF COMPLAINING FOR IRISH DADS?

SOME EXPERTS would argue that no period of upheaval can possibly match the Celtic Tiger-era crash for being a generator of apoplectic rage with curmudgeonly and discordant bitterness for Irish fathers.

But those same experts who made this assessment couldn't have predicted a pandemic, inflation, war, refugee crisis and fuel price hike quintuple whammy.

To find out if this is indeed the golden age of complaining, moaning, grousing and arguing, we spoke to the nation's dads.

'I want to cry every time I pass a petrol station and what have the clowns in Leinster House done? A cut in excise duty? They're laughing at us,' offered Tom Doland (64), absolutely revelling in the misery.

'I honestly don't know what to do with all this additional adrenaline I'm generating from being mad as a bull being hung upside down from his bollocks. Don't forget there was the minimum alcohol pricing too. Jesus wept,' chimed Derek Farrell (57), who is so perpetually outraged by current events that he could cry tears of joy.

Recent events have created a confluence of complaining among Irish fathers that simply can't sustain itself, such is the bountiful harvest of harping on and haranguing anyone within giving-out distance.

'Tell them, Margaret, didn't I say this exact thing would happen? I called it from the start, but would anyone listen?' opined Liam Tynan (70), who

seemed to be suggesting that he had predicted all major economic and geopolitical shifts of recent years, as well as a global pandemic.

'And they want us to take in how many? And how will we pay for all that? Take one wild guess – it starts with "R" and ends with "iding the hole off the taxpayer",' offered John Cormley (52), 'and mother-of-all-that-is-unholy, the inflation, they'd rob the sugar from your tea the bastards.'

'I'll tell you exactly how you deal with that Putin gobshite, you look him dead in the eyes and you just tell him you're launching nukes. I'd pay to see his face. Wouldn't be such a big man then.

'Anyway, young people don't know how good they have it. It's time they

Predictions for 2023

Ireland will have another year of unseasonably mild weather, which will be followed by Irish people somehow remarking they've 'never seen the weather so bad'.

My highlight of 2022: Ariana Grande

'When that middle-aged man on Twitter finally admitted he'd heard of me.'

experienced a good war on the front lines just like I didn't when I was a kid,' added Terry Finley (61), who might still be processing the anger he feels over his grandchild attending an Educate Together school.

'The world can't go on like this,' shared Brian Warren (66), who prays every night for all world turmoil and uncertainty to carry on, as his moaning hasn't even gotten out of first gear.

RELATIONSHIPS

MAN DOESN'T TRUST WIFE TO USE BREAD-SLICING MACHINE IN SUPERMARKET

SUPERMARKET CHAINS around the country have admitted that they only install customer-operated bread-slicing machines as a way to keep married men involved in the grocery shopping process – men like Waterford dad-of-two Cathal McGinnion, 43.

'Oh now, I'd never let Sharon near the bread slicer, that's my job,' McGinnion told us, in line with data relating to male grocery shopping patterns that supermarkets had previously shared with us.

'We have a system in place. She points out the bread she'd like, tells me how thin she'd like the slices, and then I take it from there. Sometimes I have to wait to use the machine, as there's usually a long queue of middle-aged men using it, and let me tell you, some of these lads have no clue what they're at! They need to watch me if they want to know how to properly put a loaf of bread in the hatch and press a button, I tell you.'

As McGinnion demonstrated the proper way to get the sliced bread from the machine into a paper bag without it 'going everywhere', his wife Sharon confided in us that she lets her husband handle the bread situation in a bid to 'get him out of the way'.

'Installing a machine that men gravitate towards is the greatest supermarket innovation since the introduction of the middle aisle full of power tools,' Mrs McGinnion told us.

'He's happy to mess around with a knife-based machine for up to 20 minutes, and I'm delighted because I can get the shopping done without him second-guessing everything that goes in the trolley.'

Mr McGinnion also admitted that he just really likes the 'unce-unce-unce' noise the bread slicer makes and that sometimes he does a little dance to it while waiting.

WE KNOW WE SAID OUR LAST FACE CREAM WAS ALL YOU NEEDED BUT NOW WE'RE TELLING YOU IT'S THIS NEW STUFF

WOMEN CAN ELIMINATE crow's feet, forehead wrinkles, unsightly blemishes, open pores and the ravaging effects of time with the new aloe-infused, *L. casei immunitas*-enriched moisturising face cream from L'Unreal, according to a press release from the skincare company that reads a lot like their last one.

'Unlike the other top-selling face creams on the market, this one actually does what it says on the tube,' reads the statement from L'Unreal, seemingly forgetting that they are the other top-selling face creams on the market.

'This will finally give women the confidence that we've been telling them they've been lacking since they were old enough to buy cosmetics.

Couple with these nine other L'Unreal products for best results, and don't miss a single application or it doesn't work and that's not on us, that's on you.'

L'Unreal is rolling out its new face cream with a multimillion-euro campaign that includes paid promotions with Instagram and YouTube make-up influencers, helping them get around those pesky 'don't advertise to kids' laws.

'Maybe this will finally help my face not look so haggard and old so that I'll feel a sense of self-worth for once,' said one 13-year-old, after watching a 30-minute YouTube tutorial explaining how the new cream from L'Unreal is the difference between happiness and a lifetime of cat ownership.

SOON-TO-BE-NEWLYWEDS Caroline Mannagh and Seán Morrisey have stumbled on the perfect idea for keeping their upcoming wedding rolling into a second day – throwing a fucking barbecue the next day, much to the delight of their guests.

'Oh great, it's a two-day thing,' said one overjoyed friend who hasn't seen the pair in well over two years and honestly has no idea how they got a full invite to the Mass and everything.

'I suppose I'll ring my mam and ask if she can babysit the kids for another day,' sighed Mannagh's cousin Alice.

'That's great. That's wonderful. So rather than paying for one night in a hotel, I have to pay for two and take the Monday off work – marvellous,' said one of Morrisey's old college friends from the far side of the country, possibly sarcastically.

'There's no fucking way I'm paying for a second day, fuck that,' added the bride's father, emphatically. 'You want a barbecue for this lot, buy it yourself. I won't be there, I'm 78 for Christ's sake. So are all your aunts and uncles. Just keep our names off the

WEDDING NOT ENOUGH, COUPLE THROWING FUCKING BARBECUE NEXT DAY TOO

invites – we hate barbecues at the best of times.'

The couple is to press ahead with their barbecue plans, seemingly

unaware that this is the kind of thing people got sick of five years ago, which many had hoped 'died off with the Covid'.

SOCIAL MEDIA

LOCAL WOMAN JUST GOING TO SEND YOU A VOICE NOTE, IT'S QUICKER

DUBLIN WOMAN Shannon Cannings has opted to send an eight-minute voice note as it's 'quicker to say rather than type out', much to the joy of her friends on their WhatsApp group.

'Before she discovered voice notes, she'd send normal text messages that were short and to the point, but of course now that she can record her voice she doesn't have to worry about typing and can go on for as long as she wants,' grimaced one of her friends as they sat through Cannings' latest diatribe.

'There's no denying the fact that it is certainly quicker for her to say it than to type it out, that's a 100 per cent truth. As for how long it would take us to read a response rather than listen to

this stream-of-consciousness ramble in a hunt for whatever her request might be, well that's not the point. It's easier for her, and that's all that matters.'

Analysis of an average 10-minute voice note from the 26-year-old has revealed:

- The opening two or three minutes is a monologue about how it's easier to send a voice note, usually down to the fact that she's currently driving and 'doesn't want to use her phone'.
- At least four minutes are attributed to 'ums', 'ahs', long silences and comments on things that the listener can't see.

- Maybe 30 seconds of pertinent information.
- A closing three or four minutes of a vocalised internal discussion about whether or not she has anything else to say, followed by nine separate goodbyes.

Meanwhile, the government is being urged to push through legislation that would outlaw any voice notes that run longer than one minute, tops.

> **My highlight of 2022: Leonardo DiCaprio**
>
> 'When I made the decision to date older women like my current girlfriend, who's 26 and a half.'

MAN CRAMS IN SIX MONTHS OF BRUSHING TEETH 30 MINUTES BEFORE DENTIST APPOINTMENT

HOPEFUL THAT SIX long months of treating his mouth like a radioactive bin and with the sort of neglect that should probably be a crime is easily reversible, local man Ciarán Faolin is now frantically brushing his teeth in a vain attempt to counteract the self-inflicted abuse.

Adding a second brush into the mix while spilling more blood than a front-line trench during World War II, Faolin continued the manic, machine-like arm movements, prodding into his gob in a fruitless attempt to find a loophole in oral care.

'Surely she'll be none the wiser. Yes, my sugar consumption looks like

the coke pile in *Scarface*, but on the plus side I gave the teeth a quick go

there before running out the door,' Faolin told himself, fearful of being read the riot act by his dentist and feeling like a child again.

Gargling mouthwash while Googling 'how many teeth does a person even need anyway?' Faolin began sweating at the thought of being stuck in the dentist's chair with no escape from a flurry of 'what did I tell you the last time you were in here?' admonishments.

'Fucking hell,' remarked Faolin as he passed what felt like chilli-coated barbed wire between his teeth, which was in fact dental floss.

Grinning at his image displayed on his phone's camera, with his smile obscured by industrial quantities of blood, Faolin concluded, 'Ah yeah, that should fool her' before setting foot in the dentist's reception.

MOTORING

MEET THE SICKOS WHO LIKE TO WATCH OTHER PEOPLE DRIVING THEIR CAR

'I LIKE TO LAY down on the backseat, peer between the front seats and watch them change the gears,' explained self-confessed cuckdriver Martin Felps. 'Sometimes I ask them to purposely miss a gear, so it makes that awful grinding sound – it really tingles my wobbly bits.'

'Cuckdriving' has been a taboo subject with most up until now, but people who get off on other people driving their cars have started coming out of the woodwork, organising mass drives around unsuspecting towns and cities across Ireland.

'I usually rent a car, park up a few metres away from my own car and leave the keys on the back wheel,' explains Derek Murphy, chief organiser of the group CuckDrivers

Ireland. 'I'd pay anywhere up to €500 for someone to come along and drive off in it before I follow them. The best part is overtaking them and egging on the driver to beep at me and flash the lights. Oh God, there's nothing like being beeped at by your own car. There's something filthy about it.'

Starting in 2017, Murphy remembers the first time he realised he wanted other people to drive his car.

'The mechanic was reversing her out of the garage for me after a service. It felt odd, wrong even, but in a nice weird way, so I told him to check the undercarriage so I could see him drive that cunning little minx out again,' he recalled. 'I knew I was in trouble then.'

However, it hasn't been all plain sailing for Ireland's cuckdrivers, with an anti-cuckdriver group now actively protecting nationwide.

'They're sick bastards who need to be named and shamed,' voiced concerned Tramore resident Mark Haley, who witnessed a cuckdriving event last year down the prom car park that he's still mentally recovering from. 'They were all just parked up in each other's cars, staring out, doing God knows what in there. I can't get those imagined images out of my mind.'

Gardaí confirmed that the number of people being caught driving other people's cars without being insured has quadrupled in the last year due to the surge in cuckdriving, and advised cuckdrivers to get fully comp insurance if they are partaking in this act.

'Lately, these sickos seem to be targeting learner drivers for that extra thrill of the person driving their car being unaccompanied,' a Garda spokesperson stated. 'In one instance a 12-year-old boy was driving a farmer's tractor as the farmer drove along behind him in a jeep. Where this depravity ends is anyone's guess.'

On This Day

1501: Nude model posing for sculpture asks Michelangelo, 'And you're doing my dick to scale, right? It won't be comically small?'

8 June

113

COOKING

MUM COOKS HER SIGNATURE POMPEII PASTA

A COUNTY WATERFORD MOTHER who has been up to her eyes pottering around the house has unknowingly whipped up her signature Italian dish, Pompeii pasta, *WWN* reports.

Coined due to its charcoal-black appearance and unforgettable ash aroma, the fragrant recurring meal gave the O'Neill home a smell like it had just been preserved in volcanic debris, sparking full-time son-of-two Damian O'Neill to intervene.

'Mam, I think the pasta is done,'

the 13-year-old updated the bed-changing chef/cleaner/gardener, Sheila O'Neill, who cannot for the life of her remember putting on the classic carcinogenic meal. Now cursing manically from the bottom bedroom, Sheila delivered her signature 'Aw for fuck sakes' response, no doubt a fitting slogan if her Pompeii dish ever made it to the supermarket shelves.

'Fucking cunt on it anyway,' the mother of three added, now removing a blackened stainless-steel saucepan

to the bin. 'Lads, ye're going to have to start learning how to cook your own pasta. Mammy can't be doing everything all the time,' she added, knowing this will never happen as long as she can walk on her own two feet.

Despite its exotic name, Pompeii pasta is relatively easy to make, requiring just 200 grams of penne pasta, barely enough water to cover it and running like saucepan for 45 minutes and the top gas mark on your stove.

MAN FORGETS TO DOUBLE-TAP CAR ROOF WHEN SAYING GOODBYE TO FRIEND

FEARS ESCALATED in a Waterford man today over the welfare of his long-time friend after forgetting to give a friendly double-tap of the car roof before he left, leaving the vehicle open to all sorts of bad luck and certain catastrophe, *WWN* can confirm.

Jonathan Lyons said he completely forgot to make the secret gesture for 'safe home', stating that he was so engulfed in conversation with Tony Hanaway that he only remembered after his friend had already departed.

'I tried ringing him and then texted that I was sorry for not double-tapping the roof, but there was no reply,' Lyons said, recalling the horrific incident. 'I was left feeling very anxious at the thought of me mate Tony just driving along on his own without having the kind of security and confidence a friendly double tap on the roof of his car would bring.'

Confirming his greatest fears, it was later found that his friend had indeed veered off into a ditch and overturned the car onto its roof, a sure sign and indicator that his friend's lack of taps was to blame.

'I saw my phone ringing and I tried to answer it, but the thing slipped down between the car seat and the handbrake panel,' said crash victim Tony Hanaway, who was now recovering and in a stable condition in hospital. 'I thought it was an urgent

call, as it was followed by several texts, so I tried getting the phone out with my fingers, but lost my concentration on the road and ended up in the bloody ditch. It wasn't until I got to the hospital that I saw the text and calls were from Jonathan – which of course then explained everything.'

Gardaí at the scene of the one-car collision later confirmed that it was the lack of the double-tap that caused the crash and urged people saying goodbye to their friends to always remember to double-tap the roof or driver's door for good luck before departing.

Tips for Ignoring Climate Change ☼

Live in a country with a Green Party in government that rolls out the red carpet for data centres.

PARENTING

LOCAL BUSYBODY Eimear McGuinlan is fairly certain that her neighbour up the road must have undergone a lengthy and quite possibly emotionally draining IVF journey to conceive her twin baby girls, and has outlined her thoughts on the matter to anyone who will sit with her for 10 minutes.

'And of course, it's not like she's all that young, is it?' mused McGuinlan, speculating on the ovarian capabilities of the woman in no.38, whose name is as yet unknown.

'So if you ask me, herself and the husband – I think it's her husband, they might just be partners … remind me to do further research into that – must have spent thousands upon

OLDER WOMAN WITH TWINS 'MUST HAVE HAD THE IVF', CONFIRMS LOCAL GOSSIP

thousands on IVF. Because a woman over 35 with no kids couldn't just suddenly have twins, could she? Anyway, that's my thoughts on the matter, based on what I've seen from the front window here.'

McGuinlan prides herself on her knowledge of the reproductive behaviour of her neighbours and has also noted that:

> **'It's not like she's all that young, is it?'**

- The second eldest in no.14 around the corner must be adopted, as he looks nothing like his brothers or sisters.
- The newlyweds in no.81 are having trouble conceiving a child, given that they got married nearly a full

year ago and there's no sign of a 'bump on her'. McGuinlan has no evidence as to why said couple isn't pregnant yet, but has decided to herself that it must be the man shooting blanks, as he's 'a watery-looking yoke'.

- The lady in no.41 isn't breastfeeding her child, so it will almost certainly end up in jail.

Mrs McGuinlan also mentioned that she's available for freelance nosiness in your area, and if you want some wild speculation about your neighbours then just give her a call.

HEALTH

ONE TWIN WENT VEGAN, THE OTHER ATE MEAT. THIS IS WHAT HAPPENED.

IDENTICAL TWINS Peadar and Jimpie Lacey from Co. Offaly took part in a scientific study to finally settle whether a vegan diet is healthier than eating meat. This is what happened to them over a six-month period when Peadar ate strictly vegan food, while Jimpie continued to eat meat and dairy products.

'I noticed I started crowbarring the fact that I was on a vegan diet into every single conversation,' Peadar recalled in the recently published study. 'I remember I was at my aunt's funeral in Tipp and telling the church that she probably wouldn't have died if she went vegan, but in fairness to me, I did warn everyone to drink plenty of

'I noticed I started crowbarring the fact that I was on a vegan diet into every single conversation'

water if they went down the vegan route, as the turds were like passing a small child sideways.'

Brother Jimpie, who remained eating meat, reported something called 'sympathy pangs', which he believes he was channelling from his meat-craving brother, instinctually forcing him to try everything in his power to get Peadar back to eating animals.

'I'd found myself ordering double quarter pounders with bacon, just to entice him,' Jimpie admitted. 'I would make orgasmic sounds and say phrases like "lovely meat" or "jaysis, imagine not being able to eat meat for six months like a dope". I think this was more a survival thing, trying to coax my brother back to meat to save his life.'

In several instances, Jimpie would leave

delicious images of meat-based dishes around their shared accommodation, and would sometimes fry meat without turning on the cooker vent, just to fill the apartment with that irresistible smell, stating that he 'wouldn't even eat the meat himself', instead leaving cuts on a plate in the fridge 'for show'.

Eventually, it got to the stage where Jimpie would WhatsApp his brother daily with several hundred videos of steaks being cut up in slow motion by Salt Bae, ultimately forcing Peadar to move out of the apartment, block his brother's phone number and apply for a restraining order through the courts.

'It all came to a head when Jimpie went out, bought a hot dog van and followed his brother around everywhere he went,' lead researcher of the study Dr Cathal Ryan revealed. 'Then one day Peadar snapped and ended up in a high-speed chase to get away from him, before fatally crashing into a tree.'

'Look, I told him he'd end up dead if he kept up this meat-free diet craic, and in a way, I was 100 per cent right,' Jimpie now recalls from Mountjoy Prison, where he will spend the next three years for manslaughter. 'Hopefully, it wasn't all in vain, and people will take heed now before opting to go vegan.'

Classifieds

Calculator needed

Calculator needed urgently in Waterford restaurant to settle a bill. Some of us only had tap water and no starters, so I don't see how this is just a four-way split. Ridiculous.

Mark, Emilio's Restaurant, Table 8

BREAKING

TENSIONS MOUNT IN HOME AS KITCHEN BIN CLEARLY NEEDS EMPTYING

THE ATMOSPHERE at a Dublin house share is tenser than an Israeli checkpoint at the Gaza Strip as housemates are caught up in a silent, ever-escalating, passive-aggressive war over an overflowing kitchen bin.

'We had a cleaning chart but someone doesn't honour it so it's all devolved into chaos. The least they could is empty the bin once in a while,' shared Clíona Connell, intentionally speaking loud enough to be heard by perceived instigator of the Great Bin Standoff of 2022, Ellen Hegarty.

'I love nothing more than to empty full bins, but not when it's full of recyclables that someone is too lazy to put in the green bin. Don't sweat it, it's only the planet suffering,' remarked Hegarty through gritted teeth.

The conflict has been further complicated by the presence of a third housemate, John, who is a pacifist by nature and refuses to take sides.

'Best just to keep the head down. I'm Switzerlanding this shit until they sort it out between themselves,' added John, who has defied stereotypes by being fairly decent around the house.

Delicately placing a tea bag on top of the unstable pyramid growing up out of the bin that rivals the Burj Khalifa in height, Connell made the movement as deliberate as possible before sitting down and saying, 'You're heading out tonight, aren't you Ellen?' in a clear attempt to trap her housemate into a 'take the bins out on your way out so' scenario.

'I wouldn't want to be around there when it all kicks off, and I served in Afghanistan,' shared one conflict expert watching on, fearful of the seemingly unavoidable and vicious spilling of blood.

PUCE RED, one incredulous local woman has dramatically cancelled an online shopping spree at the 'checkout' phase after a sneaky bastard of a retail company tried to heap an exorbitant delivery charge of €8 onto her order, which totalled €350, *WWN* has learned.

'The cheek, that's taking the piss,' shared Jess Rafflin, backing out of the €350 spend on account of the fact that she doesn't like being ripped off.

'I was only on the site for a pair of socks, blacked out and woke up to a new wardrobe in my basket, but I just can't justify it now – that €8 is fierce steep. For delivery from several different depots in different countries? As if it costs that much,' added Rafflin.

Rafflin is one of many consumers sick to the teeth of hidden last-minute delivery charges that tip the cost of purchases over into the 'too expensive' category, robbing them of essentials

WOMAN BACKS OUT OF €350 ONLINE SHOPPING SPREE AFTER BEING HIT WITH €8 DELIVERY CHARGE

like 10 more pairs of trousers that'll sit in their closet for the year unworn.

'Four and a half grand on the new couch, sound system and TV, okay, fine, I've made peace with that. But these cowboys want to be paid 30 quid to bring out the thing I've bought from them,' shared one incensed man, who had never heard of such a ridiculous attempt to bankrupt a person in his life.

Asked to explain this peculiar behaviour exhibited by some consumers, a leading behavioural scientist remarked, 'Fucking tell me about it pal, everything is a fucking rip off and con job these days.'

Tips for Ignoring Climate Change

'Climate change' used to be 'global warming'. Wait a few years and they'll call it something even less alarming to ignore.

FASHION

WOMAN KNEW IT WAS ONLY A MATTER OF TIME BEFORE DOUBLE DENIM CAME BACK IN FASHION

'STYLE NEVER GOES out of fashion,' beamed a delighted Aoife Herity as she took to the town unashamedly rocking full double denim for the night out.

The look, often referred to as a Canadian Tuxedo or a Culchie's Shroud, has not been popular since the days of B*Witched, and most fashion experts would agree that even then it was more tolerated than admired.

Nevertheless, long-time double denim fans such as 39-year-old Ms Herity knew that all they had to do was bide their time and it would be socially acceptable once again to head out wearing double (and indeed sometimes triple) denim.

'For years I had to wear either jeans or a denim jacket, not both,' said Ms Herity, looking like something out of a line-dancing class for impoverished orphans.

'But some TikTok star wore it once and then all these wee teenyboppers went nuts for it, so I'm taking that as a sign that we're back, baby. Wrangler up top, Wrangler down below. It feels so good to know that my outfit is 100 per cent coordinated, and required absolutely no thought. I'm never going back!'

While double denim may be somewhat acceptable for the moment, men are still waiting patiently on the day when it's okay to wear boot-cut jeans and brown dress shoes again.

UNSURE AS TO WHEN she precisely entered the phase, which is really of no importance now to 28-year-old Jessica Handly because she just has to act cool, not make eye contact, oh my God oh my God are they following her?

'I just know they're looking at my clothes and judging me. They must think I look fit for a nursing home,' Handly said, making yet another daring dash to her local Tesco despite the routine presence of the most

28-YEAR-OLD ENTERS 'AFRAID OF GROUPS OF TEENAGE GIRLS' PHASE OF LIFE

intimidating group of terrorists this side of ISIS: teenage girls.

'Their giggles, whispering and pointing haunt my dreams,' confessed Handly, who always has to hype herself up to source the confidence required to walk past a gaggle of 13-year-olds.

Handly was forthright in her assessment of herself as 'so uncool she might as well be a jumper knitted by Twink', something that reduces her insides to somersaults when she sees her local supply of teenagers.

Reaching your late 20s usually marks the end of a person's carefree 'younger people think I'm cool' phase of life, plunging them into self-doubt and second-guessing themselves.

'They "know",' a jittering, jangling bag of nerves that looked like Handly said, unclear as to what it is exactly that they know.

'They could strike at any moment; it could be with a knife or, worse, a withering put-down about my fringe, which will require years of therapy to overcome,' Handly explained.

Meanwhile, the group of 13-year-old girls currently necking the one can of Red Bull between them while swapping scrunchies have explained that Handly has never registered with them, not even once in their peripheral vision.

COOKING

PANIC AS CAVAN MAN UNSURE WHICH STEAK HE COOKED IS SMALLER, TO GIVE TO WIFE

'ONE OF THESE was definitely bigger than the other when I started cooking, but which one now?' a panicked Jeremy O'Meara barked at himself, searing all sides of two unevenly cut pieces of beef, which made it difficult to gauge. 'I know I asked the butcher for a "his and hers", but they're two different cuts and I've no scales to check.'

Fearing his wife may get the marginally bigger steak, the Cavan man tried weighing each cut by hand using the spatula, switching from left to right, bending down to see their thickness, before scratching his bewildered head.

'Now, there's a bit of grizzle running through this one, and I don't mind that, but it's throwing me off now and can't decide if that's my one,' the one-not-to-be-done-out-of-steak-meat continued.

O'Meara is one of the thousands of men who believe a man should get a bigger portion than a woman because he's bigger and stronger, something bred into him since living on a farm from a young age.

'What if the father calls in and sees I'm eating a smaller steak than Tina? He'll laugh at me 'til his grave,' he said, panicking more, frantically plating up the pair of medium rares onto a white plate, staring intensely before calling his wife in for dinner. 'Right, fuck it, I can't decide, I'll just lob more potatoes and onions on mine to save face – problem solved.'

Now finishing up his meal like it was his last, while his wife slowly picked away, O'Meara couldn't help but still feel a little cheated, before doing his usual play.

'Are you finishing that, love?' he asked, knowing his good-natured spouse would comply.

''Tis lovely, Jer, but way too much for me. Do you want some? Have the rest of this,' she replied, secretly cursing the greedy bastard to hell.

SIGNS YOU'RE NOT A MORNING PERSON

THE MORNINGS aren't for everyone. *WWN* Business brings you some subtle signs that you might be a terse, morning-averse person:

- You'll be fucked if you're arsed reading this before 6 p.m.
- Hissing out at sunlight breaking through the curtains. (Note: this may mean you are a vampire, and *WWN* is not liable for any loss of life should you burst into flames.)
- The snooze button on your alarm has become sentient and knows to turn itself off every five minutes.
- Bludgeoning to death anyone who says 'I'm not right until I've had my morning coffee'.
- Adopting the life endorsed by monks who have taken a vow of silence, until at least 11 a.m. in your case.
- Never uttering the phrase 'I'm not a morning person', because you're too busy managing your pent-up rage at being forced to adhere to a fabricated capitalist-mandated nine-to-five daily drudge that has no end.
- You completely reject 'morning' as a concept and have existed in a timeless void you entered when you refused to get up for school when you were 10 – condemned to travel the universe, completely untethered from 'night' and 'day'. After years in the space wilderness, a thought occurs to you: it's not that you're not a morning person, it's that morning is not a you person.

119

PARENTING

PARENT JUST MAKING SCHOOL LUNCHES FOR SHOW AT THIS STAGE

A COUNTY WATERFORD MOTHER has admitted to just making school lunches for show, despite knowing it will end up straight in the bin, *WWN* has learned.

'I stopped asking my daughter why she didn't eat her lunch two years ago,' Janice Rielly confirmed, emptying the contents of yet another uneaten lunch. 'I'm caught between a rock and a hard place, as if I stop giving her lunch, it looks like I'm neglecting her, so it's just best to waste buckets of food and money ▨▨▨▨ ▨▨▨ ▨▨▨▨▨▨

Citing things like 'I wasn't hungry, but I ate the bar,' nine-year-old Alison Rielly defended her blatant wastage, calling on mams across the world to learn how to make nicer lunches, like chicken nuggets and chips, and if they could include open sachets of ketchup with them too.

'And a can of Coca-Cola,' the daughter of two added, making an icky face at the now spent ham sandwiches wrapped in tinfoil her mother was now cursing over. 'I don't like the chunks of butter in them,' she said, defending her reasoning with an almost valid point.

'Oh, but you ate the Kit Kat bar handy enough,' her mother retorted, knowing deep down that if she didn't include the chocolate treat her child would starve to death in school, and she would face criminal neglect charges and the possibility of social services taking her daughter away.

'Now, that doesn't seem like a bad idea, but I'd miss having to rush together a packed lunch at 10 to nine in the morning while trying to get ▨▨ ▨▨▨ ▨▨▨ ▨▨▨▨▨ ▨▨▨▨▨ ▨▨▨▨▨▨▨▨ before deciding to just repackage today's lunch for tomorrow. 'It's not like she's going to eat the bloody thing anyway, the ungrateful little …'

SCIENTISTS 'VERY CLOSE' TO DEVELOPING TV REMOTE CONTROL THAT DOESN'T LOSE BATTERY COVER

SCIENTISTS AT MIT have confirmed that the world will see television remote controls that don't end up with a lost battery cover in just a matter of decades, *WWN* reports.

Missing battery covers have long been the bane of man's existence, and experts now believe a new technology in development will eradicate the problem for good.

'We've been working on this since the late 1970s and have finally solved the issue, but the technology is just not quite there yet,' lead researcher Dr Daniel Reeves told *WWN*.

It is understood that most television remote controls lose their battery cover within the first year of use, with a usual duct or Sellotape solution improvised by the user until the sticky side fades and eventually falls off, leaving behind a sticky dirt-loving rim around the casing.

'The batteries then fall out very easily when knocked over and can cause high levels of stress and cursing in the user in question,' Dr Reeves explains. 'Sometimes the batteries are then put back in the wrong way

and damage the remote control itself, leading to further fucks being given.'

The new technology in development will prevent the battery case from coming loose by quantum fusion, however, such a process is costly, and scientists expect the first TV remote control that doesn't lose its case will cost well into the thousands of euros.

'It could cost anywhere up to $7,000, but we believe it is worth it to avoid the stress of losing the batteries and trying to find them under the fucking chair,' Dr Reeves concluded.

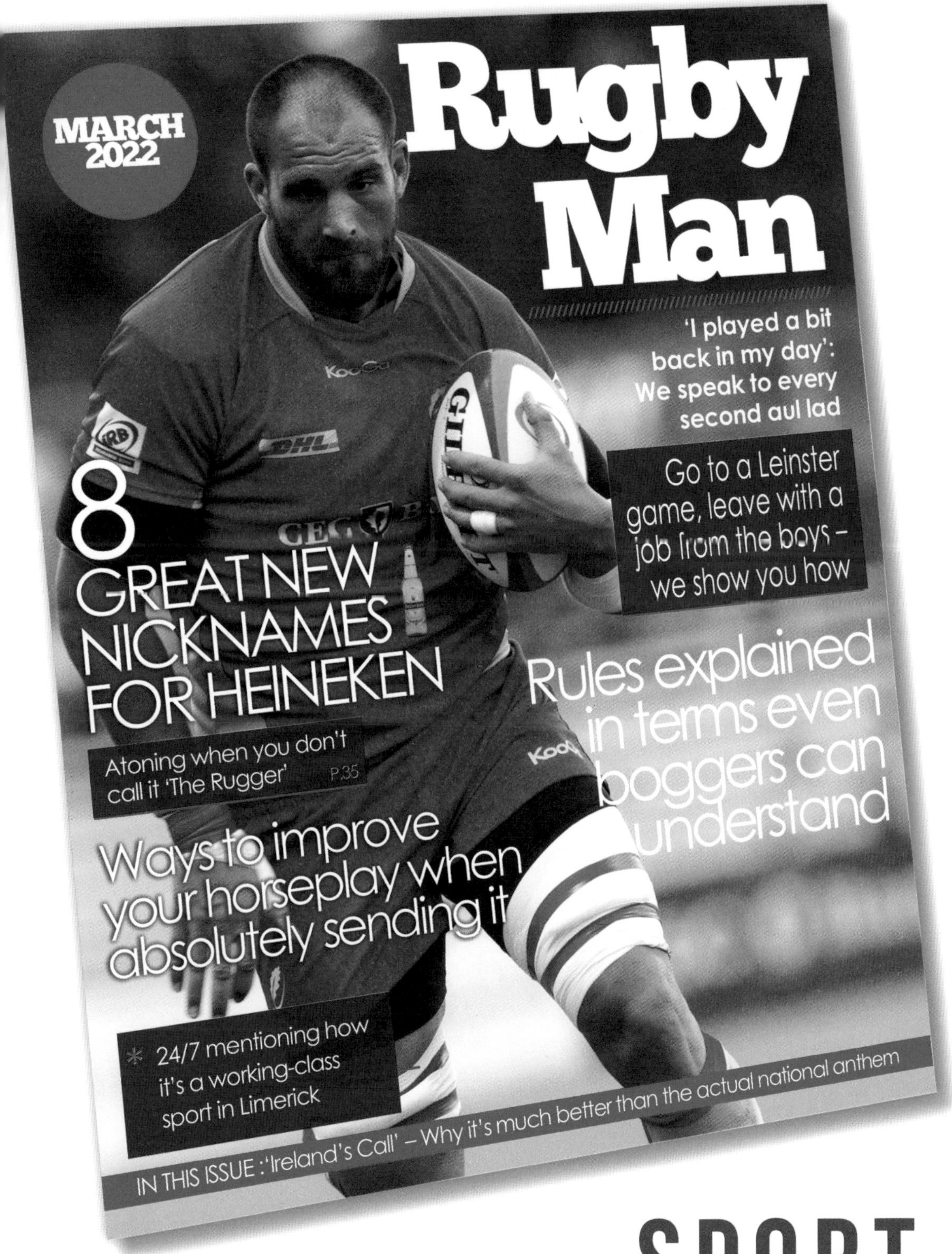

MARCH 2022

Rugby Man

'I played a bit back in my day': We speak to every second aul lad

Go to a Leinster game, leave with a job from the boys – we show you how

8 GREAT NEW NICKNAMES FOR HEINEKEN

Atoning when you don't call it 'The Rugger' P.35

Rules explained in terms even boggers can understand

Ways to improve your horseplay when absolutely sending it

* 24/7 mentioning how it's a working-class sport in Limerick

IN THIS ISSUE : 'Ireland's Call' – Why it's much better than the actual national anthem

SPORT

BOXING

'I WON'T TAKE MONEY FROM DRINK OR GAMBLING BRANDS' SAYS PAL OF KINAHAN CARTEL BOSS

SPEAKING at the launch of his new energy drink, pillar of the boxing world and mental health enthusiast Tyson Fury revealed he will never endorse gambling, alcohol or drug brands, excluding his close pal and cartel boss Daniel Kinahan.

'I won't take money from drink, gambling or CBD drug brands, as they cause mental health issues,' Fury began, 'but I have no problem hanging around and getting pictures taken with someone the High Court in Ireland called a senior figure in organised crime on a global level,' he added, holding up his new energy drink containing questionable ingredients

to be marketed to the 16–25 demographic.

Speaking with his mouth at the launch of his latest merch, the son-of-two turned down 'millions of dollars' in recent years to advertise alcohol, gambling and CBD brands, but didn't expand on whether he'd continue to advertise Mr Kinahan as a reputable boxing promoter, knowing full well his real position in society.

'Yeah, the Kinahan cartel is allegedly responsible for thousands of deaths from drugs, not to mention the murders, beatings, money laundering, tax evasion, racketeering, extortion and its stranglehold on the boxing

world,' a source close to the Gypsy King stated, 'but as long as the cartel is not affecting mental health, then Tyson is on board.'

The boxer's Furocity energy drink will go on sale in Iceland stores on Wednesday, and comes in a number of flavours including Sour Apples, Black and Blue Kneecaps, Cherry Picked Morals and Total Hypocrite.

'WE'VE NOTHING TO HIDE', CONFIRM QATAR WORLD CUP OFFICIALS DRAPING COVERS OVER DEAD CONSTRUCTION WORKER

SPREADING OUT THEIR ARMS and legs as much as possible to obscure the view of anyone who happens upon the scene, Qatari World Cup 2022 officials have stressed once again that zero human rights issues have been experienced by migrant workers after some minors reforms.

Fresh from arresting and releasing two Norwegian journalists for 'trespassing', Qatari officials were keen to highlight the official version of what workers' lives are like in the country, describing it as a cross between *Sex and the City* and *Friends*.

'That? Oh it's just a decorative cloth we keep our footballs under, and before you ask, no, you can't see them,' said World Cup official Hassan Al

Thawadi. 'Anyway, what was I saying? Oh yeah, the workers, they're like the friends on *Friends*, they have so much spare time, they just hang around in nice big apartments all day. It's like, do they even have a job? Haha.'

'No, this other cloth is where we keep the cones and bibs for training,'

added the official, before parachuting in an emergency supply of famous ex-footballers to act as ambassadors for cover-ups.

'We wholeheartedly deny that David has been paid €130 million to endorse the Qatar regime. He sold out his morals and soul for significantly less than that,' confirmed a spokesperson for David Beckham, who was in Qatar to speak highly of the quality of Qatari sheets, which absolutely aren't covering any bodies at this moment in time.

Qatari authorities then arrested several more journalists for damaging 'private property' after they checked the pulse of a Nepalese construction worker who had died of heatstroke.

SCIENTISTS UNCOVER LONG-LOST IRISH FOOTBALL LEAGUE

RESEARCHERS from across the country claim to be close to proving the existence of an Irish football league, after decades of searching for what many believed to be the 'Bigfoot' of football.

'You would hear rumours, campfire stories and urban legends about this so-called League of Ireland, where teams would compete in much the same way as teams in other countries,' said Dr Owen Goll, head of the team that uncovered irrefutable proof of the league.

'A snippet of footage would appear on social media, a headline here, a GIF there. People would claim to have a cousin who had a try-out for Shamrock Rovers, aul lads would swear blind they played half-

back for Bohs in the '70s. That kind of thing. Turns out, they may not have been lying.'

Although evidence mounts of the existence of an ongoing multi-division footballing league right here on the island of Ireland, sceptics point to the lack of mainstream coverage of any of the games as ongoing proof that the whole thing is 'mere fairy stories'.

'You mean to tell me that there's live football on a constant basis here in Ireland and RTÉ just happens to never show any of it?' scoffed one fan, who supports Manchester City because

> **'You would hear rumours, campfire stories and urban legends about this so-called League of Ireland'**

there are no home-grown teams for him to follow.

Meanwhile, RTÉ has stated that, should the existence of a League of Ireland be proven, they'll gladly televise it, providing it draws decent viewership figures in a number of key demographics and at a time that suits their schedule, nobody else's.

Cost of Living Tips

Only use electricity for special occasions like Christmas Day.

WHAT WOULD A SUPER BOWL-STYLE HALF-TIME SHOW LOOK LIKE AT THE ALL-IRELAND FINAL?

GROWING our indigenous sports is important, and what better way to get more eyeballs on them than with a stunning high-octane half-time show like they have at the Super Bowl?

WWN has obtained declassified documents from the GAA that outline their plans for such an event, and you will see from the details below that it's set to be a mind-blowing entertainment spectacular!

The show would be introduced by Marty Morrissey from the Croke Park skywalk. Marty suddenly leaps from the edge as the crowd gasps in horror. But fear not, Marty unfurls a parachute with a canopy reading 'It's GAA Time, Bitches!'

A series of parade floats showcasing the peak of Irish and GAA culture make their way onto the pitch, including floats made entirely out of coleslaw, turf and tinfoil.

Dancers carrying petrol-doused hurls gyrate to a specially penned All-Ireland Final song performed by Daniel O'Donnell. Daniel then launches several sliotars that have been set on fire by the hurls. Casualties are expected, but what a spectacle it will be!

The lyrics to Daniel's 'Puc Me Now' finish, and rumours are it's a banger worthy of Cardi B.

A shape-shifting stage will prove a visual delight, as it converts for a moment into a giant UFC octagon

to pay tribute to the GAA's treasured pastime of shemozzles.

And just when you thought it couldn't get any better, the goals at either end begin to rumble as rockets fixed to the posts free them from the earth, setting a course for the International Space Station, where the two captains on the day will contest the throw-in before descending back down to earth.

MOTOR RACING

F1 PIT TEAM HIRE MOTHER WHO HAS SCHOOL DROP-OFF DOWN TO 5.5 SECONDS

MERCEDES HAS HIRED Dublin mother-of-three Bernie Phelan to head up their pit crew after being impressed by her showings at the front gates of St Andrew of the Blessed Breakfast Roll National School.

'There are so many minor adjustments that rely on quick, precise processes to avoid complete disaster,' Mercedes CEO Toto Wolff said of dropping and picking up kids as part of the school run, identifying clear transferable skills that make Phelan the ideal hire.

'I'm usually shouting, "Belts on now yis little pricks! Right, have ya got your lunch? Coats on. Get in now or I'm leaving without you" at the kids, so I'll see no real change when I'm working with the mechanics and drivers in the pit lane,' a happy Phelan revealed.

A rare school-run talent, Phelan's airtight 5.5-second drop-off routine manages to still include small talk with other parents and warm, appreciative nods to her children's teachers and threats of violence to her little darlings if they act up, leading to speculation that changing four bald tyres in under six seconds should be a piece of piss.

'And if Lewis Hamilton gives me any lip, he'll be getting the same death stare I gave my youngest this morning when he told me at the school gate he forgot to bring his autumn leaf poster with him,' offered a cleared-eyed Phelan.

UPDATE: Phelan has already got into a heated altercation with Hamilton after he forgot to bring his helmet to the track. However, the Dublin mother had a spare one on her for these exact circumstances.

WITH THE ANNOUNCEMENT that he is to compete in Waterford's inaugural MudderFucker triathlon contested on land, sea and saddle, local man Gary Lymons has been open about his hopes of developing an entirely new personality.

'I could become one of them lads who always talks about doing the triathlon. People will say, "Jaysus fair play to ya", and then they'll ask me about all the training I do,' said Lymons, in the sort of monotone voice that only a dedicated athlete who has

MAN COMPETING IN TRIATHLON HOPING IT HELPS HIM DEVELOP PERSONALITY

used up all their natural serotonin could muster.

Lymons is the first to admit that he has failed over his 32 years to craft any entertaining anecdotes or witty observations to deploy during conversations, but triathlons could now propel him to the forefront of entertainment.

'On the plus side, training for them will distract from the fact that we're all going to die someday,' the laugh riot continued.

In preparation for his new role as an interesting person, Lymons is trial wearing the free T-shirt you get for doing a triathlon at every social engagement over the next year.

EXCLUSIVE

EXTREME CROAGH PATRICKING: INSIDE IRELAND'S MOST ELITE SPORT

CROAGH PATRICK ain't your Mam and Dad's staunch Catholic pilgrimage anymore; it's 760 metres of gruelling, adrenaline-filled endurance that will push even the hardest of hard bastards to their limits. This Is Extreme Croagh Patricking!

Devised by Mayo's tourist board following years of dwindling crowds to the site for a bit of a pray and a steep walk, Extreme Croagh Patrick (or XCP for short) has revolutionised The Reek thanks to a growing market of extreme athletes who also happen to be devout atheists.

While these people were initially more inclined to test themselves with 'Hell and Back' and 'Tough Mudder'-style events, the opening of Croagh Patrick to non-Catholics has them trekking to Clew Bay in their thousands, although some religious traditions remain to push people out of their comfort zones.

'Devout Catholics would sometimes climb Croagh Patrick barefoot, so we've kept that because it is metal as fuck,' said Arthur Murran, one of the originators of XCP.

'Legend tells of St Patrick banishing snakes from the area, so at around the 300-metre mark, we unleash a bunch of vipers into the grass to keep people on their toes. You must complete the climb without water, except for what gets flicked on you by a priest along the way. You have to carry a cross up the last 100 metres, and then at the top we have a bunch of lads dressed like Cromwellian soldiers who chase you back down to the bottom at high speeds. Say your prayers, this is one wild ride!'

Competitors who manage to complete the gruelling feat are awarded a special green cloak and mitre hat, as well as all the communion they can eat.

NEGOTIATORS CALLED IN AS CODY STILL HOLDING ONTO SHEFFLIN'S HAND

SKILLED POLICE NEGOTIATORS are making no headway with Kilkenny hurling manager Brian Cody despite entering a third day of pleading with him to let go of Galway hurling manager Henry Shefflin's hand.

'Intense death stares that would reduce a man to a teary, terrified puddle usually only last 15 seconds max, but what Mr Cody is doing here is unprecedented,' explained an FBI expert flown in to assist Gardaí.

The heated handshake occurred at the end of Galway's victory against Kilkenny, secured by a controversial last-minute free, but Cody remains in place on the turf of Pearse Stadium, fused to his former player.

'There's no way to sugar-coat this – it's day three. He's soiled himself several times, and yet has displayed no need or desire for food or sleep. Mr Shefflin, on the other hand, hasn't stopped screaming "help" since this started,' added the FBI agent.

A number of elaborate ruses have been employed by Gardaí in an attempt

to extract Shefflin safely. 'We had one of the lads dress as the Liam MacCarthy Cup, we offered him a lucrative after-dinner speaking engagement, but he's falling for nothing,' explained one desperate guard.

FOOTBALL

HOW WE THINK THE WORLD CUP PANNED OUT

WWN HAS PUSHED print news to its very limit, bringing the medium to new, never-before-reached heights.

However, try as we might, we have struggled to figure out how to live report new ink onto pages, detailing the exploits at the 2022 World Cup in Qatar as they unfold.

So we have used our rudimentary foundation in quantum physics to bring up uncannily accurate predictions for the tournament. Here's how it will go:

- Having hundreds of thousands of football fans descend on an area the size of Dublin will go off without a hitch – congrats in advance, Qatar.
- Fans will struggle to watch their teams play knowing they're playing in stadiums where migrant workers died. No, sorry, that's a typo; they'll be fine with it.
- Elsewhere, FIFA executives' bank accounts will look fantastic.
- A high-profile player will be sent home by their coach. This will be due to a highly scandalous incident … We'll go with being caught wiping their arse with the Qatari flag shortly after sleeping with the manager's wife?
- England will be unbearable. A player will write on social media, 'Dear Santa, all I want for Christmas is the World Cup'. You will vomit in your mouth.
- Media reporting will insist on how Qatar is actually lovely, and not at all the intolerant country people made it out to be – in a direct repeat of their coverage of the 2018 World Cup in Russia.
- There will be a monumental referee blunder, an injustice greater than all in human history. There will be a very rational reaction to this by pundits and supporters, and it will not be blown out of proportion.
- Goals will be scored. Shots will be saved. At the very end, a group of multimillionaires will raise a gold trophy in the air as they celebrate the fact that before the tournament they agreed to a deal with their FA to be paid even more millions if they won the whole thing.

> **'Dear Santa, all I want for Christmas is the World Cup'**

On This Day

1760: The Battle of Carrickfergus sees French forces capture the town, with locals forced to live under the hell of nice food, good wine and beautiful women.

21 February

127

FOOTBALL

PACKIE BONNER ADMITS HE SOMETIMES DIVES ONTO SOFA LIKE HE'S SAVING A PENALTY

LEGENDARY Republic of Ireland goalkeeper Packie Bonner has opened up about his struggles with leaping six feet to the right to bat away an imaginary penno, stating that he may need hip surgery if he keeps it up around the house.

Now in his 60s, Bonner admits that he probably shouldn't be recreating the iconic moment that helped Ireland reach the quarter-finals of Italia '90 but, every now and then, he hears George Hamilton in his head and goes for it.

'I try to land on the sofa or the bed or at least a few couch cushions or something,' said Bonner, walking with a limp after inadvertently landing on the edge of a coffee table earlier in the day.

'But the landings are getting rougher, so I ration them out more. I used to do the dive for people all the time if they were kicking a ball around and asking for a photo. Now I just tell them to take a photo of me standing up with my arms stretched high and Photoshop it in, I'm not diving on that hard ground in the middle of winter, fuck that.'

Bonner added that his save is not the only flashback he has to that fateful World Cup, as he also instinctively makes a fist anytime a passing bald man reminds him of 'that little Schillaci prick'.

MICHAEL TEELING from Waterford has beaten off stiff competition from around the world to secure his record-setting third World Pocket Billiards trophy this weekend, with a stunning display of testicular manipulation that wowed judges and delighted fans.

'Go on Mick, get them good and stretchy,' yelled a supporter late in the final heat of the competition, as 18-year-old Teeling skillfully fondled his balls through the pockets of his tracksuit while standing on stage in Osaka, Tokyo.

Teeling scored 10s across the board (10 for amount of ball holdage, 10 for duration of ball holdage and 10 for absolute brazenness of ball holdage when in the company of others), and his trainers praised the youth's

WATERFORD TEEN CLINCHES POCKET BILLIARDS TROPHY FOR THIRD CONSECUTIVE YEAR

dedication to the sport as key to victory.

'A lot of young lads grow out of boxer volleyball when they pass 16, but Michael here has stuck with it,' said Teeling's emotional coach, himself a two-time under-21 tonsil hockey champion.

'Look how he passed his scrotum from one hand to the other without removing his elbow-deep wrists from his pockets. Look how unfazed he is by the little old lady sitting beside him. Look how focused he is. It's just him and his balls. A beautiful thing.'

Judges awarded Teeling a €500,000 cheque and a trophy for his win but declined to shake his hand.

WWN GUIDE

PRETENDING TO TAKE UP A NEW SPORT JUST TO GET A BIT OF TIME AWAY FROM THE FAMILY, A GUIDE

STRESSED OUT, or just need a break every now and then? Have you considered completely faking a sudden reigniting of an interest in pursuing sport? Take it from these parents who swear by the clandestine life hack.

- 'I'd piled on a few pounds, and used to be mad into the cycling, so I said to the wife I'd be taking it back up on Saturday mornings, if she could be so kind as to take the girls to camogie and the boys to soccer. Sure, buying all the gear again cost a bit, but you can't put a price on sitting completely undisturbed in a café for an hour.' – Conal, Waterford

- 'It helps if you can rope in a friend as an alibi. Mine is Áine. She always mentions the tennis games when she sees my hubby, but I'm just down the wine bar cackling to myself. That reminds me, I have to buy a fake trophy. After a bottle of merlot, I said I won the Maureen McCarthy Memorial Trophy, whoever she is.' – Meabh, Kildare

- 'I'm into competitive sumo wrestling now, apparently. The times for it are very unreliable, you never know when they'll have training or a tournament, although it usually syncs up perfectly with all the movies in the cinema I want to go watch.' – Trevor, Dublin

- 'Don't overdo the stories about the sport, I made the mistake of telling himself how much I enjoyed it and being the supportive prick that he is, he wanted to bring the kids along to a netball game. Honestly, play the enjoyment part down, you've no idea how much money it costs to pay extras to pretend they're in a netball league. Netball courts are hard to come by too.' – Shona, Cork

- 'We told the kids we were playing mixed doubles, sure the eldest can babysit now, she's eight. We head off to whatever car park the dogging group is meeting at. No, she hasn't copped how odd it is for a tennis league to play at 2 a.m.' – Tom and Caroline, Meath

---

Your Census Time Capsules

'Whoever is living in my house now, don't hang up that fecking phone, I'm still on hold with Eir customer service.'
– Jenny (41), Clare

FOOTBALL

HERE ARE THE EVENTS TAKING PLACE AROUND THE COUNTRY TO MARK SAIPAN'S 20TH ANNIVERSARY

'THE SAIPAN INCIDENT' has reached its 20th anniversary, and what was once a one-day set of commemorations has expanded into a week-long festival of festering and forlorn fury for the Irish economy to properly maximise tourism revenue.

Here are all the events taking place to mark Roy Keane's controversial exit from the 2002 World Cup:

- Mass head shavings are to be offered free of charge by participating barbers.
- Acknowledging the divisive nature of the legacy left behind by Ireland's definitive civil war, there will be effigies burned of both Keane and Mick McCarthy. To find out where your nearest effigy is, go to saipancommemorations.ie/effigies.
- Rage Like Roy – anger mismanagement workshops will be held at various locations, where people with bubbling discontentment will be taught to let it all bubble over, Keane style.
- Several parades will take place across the country on rock-hard car park-like surfaces by men carrying training cones and wearing bibs. To fully replicate Saipan conditions, someone will forget to bring footballs.
- A Guinness world record attempt will take place in Cork, where Labrador owners will be staging the largest 'walking your Labrador while absolutely fucking livid' event in history.
- Some of the festivities will serve as a refresher for Leaving Cert history students, who will have an additional exam paper dedicated solely to Saipan this year.
- The government has released a stream of funding aimed at providing extra resources and medical care for football fans who still insist we would have won the World Cup if Keane had stayed on.
- A wreath will be laid by the FAI at the meeting room in Saipan where Keane attempted to assassinate McCarthy's character. A separate wreath will be placed on Irish newspapers, where teammates tried to assassinate Keane's character.
- President Michael D. Higgins will read his poem 'Shitstorm in Saipan', commemorating the darkest day in Irish history, live on the *Six One* news.
- Several large dartboards with John Delaney's face on them have been placed at various locations, although this is not believed to be connected to official commemorations.
- *The Keane Monologues* will be staged at The Abbey, where a host of Ireland's acting royalty will take turns interpreting Keane's Saipan rant, including the immortal words 'Mick, you're a liar. You're a fucking wanker. I didn't rate you as a player, I don't rate you as a manager, and I don't rate you as a person. You're a fucking wanker and you can stick your World Cup up your arse. The only reason I have any dealings with you is that somehow you are the manager of my country! You can stick it up your bollocks.'
- Enya, Bono and Daniel O'Donnell have released a charity single called 'Sorrow at Saipan', which samples Keane's rant, with all proceeds going to the victims of the war in Saipan.

TECHNOLOGY

ROONEY–VARDY TRIAL FIRST TO USE VAR

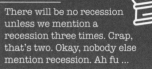

THE AUSTERE wood-panelled Victorian courtroom housing the libel case between Coleen Rooney and Rebekah Vardy, which kicks off live on Sky Sports, is to make history by implementing a first for legal technology with the use of VAR.

Replacing the usual back and forth between a judge and the legal representatives of the defence and prosecution, Premier League referees will be tasked with having the final say on any controversial legal arguments or the entering of evidence into the case.

Cameras and large screens have been installed in the court ahead of Rooney and Vardy facing off, with both parties encouraged to surround, harangue and hassle the judge, swearing blindly when they disagree with a ruling – which will prompt VAR

officials to review a decision from their remote TV van outside the courts.

'We've 40 camera angles and we're trained professionals; nothing will get past us. We'll draw red lines across WhatsApp conversations and Instagram stories to see if anything

was well offside in terms of friendship, trust and defamation,' confirmed VAR official Mike Dean.

Being a legal first, VAR's implementation has not been without its hiccups, with those in the gallery already chanting 'the judge is a wanker' when a request to enter a number of personal texts into evidence that would have been full of juicy gossip was shot down.

Earlier, stewards at the trial were criticised for their lax security measures after two streakers and one cat entered the field of legal play, with dozens more boozed-up and ticketless fans barging through the turnstiles at the courts.

PUB-TIME CONVERSATION between a number of friends in Waterford ground to a halt today after Sean McCann asked if anyone had caught the cricket yesterday, opening himself up to 45 minutes of fairly sectarian slagging.

'No, we didn't, who won? The DUP or the Royal Fusiliers?' asked Alan Wainwright, who himself has had a prod-bomb or two thrown his way with a name like that.

'I must have missed that, what channel was it on? Sky Orange?' wondered Declan Meegan, who actually likes cricket but would never do something so stupid as to admit it in public.

'Wait a second, if you were watching the cricket then does that mean you didn't get a chance to make excuses for genocidal acts carried out by the British Empire over their tyrannical reign? While sticking your tongue up Prince Andrew's hole? Because you usually never miss that,' mocked Michael Dignam, for whom talking about anything other than this fair nation is considered treasonous.

ABSOLUTE PROTESTANT WONDERING IF YOU WERE WATCHING THE CRICKET

'With talk like that, you should be forced to go around and hand back all the money you got at your communion,' added Gerry Adams, no relation to the other lad.

McCann weathered his slagging well, allowing the lads to settle down and watch the English Premier League on the pub telly.

FOOTBALL

CHELSEA FANS WAITING TO SEE WHAT BILLIONAIRE THEY HAVE TO SUCK UP TO NEXT

WITH CHELSEA OWNER Roman Abramovich tearfully selling his beloved club in a very genuine and must-be-taken-at-face-value bid to raise much-needed funding for the besieged people of Ukraine, fans of the Blues are wondering: who steps up now?

Currently on the market for a mere €3 billion, the storied London club is being eyed up by the following potential buyers:

Amal abul-Al Jawardi

With many questioning Abramovich's ties to the brutal Russian regime, many feel the time is right for an owner from Saudi Arabia such as Mr abul-Al Jawardi. The Saudi billionaire has been frequently photographed with numerous heads of state and, as such, his record in human rights abuses and the covering-up of same should be peerless.

Michael Mahon

Staying closer to home, Irish billionaire Michael Mahon could make an offer on the club he's followed since they started winning trophies. Mahon was believed to have links with the Irish drug scene but appears in recent years to have made the bulk of his money posing for pictures with boxers in Dubai. Chelsea fans can look forward to explaining that one!

John 'Big Hoss' Campbell

Yeehaw! Perhaps the club will go to Texan oil tycoon and gun lobbyist John Campbell, who earned the nickname 'Big Hoss' after realising he liked the sound of it and ordering everyone to call him that. Campbell has expressed an interest in the club, stating that it would make a nice addition to his portfolio, which includes sending rockets to Pluto 'for the hell of it'.

Broman Brabramanoviss

A late contender for owner has arrived, and this one is a mystery. Whoever Broman Brabramanoviss is, he's wealthy, likes living in London and is definitely not Russian. It even says it on his LinkedIn – 'not Russian'. Well, as long as he pumps money into the club, most Chelsea fans won't look too closely at where it's coming from. Welcome aboard!

THE MINISTER FOR SPORT has been asked to provide better support for casual five-a-side football players after one Waterford man told of his crippling PTSD, *WWN* can reveal.

Shane Trainor spoke of harrowing flashbacks to primary school lunchtime football games when he was picked last, following a similar incident at an over-45s five-a-side kickabout.

'Okay, I kick like my legs are made out of drunk space hoppers, but that's still no reason to pick me last,' explained Trainor, fighting back the tears.

'I know the lads want to win the game, but picking the worst player is an inclusive statement of intent. I felt like I was right back there when I was five being laughed at because I stepped on the ball, fell

MAN PICKED LAST FOR FIVE-A-SIDE HAS TROUBLING FLASHBACK TO JUNIOR INFANTS PLAYGROUND

over and lost a tooth,' Trainor added bravely, making a gnawing face as if remembering the pain.

Speaking of the triggering incident, Martin Grange, widely regarded as the

Zinedine Zidane of the Tramore five-a-side circuit, sympathised with Trainor.

'At the end of the day this isn't war or famine, it's much more important than that, and Trainor can go and shite if he thinks I'd pick him. Sure I could stick him in nets, but he's hands on him like melted jelly, and then what, have him out of goals? With lungs on him like an asthmatic fart?' offered Grange.

Responding to Trainor's pleas, Minister Catherine Martin has proposed an app linking the country's worst players with each other to create a five-a-side team aptly named PaddyLast.

PARALYMPICS

RUSSIAN PARALYMPIAN STANDS UP FROM WHEELCHAIR, STORMS OUT OF INTERVIEW OVER BANNING

On This Day

2015: Gay people in Ireland show straight people how to do weddings properly.

16
November

FURIOUS after the entire Russian and Belarusian teams were today banned from the Beijing Winter Paralympics after the International Paralympic Committee reversed its original decision, para ice hockey athlete Yuri Smirnoff began cursing at the assembled press before suddenly standing up from his wheelchair, walking away and flipping reporters the middle finger in disgust, WWN has learned.

The two-time gold medallist Paralympian, who the Russian Olympic Committee claimed had been wheelchair-bound since birth, stated he was very disappointed with the decision, and called the committee a 'shower of lousy bastards' while leaving his chair behind and then kicking over a metal bin on his way out the door.

'He was obviously very angry and forgot himself,' one eyewitness believes, 'so much so that he forgot he was paralysed from the waist down. His handlers later claimed he was doping, but even Russian steroids aren't that good.'

> **'Some of them could not walk unaided, and now they can – God must be on Russia's side'**

Following the decision, several more Russian Paralympians also left Beijing without their specialised sporting equipment, sparking rumours that they weren't actually Paralympians at all.

'It's a miracle!' a spokesperson for the Russian Paralympic team insisted, likening the walkout to an 'act of God': 'before, some of them could not walk unaided, and now they can – God must be on Russia's side'.

However, upon their arrival in Russia earlier this morning, all returning athletes were immediately conscripted to fight in the invasion of Ukraine.

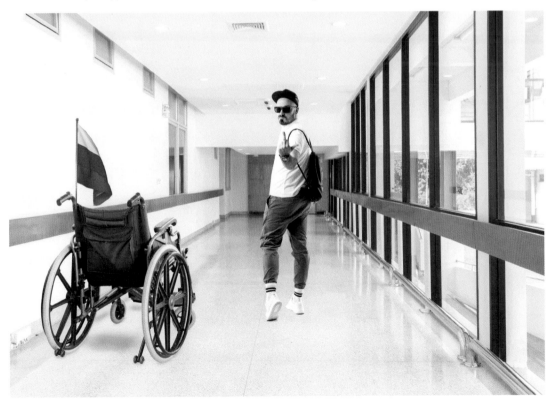

WINTER OLYMPIANS NO IDEA THEY'RE COMPETING ON TOP OF MASS UIGHUR GRAVE

HOPEFUL, determined and proud Olympians competing in the Beijing Winter Olympics, which formally launched today with a glittering opening ceremony, are completely unaware that they're competing on top of a mass Uighur grave, *WWN* understands.

'Do you mean like a figurative or a literal grave? I'm not cool with either, but obviously one is easier than the other to put out of your mind,' offered one bewildered participant, who admitted to being surprised at the great big shoulder-shrugging from the world in the build-up to a games taking place in a country that imprisoned over 1 million people from an ethnic minority.

> **'Don't expect us to grow a spine unless some speed skater trips over an actual spine poking through the ice'**

'I know that with host nations often a ski slope will be artificially constructed, but like made out of scaffolding, right? Made out of manufactured stuff, right? Or else that bumpy patch as I approached the jump might have been ...' a horrified Olympian said, a realisation dawning on them.

Leading nations vying for a place near the top of the medals table have confirmed that such human rights issues will only blight the games if their nation underperforms, in which case all fervent national pride will be discarded in favour of stressing how the games took place 'under a cloud' and, if anything, deep down they always felt that China shouldn't have been allowed to host.

'Yeah, don't expect us to grow a spine unless some speed skater trips over an actual spine poking through the ice,' confirmed every major Olympics sponsor.

Elsewhere, in response to questions over whether China is an appropriate host for the games, the uncompromising and incorruptible International Olympics Committee said 'Weather? Yes, it's lovely isn't it?'

BOXING

CONOR MCGREGOR RECALLS ASSASSINATION ATTEMPT ON VLADIMIR PUTIN

CONOR MCGREGOR has sought to clarify events around a photo of him with Russian leader Vladimir Putin that has resurfaced in the wake of the latter's invasion of Ukraine.

Humble, and not one to praise himself, the brave Dubliner revealed that there was more than meets the eye when it came to the cheerful and happy photo taken at the World Cup Final, under which he wrote, 'This man is one of the greatest leaders of our time and I was honoured to attend such a landmark event alongside him'.

'Calling him one of the great leaders of the time was actually a ploy. You see, I was going to choke him out, make him brown bread, but what you don't see on the other side of the camera is a nuke directly trained on

my cojones – the risk was too great,' McGregor now recalls.

'There was never a good time, despite being a uniquely skilled MMA assassin. That's why there are other photos of me sitting with him and watching a game. I did try, though. I offered him plutonium tea, but he said he didn't touch that Lyons muck.'

'A full stadium – that's too many witnesses. As a lethal weapon, my senses are highly attuned to these

things, so I knew he was a wrong 'un, which is why I faked looking like a pig in shit, but it isn't as it initially looked,' confirmed McGregor of a damning photo.

Supporters have come out to defend the photo.

'How was he supposed to know in 2018 that he was posing with someone who was a convicted criminal,' supporters of Russian leader Putin, who had bombed Chechnya and Syria, invaded Georgia and annexed Crimea at this point, said.

HORSERACING IRELAND TO TRIAL SPOILERS

IN A BID to increase performance using downforce, racehorses will soon have to be fitted with carbon-fibre horse spoilers, Horse Racing Ireland has confirmed today following their annual general meeting.

Spoilers will be riveted into the animal's hindquarters, allowing for the air to force down the horse's backside and maintain a better grip on the racecourse, with further attachments like alloy horseshoes and carbon monoxide boosters that build up the animals flatulence which can then be released mid-race by the jockey to increase propulsion.

'Much like Formula One motor racing, we strive to get the very best out of the animal with attachments,' a Horse Racing Ireland statement read today. 'An average of 7,000 Irish racehorses are destroyed by trainers and stud farms every year due to them not being able to run fast enough, so this will give those destined for the boat a fighting chance at not ending up on some Italian or French person's dinner menu.'

Already trialled by Irish horse trainer P.J. Bulmers, the new spoilers have shown some promising results on the test track.

'Our main goal here is to make as much money as humanly possible from these creatures by making

them run as fast as they possibly can before disposing of them like a grubby face mask,' Mr Bulmers said, welcoming the new add-on. 'We'd replace their hooves with wheels if we could, but sure look it, we have to adhere to this animal welfare bollocks.'

In light of the news, several alcohol and gambling brands have already struck advertising deals for their brands to appear on the new horse spoilers.

BOXING

TYSON FURY'S sixth-round humbling of Dillian Whyte in front of a massive Wembley crowd has been marred by supporters' criticism of the quality of illicit street drugs on offer at the fight, *WWN* Sports understands.

'Don't get me wrong, happy days for Tyson, he's in a league of his own, but I just wasn't getting much of a buzz on,' confirmed one spectator, who believes the Kinahan cartel and the sanctions imposed on them will continue to damage boxing.

POOR QUALITY OF DRUGS AT FURY FIGHT TRACED TO KINAHAN SANCTIONS

'If you can't watch the boxing while enjoying a decent baggy, then boxing selling its soul to a drug cartel was all for nothing,' confirmed one cartel fan, who won't consider attending another fight unless the

nose candy standard went back to pre-Kinahan-sanction levels.

Fans overwhelmingly enjoyed being in the presence of a fighter who is defining this era of heavyweight boxing, however the same can't be said for their enjoyment of the snow sold to them by dealers.

'I've no idea what this shit was cut with. I'd rather snort my mother's ashes. If anyone ever doubted boxing has cut its ties with the Kinahans, well I'm telling you this shit coke is proof they have,' confirmed another spectator, whose body chemistry was so unaffected by the drugs available on the night that he didn't even feel like glassing someone.

'It's got nothing to do with me, I just focus on my boxing,' confirmed Tyson Fury on his drive home from Wembley, where he passed the scene of a motorway crash and ignored an injured man begging him to ring an ambulance.

SPORTING AUTHORITIES STARTING TO THINK ATHLETES CLASHING HEADS NOT A GOOD THING

AFTER MUCH DELIBERATION, sporting authorities within the games of rugby union and football are coming round to the idea that athletes getting repeatedly hit in the

head might not be a good thing, mere decades after they were first alerted to the problem.

'We found that ignoring the problem initially made it go away,' explained one sporting executive, 'but as soon as ex-pros with signs of dementia came for our wallets, we knew we had to hire an intimidating team of lawyers, y'know, to show we're fully behind these lads.'

The issue of concussion in sport has steadily risen in priority for authorities and has, in recent years, become such a serious issue that governing bodies

have pledged to put more money and resources towards it in an effort to appear like they care.

'We care right up to the point where we'd be held liable, monetarily speaking, but we'd be happy to send out one video in a tweet on the same day every year to make it look like we care? Okay, two, surely that's enough,' added the executive.

'In the meantime, we just ask any athletes who are about to develop any debilitating conditions that can be linked to heading or tackling to hold off until we sign the next round of lucrative broadcasting and sponsorship deals.'

Elsewhere, proper hard men everywhere have indicated that the business of making the game safer for players is a whole load of flowery nonsense, and that 'the world has gone mad'.

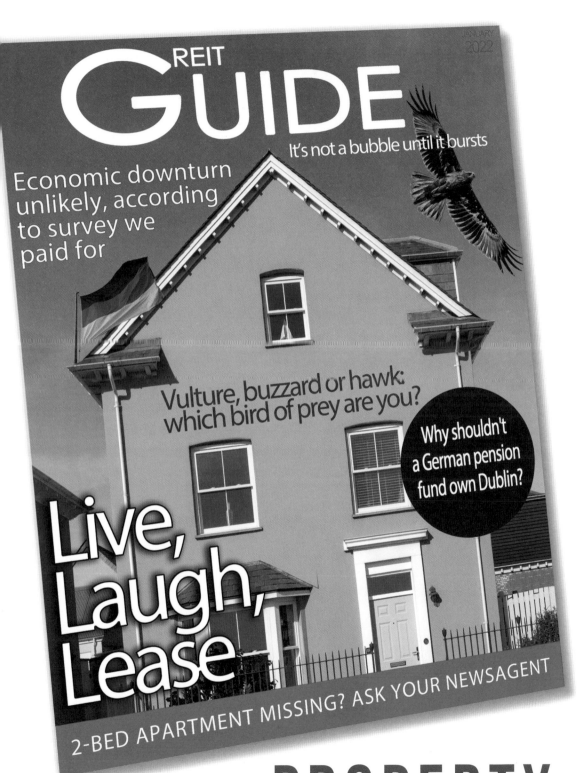

JANUARY 2022

REIT GUIDE

It's not a bubble until it bursts

Economic downturn unlikely, according to survey we paid for

Vulture, buzzard or hawk: which bird of prey are you?

Why shouldn't a German pension fund own Dublin?

Live, Laugh, Lease

2-BED APARTMENT MISSING? ASK YOUR NEWSAGENT

PROPERTY

FINANCE

'WE MIGHT BE DEAD SOON, BUT AT LEAST WE OWN A GAFF YOU FUCKING LOSER'

A GROWING NUMBER of pensioners with the mortgage on their homes long paid off are taking to the streets around the country to mock the younger generation for not owning their own homes.

'Yeah I've one foot in the grave, but at least I'm not sharing a bunk bed with a complete stranger into my 30s you fucking loser,' went just one of dozens of reported drive-by slaggings administered by elderly couples who have chosen such insults as a balm against their own mortality.

Often disregarded, condescended in and the subject of misplaced pity or infantilisation, many in their advanced years are only too happy to get their revenge on a younger generation.

'Big renting on ya!' shouted septuagenarian couple Sheila and Michael Forest, as they whizzed past a bus stop occupied by a number of people in their 30s, who they correctly presumed had been laughed out of every mortgage-offering bank in the country.

'Millennials or Gen Z, I don't discriminate, but my favourite to take the piss out of are the ones in their 30s, because they've all the hope ground out of them. The Gen Z geebags naïvely think it'll all turn out alright in the end,' explained retired homeowner Richard Fulton.

'And they really hate it when I say I'm going to vote Fine Gael even though I won't be around for the

left-wing Marxist housing takeover I pretend I'm steadfastly against. I'm only doing it 'cus I get a perverse kick out of it.'

'I can't touch my toes anymore, I go to the toilet 60 times a day, when I get up out of a chair my body creaks louder than the floorboards in a haunted house … so yes, I'm going to slag you over the fact that you'll never own a house, haunted or otherwise,' added Fulton, before chanting 'who's not getting their security deposit back and is dressed like the worst of the '90s?' at some young people.

GAA 'WIN A HOME' RAFFLES REMAIN YOUNG PEOPLE'S ONLY CHANCE OF OWNING HOME

SECRET INTERNAL EMAILS from the Department of Housing obtained by *WWN* suggest officials believe the high volume of 'win a home' raffles run by GAA clubs are Ireland's only hope of solving the housing crisis.

'We're not even going to interrogate the logic of how GAA club raffles are the only entity seemingly able to get their hands on family homes without a vicious bidding war or being usurped by a vulture fund. We would just appeal to prospective homeowners to go all in on tickets,' one department official was quoted.

GAA clubs' ability to get hold of pristine new homes during a scarcity of them has seen many desperate would-be homeowners purchase tickets in bulk, even if it is for a house built on a quicksand pit at the foot of an active volcano on a fault line.

'We need to stress: Help to Buy scheme, social housing, LDA, all that

– you'll be a lifetime waiting, so I'd honestly stick your deposit on tickets for these draws. Plus you'll be helping a club extend their clubhouse or build a cryogenics lab for their senior teams. It's a win-win for everyone,' another official said.

The department urged first-time buyers to completely ignore the recent news that houses being built this year have exceeded estimates, as only the most naïve person would think this means house prices will drop as a result.

GAA clubs remained tight-lipped on where they're sourcing these houses from and how they are so plentiful but insisted there was no voodoo magic involved.

'Okay, I didn't think there was any voodoo involved until you said there isn't,' eager young couples said as the clubs quickly hid their pentagram made out of Dermot Bannon effigies.

Predictions for 2023

Brendan O'Carroll will win an Oscar for his movie *Mrs Brown's Boys: Zombies On Mars.*

'MY WINDOW-FONDLING HELL' – DERMOT BANNON

the cold, smooth feeling of expensive liquid sand against my goose-bumped flesh and that flatulent sound my fingers made when I pushed them against the glass: fuuurp … fuuurp … fuuuuurp. I could furp for days.

'I suppose it all came to a head when I woke up a pair of former clients one morning, furping. And despite their sheer terror when they entered their sitting room at 4 a.m., I could do nothing else but laugh manically. I knew the game was up, so I guess laughing like that was a defining moment for me, as well as the later charge of breaking and entering, which they kindly dropped for an offer of free extension plans – no large windows this time, understandably.

'Don't get me wrong, I still think about large windows every day, but I don't crave them anymore. If you offered me a fondle of your window right now, I'd happily decline. That's just not me anymore. That Dermot Bannon is dead. The new DB is focused on clients who want a practical home that centres around warmth and happiness, not some sexy statement piece viewing pod glistening with an arousing blue hue.

'I guess we all have room to improve.'

RETURNING with another series, *WWN* catches up with presenter Dermot Bannon on his secret addiction to fondling large panes of glass and how he deals with his urges in the new series of *Room to Improve*.

'It got to the stage where I was caressing four, five windows a day. Past clients would come home to find me softly touching their bay window. You see, I'd always make a spare key, and I guess in hindsight this was very wrong of

me and highly illegal. I would always excuse my presence by saying I was doing a revisit episode, but there never was a revisit episode – it was just me rubbing my freshly shaven face across the ridiculously priced window I made them buy for my own pleasure. Trespassing, they called it. To me, it was more like caress-passing.

'When I look back at all the unnecessarily humongous glass windows I made clients buy, I feel ashamed. They didn't ask

for this – it was all for me and my propensity for triple glazing. I told them it was for the view, but if I'm honest, I never looked past the pane. It was all about

BREAKING

THERE WAS MORE Olympic triumph for Ireland in Japan this morning, after a bedsit on Dublin's North Circular Road was declared the winner by a panel of judges in the debut of the 'Best Dive' event.

Factors in the decision to grant gold to the apartment, listed as being for a single person but with a landlord that is 'flexible' as to how many stay in it, include:

- The proximity of the kitchen unit to the bed itself, with a mere eight inches of space between the oven and the duvet, allows the tenant to make their dinner while lying in bed (if the oven worked, which it doesn't).
- The complete lack of toilet or bathroom facilities – described by judges as 'miraculous', but described by competitors as 'suspicious', prompting calls for the apartment to be tested for regulation tampering.
- A gold-medal-worthy smell that lingers on the palate long after leaving the apartment.
- A monthly rent well above what should be expected for such a shithole of a property.

The entire podium went to the Irish dive team, with a three-bedroom house kitted out for 36 migrant workers taking silver, and a family home that gets cleared out every 12 months for the landlord's 'brother in America' to live in, only to show up on the market a week later with much higher rent, taking bronze.

The apartment will be met at the airport when it returns by Minister For Housing Darragh O'Brien, as well as Minister for Sport Catherine Martin, while Gardaí are being posted at the arrivals gate to keep an eye out for former minister Shane Ross, who has been spotted in the area.

Your Census Time Capsules

'Do they still have spice boxes in the future? If not, I'm glad I'm dead.' – Andrew (27), Galway

DUBLIN APARTMENT WINS OLYMPIC GOLD FOR BEST DIVE

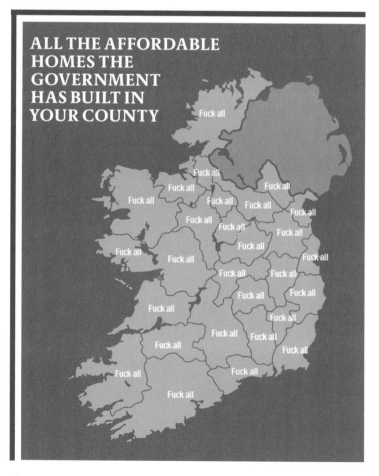

ALL THE AFFORDABLE HOMES THE GOVERNMENT HAS BUILT IN YOUR COUNTY

Fuck all (repeated across all counties on the map)

'WE NEED AFFORDABLE HOUSING, BUT IF MY HOME'S VALUE DROPS BY ONE EURO I'LL BURN THIS FUCKING COUNTRY TO THE GROUND'

LOCAL HOMEOWNER Liam Currens is acutely aware of the damage rising house prices are having on first-time buyers' prospects and is joining a growing number of homeowners calling for radical housing market interventions by the government, with one small caveat.

'My heart breaks for people like that, my daughter included, which is why I back a dramatic rethinking of housing in Ireland that'll deliver affordable housing. It's clear the government sides with speculators and foreign investors over people. Fresh thinking is needed, but if any of them so much as nip a single euro off the prices in my area I'll go full Rambo on everyone. No one will be spared,' Currens said, issuing a steely death stare.

Currens observed that once upon a time, house prices were at a loan-to-income ratio of 3.5 times a single person's gross salary, but today's market seems geared towards providing foreign pension funds with a high rent yield over a period of 40 or 50 years.

'What a broken system, couples earning €100k plus priced out of Dublin, outbid by funds. Prices are up over 14 per cent in a year outside Dublin. It's soul-eroding for the people, but at the same time if my own home, which I bought for €205k, drops a cent below its valuation today of €585k I will unleash a fury so violent it will take the army to stop me,' added Currens.

Currens' heart-rending plea for politicians to step up is part of the growing solidarity witnessed across the country, as pressure to pursue genuine efforts to address the housing crisis grows.

'I'm not asking for the impossible. I want house prices to rise in value and never stop rising, and I also want the younger generation to be able to afford homes. We need to give these kids a hand, and I'll write to my local TDs to explain how

> **'If any of them so much as nip a single euro off the prices in my area I'll go full Rambo'**

I'll vote them the fuck out if any solution involves a dent in value for my home and the one I rent out across the city,' Currens stated.

'I will wreak havoc so unspeakably horrifying and catastrophically vicious that it will render anyone who witnesses it a haunted husk of a human being. I will stretch out your entrails so they become strings on the cello I've made from your corpse,' concluded Currens, pointing to a shed in his garden marked 'weapons depot – open in case of a drop in housing prices'.

A LANDLORD'S GUIDE TO CALCULATING RENT FOR A TENANT

JUST BOUGHT your first property or found yourself an 'accidental landlord' after inheriting a house? It can be tough becoming a landlord, especially when the Department of Housing offers no support whatsoever.

The Irish Landlord League, a fantastic registered charity, is here to help. The ILL can guide you, and you're not alone – there are loads of us. Some of us are your local TD. Okay, here's some advice:

See what others are charging in rent in the area

Have you seen a lovely modern apartment with no wear and tear? Does it have parking, security, plenty of natural light, meets all fire safety standards, y'know, everything your apartment isn't? Well then, just charge the same rent with a little €100 bonus thrown on top. You've got to treat yourself in this game.

What about rent pressure zones?

Don't worry, local councils in charge of overseeing such things, and punishing landlords who don't comply, don't resource these positions. Currently the person in charge in Dublin City Council is a stapler with googly eyes pinned to it.

Should I link rent to inflation?

Again, don't stick to the rules when no one expects you to. We'd say 10 per cent should do it. And if you think 20 per cent has a nicer ring to it, go for it.

Should I make any other specific demands?

Yes, and throw in many unspecific demands too, like 'don't even!' This is the perfect amount of vague and should help turn your tenants into meek 'yes' people too afraid to speak out.

My tenant is asking for the rent book and wants to pay via direct debit

You mean your newly former tenant. Get yourself a tenant who knows that paying in cash is the only way.

Am I forgetting anything?

Oh yes, you should feel very sorry for yourself at all times and write letters into the *Irish Times* about how, if anything, you have it harder than the tenants you're gouging.

EXCLUSIVE

RESIDENT PROPERTY EXPERT, chairman of the Irish Landlord League and *WWN* deputy sub-editor-in-chief Bill Badbody pens some of his thoughts on, and solutions to, the current housing and rental crisis in Ireland, not that anyone asked:

'Okay, I'm going to make this very brief as I'm a very busy man and time is money, so excuse my bluntness – people here need to be told straight, as they seem to think this housing crisis is everyone else's fault but theirs.

'First of all, you don't have a housing crisis, you have a population crisis, but fear not, there are solutions, which I will go through here free of charge.

'Many of you will remember several years ago when drug-taking was made legal for an entire day in Ireland. Well, I see no reason why our government can't also legalise murder for a similar period, allowing everyone earning under €100k per year to exterminate a peer of their choosing

'IF EVERYONE KILLS AT LEAST ONE PERSON, THIS RENT CRISIS WILL BE OVER'

(note: landlords exempt), halving our entire population overnight and freeing up 50 per cent of properties across the country for investment funds to take.

> **'I think the act of murdering someone would give everyone on this island a newfound perspective on life'**

'Obviously, a rental cap will have to be implemented before D-Day, and I don't mean a rising rent cap, I mean a floor, whereby the rents will be guaranteed to never fall below a certain threshold again. This is a non-negotiable clause, as it was my idea.

'Yes, it will probably take everyone some time to get over the initial trauma of murdering someone or indeed losing someone they loved, but if history has taught

us anything, deep-set traumatic experiences drove this nation to where it is today – a subservient race of moaners too lazy to protest in the cold.

'Civil War, the Troubles, all the sexual and physical abuse carried out by religious and government-backed institutions – it's what makes us who we are today, and I think the act of murdering someone would give everyone on this island a newfound perspective on life going forward and, more importantly, an extra 6×8 box room they could rent out for a guaranteed €1,000 per month.

'NOTE: In the event of the mass murder idea being embraced, I have acquired dozens of potential allotment sites across the country for graveyards, pending planning and consecration.'

RENTING

FINE GAEL COUPLE WHO OWN HOME OUTRIGHT SINCE 2013 THINK AVERAGE €1,972 RENT SEEMS FAIR

NEWS that the average rent for a new tenancy in Dublin stands at €1,972 has been greeted with a vast ocean of expressionless acceptance by local Fine Gael voting couple Martin and Nuala O'Laudlin, *WWN* can confirm.

'We're not exactly big fans of Leo, Simon and Paschal ourselves,' explained the couple, who are such massive fans of Leo, Simon and Paschal that they make Eminem's video for 'Stan' look tame, 'but €1,972 sounds very reasonable to us'.

'Without ever personally talking to any renters since my children briefly "rented" by living in the apartment we own rent-free, I can say the following

– there are plenty of affordable options out there. See, the average is probably skewed by one person renting a house out for €140,000 a month in Dalkey, as is their right by the way – this isn't Fidel Mary Lou's Cuba,' Nuala explained.

'Anyway, the market will course correct vis-à-vis cyclical trends, with supply coming on stream from stakeholders in the property space,' added Martin, who hasn't blinked since 2003.

'And renters are no angels, let me tell you. Nuala knows this – remember Geoff from the club? Rented his apartment to some Eastern

Europeans … they put the apartment in their suitcases and took it back to Lithupolangaria or wherever. Honestly!'

While noting it's scientifically proven that young people love living four to a room at that age anyway, and that liveable conditions would be wasted on them, the couple said they were unaware of anyone over the age of 25 renting.

'I heard on Newstalk that people love renting now and don't want houses, which is why I felt it was my duty to object to those houses being built down the road,' nodded Martin as vigorously as he shakes his head whenever a left-wing politician appears on TV.

The couple was careful to note that they're not saying it's easy out there, and would-be homeowners absolutely have their sympathy, but at the same time it is very easy and people only have themselves to blame.

'I don't know what some people are complaining about. I saw a lovely one in the *Irish Times*, studio apartments called – what was it Martin? – "The Pinnacle". Had a gym, the whole thing was designed by Vogue Williams's nanny's interior designer and each kitchen comes with a Happy Pear twin. Now it wouldn't be legal to call something "The Pinnacle" unless it's true, there are laws,' Nuala said of a build-to-rent development with a starting rent of €3,200 for a one-bed studio that has sat unoccupied for three years.

'No really, and people still complain?'

FINANCE

HANDY TIPS WHEN SAVING FOR A MORTGAGE

SO YOU'VE STARTED on the road that you hope will end with you becoming a homeowner/saddled with debt for 30 years. But did you know that many first-time buyers fail to identify simple and effective ways to save for that all-important deposit?

WWN's financial expert Freddie Knobbs has those vital tips that could get you to your savings goals all the quicker. Knobbs' nuggets of wisdom include:

- Invent a texting time machine that allows you to send the message 'spend everything you have on Bitcoin' to your 2010 self.
- Mug the elderly couple in front of you in the ATM queue.
- Don't spend money on socialising, premium-access television channels or gambling. It's important that this journey be as joyless as possible.
- Think long and hard about which bank to go with and really put the required research into it before realising they are all equally useless.
- If you hadn't already thought about being born into a family wealthy enough to chuck you €50k on the sly, you'll be feeling pretty stupid now. The alternative is to check under your cushions for spare change, and when you've finished that, break into other homes and do the same.
- Don't just skip meals to save on money, completely shed your human form and become an amorphous cloud-being; that way you no longer have to pay for necessities like rent, clothes, travel and food.

- Everyone talks about adopting in-need children. Well, have you considered adopting an elderly bachelor farmer with a terminal illness who also has no living relatives?
- Selling your organs on the black market is a stupid idea now. The market has been flooded by fellow first-time buyers doing the same, with the prices being driven down as a result. Do you really want to go through the pain of selling your liver when all you'll get is a One For All voucher worth €20?
- Set up 'vaults' in your Revolut account – this way you can regularly feel deep shame when you extract money from the vault marked 'savings' to buy another round of pints or pay an essential bill. This shame will help grind you down to the point where you no longer possess the hope or belief that you have what it takes to be a homeowner. Now, doesn't that feel better*?

* significantly worse

Your Census Time Capsules

'If you find any money in my house after I'm gone, under no circumstances donate it to charity.' – Martin (67), Cavan

FINANCE

HOW I MANAGED TO BUY MY OWN APARTMENT AT 22 WITHOUT HELP FROM MY PARENTS

IF IT'S ONE THING that people struggling to get their foot on the bottom rung of the property ladder like to read, it's another newspaper article centred around a young person who has just bought the home of their dreams with absolutely no help from anyone.

No help aside from an immense inheritance, or with well-to-do parents providing a deposit or just buying a house outright for them.

Today's subject is a 26-year-old Waterford man who has lived in a two-bedroom apartment of his own since last year without help from anyone at all.

'It was four years ago, I was in Waterford IT but still living at home on the other side of town, and I remember thinking, God, it'd be so much easier if I just had a place of my own, so I could go on the proper tear whenever I wanted without the aul lassie giving me shit all the time,' remembers Conall Mulhearn, sitting in the window of his apartment, looking out over the city.

'Nine of the lads in my course were all living in the one two-bedroom house on the QT paying cash to the landlord off the books, a pure zoo, but they didn't mind because they were on the lash five nights a week.

'Meanwhile, I'm still at home, getting the odd quiet ride here and there, but did you ever get the ride without moving at all? It's not it, let me tell you. So I'd always be on at the lads to let me move in with them, but they'd say no, nine in the one gaff is pushing it as is. Bad and all as their

> ## 'The drug gang found me, of course – they always do'

landlord was, he had a limit to how many 20-year-olds he'd ram into the one place. And there was no way I could afford a place of my own, not even the rent. So it was looking bleak.'

With only the income from his part-time job stacking shelves at Tesco to keep him in cans, Mulhearn's prospects of owning property before he was 40 looked grim until fate smiled happily on him one day.

'I was on the way home from work and cut through this industrial estate that's a bit of a shortcut. You wouldn't go through it at night usually, but I was in a rush to get home. I passed a parked car that was on its own, and that's when I noticed there were holes in the side window,' explains the 26-year-old, as he shows us around the spacious open-floor area that serves as a kitchen/dining room, ideal for entertaining guests, which leads on to the living area.

'Two lads inside, one on the passenger side, one on the driver side. Bullet to the side of the head apiece, you could see they'd drawn guns on each other and pulled the trigger at the same time. "Deal gone wrong" shit for sure, and in the back was the reason. A hold-all of grass and a hold-all of cash – 300 grand, just sitting there. So I did what anyone looking to get on the property ladder would do. I took the bag and put a match to the car. The lad in the passenger side wasn't all the way dead yet. He had enough in him to turn his eye and watch me the whole time.

'As the flames leapt up, you could see the look on his face turn to one of acceptance, as if to say "Yeah kid, it's hard out there, I can't blame you". I'd love to say that the image haunts me to this day, but in actual fact I've never given it a second thought.'

'The days afterwards seemed like a dream. The cops came along and called it as they saw it; drug dealers

My highlight of 2022: Elon Musk

'Solving world poverty, in a manner so subtle you probably didn't even notice it.'

ran afoul of someone, gangland execution, car burned out, no mention of money. Meanwhile, I had the price of this apartment sitting in an Adidas bag in my wardrobe at home. I was smart enough to know I couldn't spend it straight away, but I was still "22 enough" to make some stupid decisions.

'I found an estate agent who was willing to let me buy a €220k apartment for €300k cash and would sort everything out in my name, no questions asked. There are still a few of them around if you don't mind paying them the extra, although if I were to be an honest buyer, I'd probably still have paid 80k over asking anyway, hahaha. I told my mam and dad that I'd rented the place and moved in a month later. They think it's a bit bigger than I should be able to afford, but they don't really know any

better because they bought their house on a single salary in 1981 and haven't followed the property market since.'

As he walked us through the two-bedroom apartment, he pointed to the spare room, which is currently let out to six Brazilian workers employed nearby, a handy supply of weekly cash that Conall claims he 'may as well' collect.

We're enthralled by our host's tale, although he adds that 'nothing is free' in this life. 'The drug gang found me, of course – they always do,' laughs Conall, as bright sunshine beamed through the floor-to-ceiling windows.

'The estate agent gave me up straight away after they interrogated him about anyone making large cash purchases in the weeks after the deal went wrong. So now I work for them and have done so for years. Otherwise, they say they'll kill me or

On This Day

In 1960, Che Guevara posed for *Playgirl*.

2 July

my mam and dad, or, worse, burn this place down and put me right back into the rental market.

'They made me shoot a man on his doorstep last week, one in each leg as his wife screamed from inside. I just had to bury it deep down and remind myself – you're a homeowner now, just be thankful for that. Whatever else happens, whatever else your life becomes, you own your house. There are a lot of people who would gladly swap places with you.'

Next week, we ask the question: are evil spirits real? We're talking to a family of four who just moved into a three-bedroom semi built on a famine graveyard who hope the answer is no!

Waterford Whispers News

VOL 1, 20156136   WATERFORD, SATURDAY, 9 SEPTEMBER, 1979   12p

Referendum Results Split on Colour of Salt and Vinegar Crisp Packets

CRISP manufacturers have been left in limbo today after referendum results officially tied 50/50 on what colour salt and vinegar crisp packets should be, WWN reports.

The blue side expressed their disappointment, with some suggesting that another referendum be held on the matter, while producers of green salt and vinegar crisps welcomed the results.

'Everyone in Ireland knows blue is the go-to colour for salt and vinegar crisps and that the green packaging is a protestant concoction designed to undermine the Irish way of life,' Fianna Fáil Taoiseach Jack Lynch stated after backing the losing side. 'The British government are trying to cause confusion over the colour's true meaning by making their salt and vinegar packs green.'

Defending their green-coloured packets, Walkers salt and vinegar spokesperson James Smith denied any wrongdoing, calling the referendum results a fair reflection of how deep-fried potato chips laced in sodium and fermented yeast should be packaged.

'We like to keep the blue packet for cheese and onion flavoured crisps, and if people get upset over that then fine,' Smith explained, 'I find it appalling that some Irish crisp manufacturers use the colour red for their cheese and onion packaging, but you don't hear us Brits complaining about that sick shit.'

Following the referendum results, Tayto have agreed to package their cheese and onion crisps in a separate yellow, more neutral packaging for Northern Ireland customers only.

THE LAW

IF YOU SEE A LANDLORD ASSAULTING TENANTS, CALL THE COPS WHO ARE RIGHT OUTSIDE

FOOTAGE of a landlord assaulting tenants has been described as 'shocking' by a number of people who have no idea how common that sort of thing in Ireland is, or indeed 'how these things work'.

If your landlord (or an appointed associate) happens to burst into your accommodation some evening demanding money or just physically threatening you for whatever reason, you may wish to call the police for assistance. Here's how:

1) Just stick your head out the window

It's very possible that while you're being violently evicted, there are a few uniformed Gardaí outside your front door deterring anyone from helping you or minimising the risk to the safety of the balaclava-wearing men who are currently rendering your apartment unliveable.

Just give them a quick shout to see if they want to do anything about the court-approved mobbing that's taking place, although don't hold your breath. Unless your head is shoved underwater, that is.

2) Lodge a formal complaint against your landlord

If you have a complaint against a landlord or letting agent, then you should report this to your local Garda station immediately.

Guards have entire departments dedicated to ensuring renters' rights are protected, and that no harm comes to them. They've got droves of people standing by to help you. No renter in this land will ever feel they can't speak up about abuse, harassment or unfair treatment when these guys are on the case!

3) Take your beating – you've earned it

Look, if your landlord is angry with you then we're sure you've earned it. Were you late with the rent? Did you not adhere to the list of demands laid out when you rented the place to begin with? Whatever it was, you've clearly angered your landlord, and as such, we've no sympathy for you. If you don't like it, buy a house. Simple as that.

HOUSE PRICE INFLATION RISES TO 'WAIT UNTIL THE NEXT CRASH TO BUY SOMETHING' PHASE

HOUSE PRICES across Ireland have reportedly risen to a phase previously reached in late 2007, known as the 'wait until the next housing crash to buy one' phase, WWN reports.

According to the latest research from property website MyHome.ie, the annual asking price inflation for housing is now running at 12.3 per cent, or 'we're all fucking doomed again' levels.

'It's gas, we'll never learn,' said recent successful mortgage applicant and father of two about to emigrate to Australia in a year, Donal Spike, 'I know I'll be in negative equity in a couple of years, but fuck it, we're suckers for punishment,' Spike added, smiling manically at his future financial fate. 'Hopefully there will be another bank bailout and we can apply to have some of our mortgage written off – the usual Irish craic.'

Outside Dublin, asking prices were 2.7 per cent higher in the first quarter compared to the same time last year,

with the annual rate of house asking price inflation in rural Ireland sitting at 14 per cent.

'Will my €250k home be worth even half that in a couple of years? Who knows!' voiced another recent large debt acquirer. 'But thanks to modern technology and government incentives, I'll be able to remotely draw the dole, all from the comfort of my overpriced house that I'll eventually default on, yay!'

Experts believe Ireland may have developed a little-known condition called 'Ostrich Syndrome', an ailment handed down from one home-owning generation to the next.

'Sufferers experience zero tact when signing up for large mortgages, despite knowing the real cost of the house they're buying,' one expert stated, before concluding, 'however, it's not sand they have their heads in – it's their arse.'

RENTING

RENTAL PROPERTY STINKING UP THE ENTIRE STREET

A RENTAL PROPERTY in Waterford has come under fire over its dilapidated condition and the general messiness of its inhabitants during an annual meeting of the local resident's association of Tobin Street, *WWN* has learned.

Number 34 quickly became a bone of contention among neighbours when it was discovered it was to be rented out on the HAP scheme, following the death of its previous owner, Jack Power, 'who kept it lovely in its day, so he did.'

'I always see yer one smoking fags outside in her pyjamas, head on her like she was dragged through a briar bush,' offered Molly Rochford from across the street, who bought her home for £IR3,000 back in the day and openly resents those not on the housing ladder. 'The bins are always out the front, too lazy of course to bring them around from the back every week – typical sponger,' added Rochford, who is allowed to park her car and block the path because she owns her home.

The property, which was quickly rented out without any refurbishment or desire to update, soon became an eyesore for the homeowners of Tobin Street, who didn't hold back on their tirade.

'She has kids' toys all over the front garden now, and the grass growing up through them. You'd think she'd give the place a lick of paint,' said the chairman of the resident's association and rightful heir to number 56 when his mother dies, John Baker. 'She probably got the whole place for nothing – and where's the father, is what I'd like to know?'

Unaware of the ridicule, HAP tenant, widow and mother of two, Triona Wall, began touching her now burning ears, wondering if it was her MS medication or something else afoot.

'Could be the damp walls getting to me here. I've been asking the landlord to fix up this place for months now and no answer. People must think I'm a right filthy mare,' she thought. 'I'm sure they understand my situation considering a third of the country is renting homes. People wouldn't be so fickle.'

> **'She has kids' toys all over the front garden now, and the grass growing up through them'**

On This Day

28 December

2002: A horde of pandas met to discuss forming a recycling company in Ireland.

BREAKING

YOUNGEST SIBLING BAGSIES THE FAMILY HOME

UNDER THE FALSE IMPRESSION that the family home is now his because all his brothers and sisters have moved out, Niall Cantwell casually began redecorating in his head despite both parents still being alive and well.

'If I knocked that wall out I'd have a nice open-plan kitchen and living room with a huge skylight in the roof, conservatory too,' the 26-year-old thought to himself as his mother Jan handed him his lunch on a pillow for his lap, warning him that the plate was hot. 'They must have, what, five, maybe seven years left?' he continued, now shooing his mother out of the way so he could imagine his new arrangement.

The full-time stay-at-home son-of-two laid claim to the family home last Christmas, much to the utter contempt of his three siblings.

'I'm will they'll warm to it when Mam and Dad pass. Like, I'm the one taking care of them now in their old age,' he said of his parents, both 52, before shouting into his kitchen-bound mother for salt. 'Jesus, I'll have to get a quare one in to feed me too, take care of the clothes and beds and all that house shite.'

Ignoring several previously heated arguments about 'who gets the home when Mam and Dad are gone', Cantwell remains oblivious to his siblings' torment over his claim, excusing their beef as jealousy, pointing out that they already have homes of their own.

'Sure, I've been living here rent free since I left school and haven't worked a single day in my life, but those pricks just fucked off and left me here to be mollycoddled by Mam and Dad while they swanned about making their own lives for themselves, so who's in the wrong here?' he posed.

A recent study found that 99 per cent of youngest siblings believe the family home should default to them.

'It's a bagsy mentality; the same hoors would find a lost wallet on the street and keep the money and throw away the cards,' the study concluded.

Tips for Ignoring Climate Change

They were talking about this craic back in the '80s, and we're still here. The '80s! Sure that was a hundred years ago.

PROPERTY MARKET

LEITRIM HOME GIVEN DUBLIN EIRCODE BY MISTAKE NOW VALUED AT €1.4MN

THE IRISH PROPERTY MARKET is reeling from an An Post error that has seen one rural Irish house given a Dublin Eircode, sparking panic and delight in equal measure in property industry circles.

'I'm sorry, I know it's a converted cowshed on a floodplain built on a secret nuclear weapon testing site, but its Eircode begins with D04, so you know the rules,' a gleeful estate agent said as he showed a couple around the modest home.

First appearing like an inconsequential error with a simple solution, property speculators have spied the Leitrim case as a way to

combat a downturn in Dublin prices as a result of the advent of remote working.

'Yes, all we needed to up prices outside of Dublin by 10 per cent was just a dozen examples of people leaving the capital for a better quality of life, but if we just issue everywhere with Dublin Eircodes we can artificially inflate prices at a much quicker pace,' shared one speculator, who was worried there for a second.

The Drunamore home's online listing has been changed to reflect its Eircode, with the property now described as '5 minutes from the Luas, within walking distance of Dublin city centre and Wicklow, and deceptively spacious'.

'I know this makes no sense and yet I can't seem to stop myself, it's like I'm under a spell,' said one couple attempting to outbid a €1.4 million offer on the pitiful piece of land.

WITH THE TAXPAYER on the hook for the improved €2.2 billion mica redress scheme, which remains utterly deaf to the concerns of the homeowners affected, *WWN* can confirm that those involved in acquiring and supplying the defective blocks have had another flawless night of uninterrupted sleep.

'None of that mindfulness app "whale sounds of the sea" shite

PEOPLE DIRECTLY RESPONSIBLE FOR MICA SCANDAL ENJOY ANOTHER PERFECT NIGHT OF UNINTERRUPTED SLEEP

needed to help me nod off,' boasted one person, who only had to see the words 'self-certify' in building regs to know they could squirm out of this consequence-free.

'Consequence-free isn't true at all. We've been ordered to shut down one plant by the council that also recently granted us planning permission to open another one. That's clearly a lesson learned for us. I slept like a log, despite all the screams of the families I've fucked over,' added another person involved in wriggling out of accountability.

Elsewhere, other people weren't so lucky.

'An absolute nightmare – I had the lads up all night adjusting the price of materials and labour,' shared one developer, who noticed the maximum redress under the scheme is €420,000 and has inflated prices accordingly.

Meanwhile, a distraught and sobbing Minister for Housing, snot bubbling from his nose as he blubbered like a newborn, regretfully informed Fianna Fáil's bestest friends in the construction industry that he will be bringing new regulations, decades too late, but reassured his pals that whatever body is tasked with on-site compliance checks won't be resourced properly.

STUDENT ACCOMMODATION? HERE ARE FIVE SOLUTIONS

THE CHRONIC SHORTAGE in the housing market has hit students hard this year, with many forced to defer positions or book rooms in hotels for weeks on end as they attempt to juggle full-time study with full-time flat hunting.

If you or someone you know is struggling with this problem, here are five potential solutions that'll see you sail through college in no time:

1) Be rich

Studies have shown that being rich is one of the easiest ways to avoid hassle in Ireland, including the stress of finding accommodation. It's vital to come from a rich family that can easily afford to pay the extortionate rents currently demanded by landlords, or indeed a family that had the foresight to invest in the property market and have an apartment ready for you to use. All they have to do is evict the family that lives there first and you're away.

2) Sleep around

College wouldn't be complete without a string of one-night stands to remember/forget in later years. Sleeping around not only saves you a fortune but there's also the bonus of having sex every night. We would advise students opting for this to pack light, be open to all genders to guarantee accommodation and don't forget to get regular check-ups.

3) Commute

We appreciate that college is hard and requires huge amounts of quiet time to allow you to study hard and achieve your dreams. And what better place to do that than on a four-hour bus commute every day? Sit back in minimum comfort and hit the books as you chug along on a wet motorway while developing motion sickness from reading as you fend off drug addicts looking to use your phone to make 'a quick call'.

> **Tips for Ignoring Climate Change**
>
> 'Bit of sun, you can't beat it!' to be uttered when it's 20 degrees in Mayo in December.

4) Nightclubs

With nightclub closing times expected to be extended to 6 a.m. under new legislation, we would advise students to become gold card members of their favourite clubs. Earplugs are advised here, along with some cheap Tesco vodka to help you sleep in a nice corner. This method, along with option 2 above, works best for most students.

5) Be rich

We've already mentioned this one, but we can't emphasise enough how important it is to be extremely rich if you want to avail of Ireland's 'free education system'.

RENTING

STUDENT ACCOMMODATION CRISIS: 'JUST LIVE IN YOUR OLD PAIR'S DUBLIN APARTMENT RENT-FREE LIKE I DID'

On This Day

13 January

2015: Waterford man David Devine throws a piece of rubbish into a bin from at least 15 feet away. Tragically, there are no witnesses.

ON HAND to offer his expertise free of charge to students deferring their start in college due to a lack of affordable accommodation, is a recently graduated former student and current benefactor of his parents' hard work and wealth, Jonathan Dowdy Hall.

Moved by the difficulty being endured by students, Dowdy Hall shares his indispensable knowledge on securing affordable accommodation at a time when you should be free to just concentrate on your education:

'Protests? Like, actual fucking protests over accommodation? This is beyond cringe, guys. The solution couldn't more simple and right in front of your eyes.

'Shouting until you're hoarse and holding up placards that would finish last place in an arts and crafts competition for blind squirrels isn't the answer. Here's a catchy slogan for you: "No way, we don't have to pay because the old pair has a city-centre apartment".

'Considering you're all so woke you'd think you lot would cop on and actually wake up – just give the old pair a ring.

'Seriously, what are the chances that the majority of you are peasants who mistakenly thought you would be allowed to attend third level in Ireland for "free" and not a normal average person like me? And anyway, how much is "a rent" these days – €50 per quarter? Really, that's what you presumably birthed-by-rich-parents students are protesting about?

'What is that anyway, two avocados? You can't be crying over spent rent if you're out doing extravagant things like buying food as well.

'Yeah, okay, your parents' apartment might not be the height of luxury, but if you're doing a four-year degree it'll probably be worth close to a mill by the end of your degree the way prices are going, so the potential to be slagged by the children of a property developer or an Emirati Crown Prince are slim enough.

'What parents don't have a little nest egg of an apartment lying idle? Literally all my friends' parents did, which, extrapolated out for the rest of the student population, is basically everyone! It's Parenting 101, spunk the spare spondoolas on an apartment 20 years ago so that your kids have somewhere to stay rent-free, like Eddie Hobbs told them to do with the old SSIA.

'You're only embarrassing yourselves giving the "oh it's so hard" quotes to the media, sounds like you'll barely scrape a 2.1 armed with the brain power of a broken hoover. Are you seriously advocating for affordable rents? You're talking about your inheritance here, which we all have, clearly.

'Strapping a bomb to your windfall like some sort of tenants-rights Taliban? You're clearly an Arts student with that demented logic!'

> **'You're only embarrassing yourselves giving the "oh it's so hard" quotes to the media'**

Cost of Living Tips

Instead of going to things, don't.

HOW I SPEND MY MONEY

A HOUSING DEVELOPER SURVIVING ON STATE HANDOUTS OF JUST €195,000 PER HOME

WELCOME to *How I Spend My Money*, an original series on *WWN* that looks at what people in Ireland really do with their hard-earned cash.

This week we chat with Dublin developer Martin Dunne, who lives in a modest €5 million home in South Dublin and relies on government handouts to survive while struggling in Ireland's most unrewarding industry, affordable property.

'I suppose you could say we're the forgotten ones. After the crash, many of us had to file for bankruptcy and burn all the people we owed money to. I then had to wait 12 months before my bankruptcy was over and could start all over again. People hear what you do and immediately think "chancer, always looking to pull a fast one at the expense of the buyer". They don't see the person behind all that, they just see the tax evasion, the brown envelopes to councillors and the huge stacks of money we make from fleecing the taxpayers out of billions. It's unrewarding work. Surviving these times is hard, especially with the government's new Housing for All plan. We've been reduced to handouts from the state – basically, social welfare for developers. Now we're taking just €195k profit on a €450k home financed by you, the taxpayer. It's peanuts, I know, but thank you, I suppose it's something. The poor banks are in the same boat – on that €450k "affordable" mortgage, they only make a bit more than us at €200k per unit. It's a disgrace that even the people printing the money can only scrape by. That's Ireland for you. These are indeed tough times for the industry, so hopefully the below

will give you a little insight into my struggle.'

- **Occupation:** Irish Property Developer
- **Age:** 44
- **Location:** South County Dublin
- **Salary:** €300 million+
- **Monthly expenses**
  Rent: No rent as I own all my homes outright, well, my wife and kids do (wink wink).
  Household bills: No idea, as my team of accountants sorts all that.
  Transport: Land Rover Sport or helicopter, sometimes private jet.

Monday

6 a.m.: Woken up by text from friend sending me link to some lunatics in Carlow developing sustainable homes for just €200k each. Rang friends in papers to quash story. Called source in housing department to give out.

12 noon: Chatted to some government friends to try to get affordable house prices in Dublin raised to €650k.

4 p.m.: Lobbied councillors and ministers to try to avoid them taxing vacant units, as it would cost us billions. News of 180,000 vacant homes in Ireland just sitting there would not go down well.

6 p.m.: Got confirmation government won't tax vacant homes. Will sit on lots now and hopefully increase value by another 11 per cent year on year. Will hold back on them and develop down the line into barely living pods. Win-win.

Tuesday

8 a.m.: Read a report stating that 470,000 young people in Ireland are currently living at home with parents. Co-living pods at €1,500 per unit spring to mind. Will try to get government to fund them.

11 a.m.: Ignored numerous emails from culchies wanting units developed outside of Dublin. Just what drugs are

these people on? No one's going to build at those shite profits in the sticks. Dublin is where the money is at.

2–6 p.m.: K Club with Johnny and the lads.

Wednesday

7 a.m.: Investment fund offered me $100 mill for a block of units in West Dublin. Took the arm and all off them. Government's problem now.

9 a.m.: Masturbated into *Indo* newspaper article on how rents will increase with inflation and expected to rise 11 per cent in the next 12 months. Asked my property manager to inform my sitting tenants of new increases. Masturbated again into bank statement.

3 p.m.: Bought up some refurbs to make a killing off of in another few years. This no vacant property tax is a godsend. Thanks, Darragh.

Thursday

10 a.m.: Sat down with fellow developers about the measly €4 billion we'll make out of the Housing for All plan in Dublin. Agreed it wasn't enough and told Magnier and the lads to lobby again to increase the affordable prices. We'll get them up in the end.

11 p.m.: Set reminder to pitch more units to REIT fund I'm a shareholder in. That's 20 years of guaranteed dividends for me and the lads. Every mill worth 1.5 in 20 years. Asked financial advisor to start shifting more of savings into offshore subs so Revenue can't chase.

5 p.m.: Gave myself a raise and a lovely €300k bonus while simultaneously giving out on Twitter that the government and public are riding us.

Friday

11 a.m.: Flight to Mallorca. Called Moroccan lad for a large bag of coke. Hit the town with Johnny and the boys. Good times ahead.

Build Your Own Home

JUST €1.22

FREE BRICK ATTACHED
WITH EVERY ISSUE

BUILD YOUR OWN HOME – IN JUST 300,000 WEEKLY INSTALMENTS

WWN GUIDES

DRUGS

SIGNS THE WEED IS TOO STRONG

WITH THE POTENCY of cannabis increasing due to a combination of prohibition and demand from users for more bang for their buck, whiteners have become more commonplace, where pale-faced people have been left incapacitated from the effects of highly potent, unregulated cannabis products. Here are some signs that the weed you're consuming is too strong.

You wake up covered in blood to find your car is written off in the driveway

Probably one of the most common effects of cannabis is blanking out before getting into your car and driving around like an absolute maniac while high on weed and crashing into people and random things on the road. This usually happens after the third puff of a joint.

You become so addicted you start selling your body for sex

There isn't a cannabis addict on this planet that hasn't resorted to selling their own body for sex. Cannabis and prostitution go hand in hand, and if you are to smoke this drug, make sure you always have Vaseline or some form of lubricant to hand.

The second you smoke weed, you immediately go on to try crack and heroin

Weed is a gateway drug. The very second you take a hit you will feel the immediate urge to smoke crack and inject heroin. This is normal behaviour, and cannabis smokers should get to know all the other drugs before starting. Just think of cannabis as an induction course. Did you know Bob Marley died after

injecting heroin into his toe and it became septic, and he died a junkie (it was on the internet one time)? We can't find the link now but will send it on later.

You become extremely violent and start robbing people on the streets

Just a salt grain amount of bud is enough to send even the most placid of people into a homicidal rage and end up chewing the face off of an innocent bystander. Roughly 98 per cent of all violent crimes can be traced back to lethal batches of marijuana. Did you know that Hitler smoked cannabis all the time and would sometimes inject it to give him extra energy and aggression?

You've overdosed and ended up in hospital

Whiteners, or whiteys, are when a user overdoses on too much cannabis and drops to the ground frothing at the mouth. The user has only a matter of minutes left before they go into cardiac arrest and die. Most A&E admissions in Ireland last year were people overdosing on weed. More than 50,000 people die from cannabis every year in Dublin City alone. Cannabis is responsible for dozens of world conflicts, the attacks on 9/11 and the last housing crash. Most military hardware is now made from hemp. Covid-19 is actually part of the cannabinoid family.

DRINKING

GUINNESS AROUND THE WORLD, A GUIDE

THEY SAY Ireland's most famous export doesn't like to travel and, in truth, the best pint of Guinness you'll get is in your local. But we've had many pints of Guinness on our many travels, and here are our two cents on the subject:

1) McDaid's Irish Bar, Lanzarote
A good pint in a good bar with plenty of Irish flags up around the place and the Premier League on the telly. You could be sitting in Waterford if it wasn't for the blazing sunshine and all the English lads.

2) McGuigan's Irish Bar, Lanzarote
Another decent pint, spoiled only by the baking heat and the faint taste of sun cream that ran over our lips and blended with the black stuff as we supped. But again, no sign of this 'Guinness doesn't travel' myth.

3) McMahon's Irish Bar, Lanzarote
Again, nothing wrong with this pint. And it was either drink this or drink some Spanish beer that we've never tried and sorry, that's not what holidays are for.

4) McDaid's Irish Bar, Lanzarote
There's talk that you can't get good Guinness in America or London or Australia and look, that may be the case. But from our travel experience, here in Lanzarote, it's alright. Hang on, were we in this bar already today? Did it have that pool table? Anyways, rack 'em up there, bai.

5) McDaid's Irish Bar, Lanzarote
I dunno, maybe if the editor wants us to write about how Guinness travels to Nigeria or wherever he should send us there on a job, or whatever. We're here doing this on our own time, on our own holiday with our own lads. Wait, where'd the lads go?

6) Captain Crazy's Late-Night Karaoke and Bar, Lanzarote
Fuck knows how we got here, but the Guinness is decent. Well, we say Guinness but they don't sell it, all they sell is that Spanish beer from earlier, and y'know it's not bad once you get used to it. Alright, I'm next here at karaoke – what do you mean they don't have 'Hold Me Now' by Johnny Logan? I thought we were still in the fuckin' EU here? This is bullshit.

Predictions for 2023
According to the *Daily Mail*, the 'woke mob' will be coming for you on at least 4,567 occasions.

ART

'WE PURPOSELY MAKE SHIT SCULPTURES TO ANNOY YOU': ARTISTS SPEAK OUT

IRISH STATUES, busts and sculptures divide opinion like few things in Irish life, and the artists who create them have spoken out for the first time, lifting the lid on their motivations for creating some 'awful'/'actually I quite like it' works in the wake of the unveiling of a controversial Maureen O'Hara statue in Cork.

'We are acutely aware of the dearth of decent topics of conversation for Irish people. You lot are starved of things to talk about – we simply provide a public service by creating divisive works that you can spend weeks, months and years giving out about,' shared one sculptor, who would neither confirm nor deny if they gave Molly Malone massive jugs.

'What I was hoping for with this one was to make sure it didn't look much like Maureen, but to have her bust be perky enough for one weirdo to come out of the woodwork to produce a two-hour YouTube video about being an O'Hara boob expert, a breastpert if you will,' said the artist behind the Maureen O'Hara statue, which lasted five minutes in Glengarriff before locals tore it down in a fit of rage.

'I know it looks nothing like the person I was commissioned to sculpt … but I get off on how much that'll annoy people who call into Joe Duffy,' said another artist.

'I'm driven by metaphysics – I seek to comprehend the unknowable'

Bill's Landlord Tips

If a grandparent passes away and leaves you their home in their will, do what you know they'd have loved: convert it immediately into a co-living centre and stick 18 Brazilians in it.

'We appreciate that our value as artists isn't to challenge the public, as their fragile idiot brains wouldn't be able to cope with a provocative thought without exploding, so we default to making sure the likeness of a famous person is just "off" or that a mythical creature or animal is the right amount of unsettling,' added another artist who vowed to make a statue of Michael D. Higgins out of pasta and books if commissioned.

'In one sense, I'm driven by metaphysics – I seek to comprehend the unknowable, and that is present in the discordant shapes I sculpt which

My highlight of 2022: Kurt Zouma's cat

'The RSPCA sirens outside coming to rescue me.'

seem to fight themselves from within, as we all do – but I'm actually more driven by hearing "I coulda made that" from 500 different people,' said another artist, whose parents wished they had just gone into a solid career like accountancy.

'A great big fucking head,' responded the Luke Kelly sculptor when asked what they hoped to achieve when formulating their tribute to the Dubliners singer.

FIVE THINGS TO WEAR WHEN TAKING OUT THE BINS

'BUT IT'S JUST a quick dash to the kerb and back in my PJs, no one will see me' – the words of unimaginative fashion disasters everywhere.

Life is a fashion show and everywhere is a runway, so have some self-respect. Make every day the *Ireland AM* fashion show segment!

If you don't dress up for taking the bins out, just cut to the chase and lock yourself away like a hermit, because life isn't for you, you drab idiot!

Tips for Ignoring Climate Change

Do you even know what permafrost is? No. So why get bent out of shape if there's less or more of it?

Want to regain some dignity while pushing out a bin full of shite? Here's how:

1) Sunglasses
Is it raining? Is it 7 a.m. in the depths of winter? Great, to your neighbours you look like some unspeakably suave Italian!

2) Heels
So what if the bins are carrying two metric tonnes of dirty nappies or empty wine bottles. Head up, shoulders back, six-inch heels forward.

3) Hot pants
Only do the bin walk after a spate of 100 squats – get your pump on, those

arse cheeks need to look like the last arse Kim Kardashian traded up from.

4) Statement handbag
Dragging three bins at the same time shouldn't prohibit you from pushing the very limits of style as we know it: a clear handbag with handles made out of handcuffs.

5) A bin
At the end of the day, you'd be kicking yourself if you spent so much time getting ready in the morning in a rush that you completely forgot the most important accessory of all!

Now the men's turn:
Wear whatever the fuck you want, no one's going to judge you.

BEAUTY

CHANGING YOUR LOOK WITHOUT MAKING PEOPLE SAY 'SHE LOVES HERSELF', A GUIDE

My highlight of 2022: The Happy Pear

'Probably curing cancer.'

SUBTLETY AND PATIENCE are key when reinventing yourself in Ireland if one wishes to avoid accusations of 'notions' or 'being up her own hole'. Here's how you can give yourself a makeover without incurring the wrath of the bitteratti:

1) Hair

A dramatic departure from your regular hairstyle may brighten your day, but this will only last until you hear the first whispers of 'Does she think she's going to the Met Gala?' or 'She has the head dyed off herself'. You could ignore these and live your life, but it's just easier to play it safe. If you want to change your colour, do it gradually, so the worst remark you get is a confused 'Was your hair always that colour?' Want to go from long to short? Fake a brain injury and put it down to surgery. That way, you might get a compliment along the lines of 'You know that actually suits you'.

2) Make-up

In Ireland, people will say you either have 'not a scrap of make-up' on or you're caked in the stuff. There's no middle ground. So decide where you'd like to be. Anything outside of the very basics will have you lumped in on the 'caked' side, so be very careful. Care is also needed when choosing *when* to wear make-up. You don't want to hear 'She's very done up for a Wednesday morning', now do you? You may have

better things to talk about, but these people certainly don't.

3) Clothes

All Irish women should have four changes of clothes – work, weddings, funerals/meeting boyfriends' parents and home wear.

'She's very done up for a Wednesday morning'

A fifth outfit is permissible if she plays Ladies GAA with a team that doesn't allow skirts on the pitch. After that, you're in 'she loves herself' territory. If you wish to wear something nicer than that, you may need to do so somewhere far away from that nosey little arsehole town you currently live in.

FUNERALS

'DOESN'T HE LOOK WELL', AND OTHER SMALL TALK AT WAKES

THERE ARE ONLY THREE certainties in this life: birth, death and taxes. But at least with birth and taxes, you don't have to suffer through a wake.

If you've ever found yourself struggling to make small talk with a recently bereaved person while the corpse of their loved one is literally feet away from you, here are a few dos and don'ts to see you through.

DO – Comment on how good-looking the dead body is

You may never have complimented them on their looks when they were alive, but the minute someone dies it's imperative that you fawn over them as much as you can. 'Don't they look so peaceful' works, no matter how they look. 'You'd swear he'd nearly sit up!' is good too, despite the ramifications a deceased person doing such a thing

would have. 'I hope I look that good when I die' is pushing it a bit, though.

DON'T – Take selfies

No matter how well the corpse looks, they aren't suitable for the 'gram.

DO – Take a cup of tea to be sociable

Spill it down the sink, throw it into the bushes, do whatever you want with it, but take one. No further questions will be asked. Trust us, wakes are like your mam's house on steroids.

DON'T – Order off the menu

What you see is what they got. It's ham sandwiches, custard creams and fruit loaf, and that's it. Don't kick back and ask if they have anything gluten-free, and don't tell them you'll wait while they make you a quick

quesadilla. Have an egg-and-onion sandwich, bless yourself and fuck off.

DO – Be courteous to the entire family

Even if you have previous beef with one of the family, now's not the time to bring it up. You're sorry for their loss, if they need anything just shout, and then move on.

DON'T – Try to score

No matter how hot that cousin looks in black.

TRAVEL ━━━━━━━━━━━━━━━━━━━━

HOW TO BEAT JET LAG

LONG-HAUL FLIGHTS can mess up your internal clock for days, and even shorter trips can disorient your sleeping patterns and leave you groggy and miserable – we're talking jet lag, the scourge of the holidaymaker and the most expensive hangover you'll ever have.

As you get older, having a few beers on the plane and 'powering through' becomes less of an option when combating the phenomenon, so here are some tips that might help instead:

1) Don't fly anywhere
Forget your jet lag for a minute, have you considered how much air travel is contributing to climate change? Or were you too busy watching *Better Call Saul* on your phone while on a trip to Madrid with your wife and your wife's family to care? Forget avoiding jet lag, how about you just stay home and avoid climate disaster?

2) You're killing the planet
Careless, unsustainable travel such as 'getting away for a few days' or 'taking a break from it all' is murdering the planet. If you want to travel, by all means do. But use more sustainable methods, such as bicycle, catamaran or husky sledge. After that, the blood of millions is on your hands. Plane travel should only be used in cases where organ transplants need to be shipped in a hurry or for politicians attending a summit on the other side of the world to discuss what to do about climate change.

3) Sorry to belabour the point but you're killing the planet
It wasn't billionaires taking private jets to travel 50 miles at a time that caused climate change. It wasn't airlines flying empty planes during the pandemic to avoid giving refunds, and it wasn't warplanes constantly circling the globe monitoring and bombing other countries. It was you and the lads going to Vegas on a stag. And you're here worrying about jet lag? Disgusting. You should be ashamed of yourself.

COMPUTING

SETTING UP A COMPUTER FOR YOUR PARENTS: WE SHOW YOU HOW

YOUR PARENTS have often complained about how much harder it is for them these days to carry out simple household admin, because 'everything's online' – so, like the good son or daughter that you are, you've gone ahead and gotten them a computer with access to the internet to help them do things like book an NCT or whatever. All you have to do now is show them how to use it all. Here's our advice:

1) Are you fucking high?
Are you fucking high?

2) What good can come of this?
The best-case scenario of teaching your parents how to use the internet Is that your parents can now use the internet. Your dad is radicalised by the far-right within days and your

mam is caught watching porn on day one. And you'll know all this because they're on social media, chiming in with 'Is this someone you know from work?' after every YouTube video you post. Is that what you want? Is that what you really want?

3) They can't work a computer.
Do you honestly think that the people who need you to tune the radio in

every time you visit, or to delete text messages from their phone so they 'don't run out of space' are going to understand the phrase 'just open it in a new tab'? Are you going to be able to explain over the phone how to change the WPA settings on the router? In all your time of knowing your parents, what have they done to show that they're capable of avoiding a phishing scam that sounded like it was coming from 'a nice young man'.

4) This is madness.
Just do whatever they need to be done on your own computer. Do you think giving them one of their own is going to save you time or hassle? You'll spend hours trying to show them how only to end up doing it yourself anyway. Use the money instead for alcohol – you'll need it.

HOW TO FILL THE TIME WHEN YOU'RE WAITING ON A FRIEND BUT YOU'VE FORGOTTEN YOUR PHONE, A GUIDE

FINALLY, the day you have always feared has arrived. You've arranged to meet a friend for a social engagement and they're running late but you were stupid enough to leave your phone at home.

How in the name of Steve Jobs Almighty are you going to fill this wasteland of time before they arrive? They will be here in a minute for sure, but it'll feel like 80 days now you can't jump on Instagram or stick the earphones in and catch up on a podcast.

Okay, here goes nothing. We think we can help you:

1) Relax your shoulders and breathe slow, deep and deliberate breaths. You will be fine.

2) Just stand there. No seriously. No, you don't look like a weirdo. Oh stop it now, no one is going to think you're a demented bag lady or a creepy lech. Okay, well, maybe don't have your eyes manically darting around and looking at people passing by to check for some trace of them judging you for just standing there on the street.

3) Folding your arms is perfectly natural, you're just massively

overthinking it, and so yes, maybe now you look odd because you're acting like someone who only grew arms yesterday.

4) Christ, it's only been 43 seconds.

5) Bravo, you got so anxious and desperate that you accidentally waved at someone who wasn't your friend.

6) Glue your phone to your hand next time. Some people.

7) Are you taking out a book? Okay, now you've really made things worse for yourself – are you high?

WWN GUIDE

HOW TO ENRAGE A *STAR WARS* FAN

- Call them 'laser swords'.
- Over time, *Star Wars* fans have learned not to take the bait when someone calls it *Star Trek*, so greater effort must be taken to piss them off.

On This Day

25 March

In 2560 BC, the construction firm in charge of the Great Pyramid of Egypt (already the most expensive pyramid in the world) announce that they need additional government resources if they want to be operational by 2556 BC, having already blown past the initial 2565 BC deadline.

Go for the jugular – say something like '*Stars Wars* is just a bit surface-level, isn't it? There's no great philosophical underpinning to the message.'

- Additionally, fans have built up a tolerance to others misnaming beloved characters, but an odd Dark Vaper, Luke Skywaller, Print Sets of Leah, Baby Yoga, Arturo D2 and CBD Oil wouldn't go amiss.
- Act like there's absolutely nothing wrong with Black and Asian people playing lead characters in new TV shows and films in the *Star Wars* universe – a good chunk of fans will go berserk at this. Weird, we know.

Your Census Time Capsules

'Hello dear descendants in 2122, I'm here to tell you my deepest, darkest secret: my husband doesn't know it, but he's not the dog's real dad.'
– Patsy (48), Kildare

- Simply invent a rival sci-fi franchise that you believe *Star Wars* blatantly rips off at every turn. 'The Old Republic', 'the Knights Of Ren', 'the Jedi Order'? Gimme a break, it's a most shameful rip-off of *The Klug Baton Chronicles* written by Opie M. Ultani, later adapted for the big screen in Egypt in the 1950s.
- 'It's derivative' – you don't even have to know what it means, just say it with a nonchalant disdain, it'll gnaw away at their souls.

BEING A CONTRARY LITTLE BOLLOCKS ALTOGETHER, A GUIDE

WHILE IRELAND is famously a nation that prides itself on begrudgery, it doesn't come easy to everyone. Similarly, being a contrary bollocks in nature often requires hard work and study.

Take this guide as your first foray into a life of contrary bollocksism, a stepping stone to stepping all over the joy present in life, however thankfully fleeting it may be:

Something is popular
Congratulations, you fucking hate whatever it is. But don't stop there, it is necessary to belittle anyone who likes said thing, the fucking losers.

Someone suggests an activity
You've never heard of such a ridiculous suggestion in your life. Now list off, at length, all the reasons why this was stupid.

A beloved person has died
Have they now? Well, let's just go to their Wikipedia, sort by 'controversies' and

let everyone you encounter know all about it.

Wrongs
Wrongs? In a world full of them? Poppycock! Sure aren't there wrongs everywhere, at any given time, and shouldn't people be talking about them as well at this very moment when other things are being talked about?

Rights
Similarly … Oh la-dee-da, something or someone is doing good in the world. Righting wrongs, is it? What about this unrighted wrong over here? Bet you didn't think about that, did you? Time for you to feel awful about that so your fleeting happiness doesn't outstay its welcome in my general vicinity.

Develop quirks
Really put effort into earning the contrarian label. Cement it by carrying your weekly shopping in a hollowed-out melon and declaring bicycles to be too erotic. The stranger the thought,

the madder the action, all the better.

Ah would you look at him/her/it, cute as a button
Be it an animal or a child, you've seen nothing more ridiculous in your life than offering compliments or praise to the simpletons. What have they done to deserve such things?

Approach everything with a deep cynicism
What do you do when you encounter someone being a cynic? Either double down on your cynicism, suggesting an even more dour opinion, or suddenly brighten up and suggest that being so negative will get that person nowhere.

FINANCE

BULLDOZING AN ATM FOR A HOUSE DEPOSIT, A GUIDE

FOLLOWING NEWS that the average deposit amount for first-time buyers stands at €52,100, *WWN* looks at one of the fastest ways to save up for a house in Ireland: bulldozing an ATM from the wall and using its contents as a down payment on your very first home.

It may seem highly illegal and morally corrupt to steal a JCB, rip a machine full of money from a wall, cause criminal damage and drive away with the proceeds, but which is

worse: renting for the rest of your life or the slim chance of spending three to five years in a cushy Irish jail with all your meals and board paid for while your deposit is stashed away, waiting for your release? Exactly, so let's get cracking.

Picking the ATM location is key to pulling this off; you don't want to pick a local business run by a family, so we would suggest sourcing a rural bank with an ATM outside. Preferably, pick the bank you're going to get a mortgage from. After all, these bastards are going to make €150k interest from your 30-year mortgage, so fair game. Don't forget, you bailed these buckos out, and they owe you €50–100k, at least.

For security reasons, we would suggest keeping this heist down to just you and your partner, so practising with a few ATMs around the country first is recommended. Anywhere along the border with Northern Ireland is good, as this will lead police to believe the culprits are either a Republican or Loyalist gang. They'll

never suspect a Tom and Mary from Portlaw.

Once you've got five or six practice ATMs under your belt, go for the big one on the Friday night of a bank holiday weekend, when it's full to the brim. Sure, you may already have more than enough money to pay for a house in cash at this stage from your practice goes, but what if there's another housing crash? It's better to be safe than sorry and to have enough cash stashed for a rainy day.

Okay, you've now successfully pulled off your heist and have a couple of hundred grand to play around with, but it begs the question: can you trust your partner now after everything that's happened? Will she or he blab to someone about your crimes? We suggest taking out your only known witness to make sure you don't get caught. This will also double your kitty.

Obviously, you won't be able to lodge this money anywhere due to it being flagged, so we would suggest sourcing underground investments like high-grade cocaine, cutting it up with a mixing agent and turning 100 per cent profits from everything you traffic into the country. Again, for security, we would suggest hiring dozens of henchmen and former criminals to help your investment continue to grow. NOTE: Please also ship in some automatic guns with your cocaine shipment, as insurance. We can't recommend handguns and assault rifles enough.

Finally, set up a range of legit businesses like car dealerships and chippers; these will allow you to launder your hard-earned cash and start running a legit bank account with your initial bank of choice. Run the account with steady lodgements of 3–4 grand a month for six months and then apply for your mortgage. Congratulations, you have finally made it onto the Irish property ladder.

COOKING

DOLORES CAHILL'S SIMPLE BANANA NUT FRUITCAKE RECIPE

HI PATRIOTS. *WWN* Food has managed to get our hands on molecular biologist and immunologist Professor Dolores Cahill's fantastically simple 40-minute recipe for one of our favourite pieces of confectionery, a beautiful banana nut fruit cake. Mmmmm delicious.

First of all, you're going to need plenty of nuts for this cake to rise. In fact, large groups of nuts are essential for any fruit cake to stand out from the crowd, so handpick them carefully. If this recipe is anything to go by, finding lower-class nuts like peanuts are best to use and the easiest to get a rise out of. Feel free to use broken nuts too, as these will help gel your whole fruitcake together. Yummy.

Now, no banana nut fruitcake is complete without going absolutely bananas, lol. Mash the bananas using a glossary of disputed scientific claims while maintaining a sense of intellectual superiority. Threaten the bananas with a citizen's arrest before mixing them with the prepared nuts from before. This should intimidate the bananas into a mushy submission. It says here to call the bananas paedos until they turn dark brown, and then to insult their colour.

Add vague scientific claims with some fruit and a tub of vitamin D supplements to the mix. Stir well until the nuts from earlier are unrecognisable. Turn the oven on to 350 degrees for five seconds before putting your mix into a petrol-coated baking dish.

NOTE: When your banana nut fruitcake is ready to extract from the oven after 40 minutes, please do not use any oven gloves to take the dish out, as this is actually more dangerous than using your bare hands. Rest the piping-hot baking tray on your bare lap and eat using your melted fingers.

When finished, slap the baking tray against your face for several minutes, taking care to recite two decades of the rosary. To finish, donate €500 to someone's latest 'medical freedom campaign' so they can do up their castle in Athy.

Voilà, you fucking idiot, you've made banana nut fruitcake!

AFFLECK-LOPEZ MARRIAGE INSPIRES WOMAN TO GET BACK WITH TRAINWRECK OF AN EX

INSPIRED by the re-romancing journey of Hollywood sweethearts Ben Affleck and Jennifer Lopez, local woman Gráinne Pautlin is now back with her ex, who is universally known by everyone close to Gráinne as 'that walking advertisement for celibacy'.

'If Ben and Jen can reconnect and marry, I don't see why I can't make it work with the man who insisted on wearing boxers as shorts because "shorts are a capitalist scam, more layers = more profits",' shared Gráinne, tightly hugging once-again beau Mick O'Maffey in a loving, Instagram-friendly embrace.

'He still works part time at the same deli counter he did 8 years ago, and he's still convinced his fidget spinner hustle is about to make him rich, but he's definitely grown and matured as a person,' explained Gráinne of their storied relationship, which has only received a fraction of the tabloid coverage Affleck and Lopez have.

Possessing all of Affleck's alcohol issues, questionable comments about

Cost of Living Tips

Don't have any kids.

women and apparent anger issues, but none of his money, Mick is the ideal candidate to partner Gráinne as she enters the best years of her life.

'I didn't know it was scientifically possible to live even more at home with your parents than when I was going out with him before, but Mick's managed to do it. But that's nice right? His Mam's his best friend, landlord, maid and chief bollocker,' Gráinne said, the colour draining from her face as she slowly realised what she's done to herself.

'No Gráinne, this can work. Mick and Gráinne, Ben and Jen. Graick. Bennifer. Yay to finding true love again,' Gráinne screamed at herself internally, as she said yes to Mick when he asked if she wanted to see the new yo-yo tricks he's learned since they were last together.

FINANCE

TIPPING: HOW MUCH, WHEN AND WHERE

PASSING ON a gratuity to someone used to be reserved for the movies, or when you were visiting a cousin in Boston, but now it's crept into everyday life here in Ireland.

If you're unfamiliar with the concept of generosity, you may feel a little overwhelmed by this sudden change, so allow us to bring you up to speed:

When to Tip

Giving a little pocket money to your server in a restaurant is a gateway into tipping, and has come to be expected as the norm on nights out. But when else do you tip? Do you tip the lad delivering your Chinese, even if there was a delivery fee? What about taxi drivers? Tradespeople? It's almost impossible to be right all the time, and you can't constantly be pumping out cash like a border ATM on its side. Your best bet is to just issue a blanket, no-tip policy when not in the company of friends, but tip when you're all together. That way, you can still be relatively miserly but word of it won't spread.

How Much to Tip

We heard somewhere that a generous tip is 20 per cent of the bill. However, this is madness and cannot be expected from anyone. What, have we adopted these people? Are they a friggin' snow leopard off the telly that we're saving from poachers?! We urge anyone reading this to only ever tip about a fiver or so. That way you can say you 'gave them the price of a drink', without elaborating that you mean the price of a Guinness in the midlands in 1998, not a gin and tonic cocktail so big it comes in two glasses.

How to Tip

Lastly, how do you ensure that your generosity, when forced, is noticed by everyone? This can be accomplished by stating it loudly, 'There's a few quid there for yourself' works well at a table, or by posting it on social media to show how benevolent you are. Don't subtly slip them a fiver – shout it to the heavens, even if you did only leave a few coins that were in your pocket, like when you were seven and your mam gave you 20p to put in the Mass collection basket.

DRINKING

ORDERING A NON-ALCOHOLIC BEER IN AN IRISH PUB, A GUIDE

AMONG THE MOST terrifying prospects in the modern world, and we include the impending threat of climate change or another Boyzone album in that list, ordering a non-alcoholic beer in an Irish pub is a pressurised experience like no other.

Thankfully we've made such huge strides in this country in recent years when it comes to alcohol that people who opt to drink a 0 per cent alcohol beer only face ridicule, endless inquiry and ostracisation.

Here's how to deftly order one without arousing suspicion/being chased out of town:

Whisper your order under your breath. Or, better yet, write your order on a piece of paper and hand it to the bar staff on the sly like you are trying to subtly rob a bank without anyone noticing.

Throw people off the scent by pretending to down an invisible shot, loudly grimacing and shouting, as if it was tequila.

As a member of the bar staff reaches for the bottle of non-alcoholic beer, use the walkie-talkie on your person to signal to your accomplice that it is 'go time'. Shortly after your accomplice drives a double-decker bus into the pub you're in, creating havoc and panic, quickly remove all evidence that your beer is non-alcoholic, such as offending labels identifying it as such, and pour it into a pint glass.

Still not satisfied you've thrown everyone off the scent? Slur your words, become aggressive and tell racially insensitive jokes until you're kicked out.

However, if you are an avid gym-goer, who seeks to share this fact

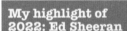

My highlight of 2022: Ed Sheeran

'Ruining my reputation after successfully proving I wrote "The Shape of You".'

with as many people as possible at all times to bask in the admiration of others for your clean living and restraint, you may prefer this alternative method of ordering:

Clear your throat, grab a megaphone, and scream with the power of a dozen irate banshees, 'No! A NON-alcoholic beer, ZERO-alcohol pal, yeah. Hitting the gym first thing tomorrow. Can't be filling my body with that poison. That's NON-alcoholic now, yeah? Nice one!'

TRAVEL

GETTING A RYANAIR REFUND, A GUIDE

ACCORDING TO A SURVEY carried out by consumer group Which?, Ryanair has received a refund rating of just 47 per cent, making it the worst short-haul airline for giving customers back their money. Considering this, *WWN* has put together this handy refund guide for getting your money back from the budget Dublin-based airline.

Kidnap the Ryanair CEO

Kidnapping Michael O'Leary and demanding your refund as ransom may seem like a very extreme road to take, but when you factor in all the stress that goes with waiting countless hours to speak to a customer service representative, filling out forms, arguing with supervisors and jumping through the many hoops Ryanair throw at you, you may reconsider. Despite his Teflon exterior, Michael is just a normal, everyday multimillionaire, and will bow down to threats of violence just like the next person, but be advised, he has a golden tongue and may charm any hostage-taker into submission. We would suggest keeping Michael gagged throughout the ordeal to avoid being swooned by promises of no-frills ransom.

Amass a Huge Social Media Following Online and Publicly Call Out Ryanair

Ryanair's social media accounts are famous for their hilarious retorts and cheeky postings, and regularly use their huge followership to instil fear in lowly customers demanding justice, so why not turn it around by amassing a huge followership of your own. Sure, it will take you several years to achieve such a status, but it's still less time than waiting for Ryanair to finally pony up. Bombard them with screenshots of your endless back and forth emails, pictures of your bald spots from pulling your hair out and screenshots of the 70-minute call waiting times. This should at least get a like from the Ryanair Twitter account, which is pure gas, so it is.

Make a Formal Written Complaint to Your Local Commission for Aviation Regulation

Probably the easiest and most effective option in our guide is the good old-fashioned letter of complaint. Now, it won't make your money come any faster, but if enough people officially complain then Ryanair's current refund rating of 47 per cent will seem more like a target for the next year.

HOUSING

MAXIMISING YOUR LITTLE APARTMENT BALCONY, A GUIDE

As a tenant, you must understand that you are responsible for the upkeep of all aspects of the apartment that someone is very kindly allowing you to rent.

CONGRATULATIONS! You've finally managed to spend a huge portion of your monthly salary on a tiny apartment in Dublin City. And even better, it's got a little balcony where you can take in the sights and sounds of the town around you.

Now, your landlord may have warned you that you aren't getting a red cent of your deposit back if you so much as Blu-Tack a poster to the walls, but perhaps you could do something to make the most out of the two square metres of outside space you have?

1) No personalising

As a tenant, you must understand that you are responsible for the upkeep of all aspects of the apartment that someone is very kindly allowing you to rent. That includes, even if not expressly stated, the little balcony. As such, you must not do anything to personalise or modify the balcony in any way. The only thing you are allowed to do is to maintain it and keep it clean, and even at that, you are not guaranteed your security deposit back. There's a wrong way to clean things, you know.

2) No smoking either

Just as your apartment is a no-smoking area, so too is your balcony. This should be easy to obey, though, as you shouldn't be smoking to begin with. Smoking leads to ill health, and ill health can lead to time off work, thus putting your ability to pay rent in jeopardy. What kind of tenant are you, that you would risk your landlord's income like that? You know, on second thought, maybe this apartment would be better off with one of the hundreds of other people who applied for it.

3) No laundry. Look, just don't open the fucking doors

Of course you're not allowed to hang laundry out on the balcony – it's unsightly and lowers the property value of the neighbourhood. Dry your washing indoors, but be sure to report any mustiness or mildew that may occur so that your landlord can take it out of your security deposit as quickly as possible. And yes, maybe just regard the door to the balcony as 'more of a big window' from now on. It's best to only ever go out if you have to wave for help if the apartment is on fire, and even then, you may need to consider how that's going to play out for you when you go to look for a reference for your next landlord.

WWN GUIDE

GETTING DEPORTED ON YOUR J1

WITH J1 SUMMER season nearly upon students, *WWN* has produced this essential guide to ensuring you never forget your magical experience by getting deported.

Here's how you do it:

1) Mistakenly talking to a US police officer the way you would a guard. 'Howiya horse?' will certainly be taken not as a genial greeting but as an imminent threat to life, and you will be subsequently deported from life itself by a trigger-happy police officer.

2) If you're on America's west coast, have you considered joining the Bloods or the Crips? Getting caught up in a gang feud will likely end in guaranteed deportation, but it will also make your Tupac-loving parents proud.

3) Availing of an abortion in a number of US states. Honestly, some states are now so proactively backwards and anti-women that it's like pre-2018 Ireland out there.
NOTE: If you publish a far-right manifesto detailing some unhinged white supremacist talking points, you run the risk not of being deported but of being defended and celebrated by Fox News hosts.

4) Accidentally sending a picture to your mother of the squalor you have reduced your accommodation to. She will happily ring immigration on you herself for the shame you're heaping on the family name.

5) Singing school rugby songs and absolutely sending it with the lads. The Irish Embassy will personally frog march you to a CIA black site, where you will be tortured for being a dose.

6) After a long day at the gun range shooting semi-automatic weapons, you can still get yourself deported for drinking a Bud Light when under the age of 21.

7) While research shows Irish students expel enough vomit in the US each summer to fill in the Grand Canyon, actually vomiting in the canyon or on any other US landmarks is an automatic deportation.